PSYCHOLOGY: PERSPECTIVES AND PRACTICE

ANNALS OF THE NEW YORK ACADEMY OF SCIENCES
Volume 602

PSYCHOLOGY: PERSPECTIVES AND PRACTICE

Edited by Sheila M. Pfafflin, Jeri A. Sechzer, Jefferson M. Fish, and Robert L. Thompson

The New York Academy of Sciences
New York, New York
1990

∞ *The paper used in this publication meets the minimum requirements of American National Standard for Information Sciences-Permanence of Paper for Printed Library Materials, ANSI Z39.48-1984.*

Cover art: *Cover art is a spatially quantized transformation (Blocpix®) of an original rendering of the brain by New York Academy of Sciences member Ed Manning of Stratford, Connecticut. This rendering is courtesy of Yuguchi & Krogstad Inc. of Los Angeles.*

Library of Congress Cataloging-in-Publication Data

Psychology : perspectives and practice / edited by Sheila M. Pfafflin . . . [et al].
p. cm. — (Annals of the New York Academy of Sciences, ISSN 0077-8923 ; v. 602)
Revised papers presented at meetings of the New York Academy of Sciences Section of Psychology, 1982–1987.
Includes bibliographic references and index.
ISBN 0-89766-601-1 (cloth : alk. paper). — ISBN 0-89766-602-X (pbk. : alk. paper)
1. Psychology—Congresses. 2. Clinical psychology—Congresses. I. Pfafflin, Sheila M. II. New York Academy of Sciences. Section of Psychology. III. Series.
Q11.N5 vol. 602
[BF20]
500 s—dc
[150] 90-43596 CIP

APS/PCP
Printed in the United States of America
ISBN 0-89766-601-1 (cloth)
ISBN 0-89766-602-X (paper)
ISSN 0077-8923

ANNALS OF THE NEW YORK ACADEMY OF SCIENCES

Volume 602
September 14, 1990

PSYCHOLOGY: PERSPECTIVES AND PRACTICE[a]

Editors

SHEILA M. PFAFFLIN, JERI A. SECHZER, JEFFERSON M. FISH, AND ROBERT L. THOMPSON

CONTENTS

[a] This volume comprises papers presented at the 1982-1987 meetings of the Section of Psychology of the New York Academy of Sciences. The papers have been updated, where appropriate, to include new information through spring 1990.

Part III. Applied and Clinical Psychology

Introduction

SHEILA M. PFAFFLIN

American Telephone and Telegraph Company
Short Hills, New Jersey

The papers in this volume were presented over several years at the meetings of the Psychology Section of the New York Academy of Sciences. They have been selected for this volume of the *Annals* because they reflect two considerations that were used in their original selection and that we feel make them of enduring value: their individual excellence and the ways in which they reflect important developments within the field of psychology. Our intention is to provide psychologists in many areas, and scientists in other fields, with a broad perspective on these developments, while at the same time presenting material of interest to specialists in a number of areas.

The volume is organized into three parts: historical perspectives; physiological, comparative, and social psychology; and clinical and applied psychology. Because my co-editors will be introducing the various sections, I shall not provide a detailed discussion of the papers here. However, I do want to give an overview to provide a context for approaching this volume.

Historical perspective is important to an understanding of progress in any field. It is particularly appropriate as we enter the last decade of the twentieth century to give consideration to the important developments in the field of psychology in this century. We have selected three papers from among many possible topics because of our view of their scope and timeliness. Let me indicate briefly some of the considerations that went into these selections.

Two developments have become increasingly important in psychology over the past few decades: increased emphasis on the biological and evolutionary background for behavior and a return to favor of investigations into various aspects of cognitive functioning, including human consciousness. Taylor's paper provides historical context for these developments in his analysis of William James's interpretation of Darwin's work.

An equally important development in psychology during this century has been our increasing understanding of the importance of social structures in determining human behavior, which has resulted in the establishment and enormous growth of the field of social psychology. In the paper by Otto Klineberg, we are fortunate to have a unique view of the establishment and development of social psychology by its founding father.

Finally, no one with any familiarity with the field can be unaware that psychology is undergoing critical changes. The spectacular growth of clinical psychology has created an entirely new structure for applied areas of the field. At the same time, developments in cognitive science and research on the brain and behavior have resulted in major realignments in research areas; much research today is interdisciplinary, so that in many areas behavioral research is as closely related to linguistics, computer science, and neurobiology as it is to traditional experimental psychology. These developments have created intense strains on the organizational structures in the field. It is fitting, therefore, that we end this section with the paper by Virginia Sexton, which provides historical perspective on the critical issues of purpose and identity facing psychology today.

The papers in the section on physiological, comparative, and social psychology reflect important trends that have evolved in this area and that complement the historical perspectives. First, we have several examples of the increasingly sophisticated explorations by psychologists of the relations between behavior and biological functions, and which reflect, among other factors, the influence of the rapidly growing field of neuropsychology. The papers presented here show the scope of such research today: They range from a discussion of the important developments in our understanding of the nutritional factors in the development of brain and behavior presented in Morgan's paper, through developments in our understanding of conditions such as epilepsy and sleep disorders, presented in the papers by Barowsky *et al.* and by Fried, which have been made possible by the strides in recent years in analyzing the relationships between brain and behavior.

Secondly, we have work on the cognitive capabilities of animals and its relationship to human cognitive functioning. Psychological views of animal behavior have undergone major changes since the days when behaviorist principles dominated the field. The paper by Swartz provides an interesting current perspective on this issue, while the paper by the Adlers presents significant recent research on a species, the dolphin, whose cognitive functioning has aroused great interest.

This section also includes papers that reflect equally important developments in our understanding of how the unique social environment of humans determines their behaviors. The paper by Chen and Yates presents recent work in an area of research long central to social psychology, while the paper by Paludi reflects one of the new trends in social psychological research inspired by the rapidly changing status of women in our society.

In selecting among the many possible areas of applied and clinical psychology, we had two considerations in mind: We have tried to select those areas that deal with issues of importance to our society at this time and that also provide innovative examples of the application of psychological principles to social problems. For example, no one in our society today can be unaware of the impact of addiction; Stanton Peele provides some challenging views on this issue from a psychological perspective. Similarly, the many changes that are taking place in child care practices as a result of changes in family structure and the increasing participation of women in the work force provide an obvious motivation for examining issues in this area, and the paper by Salzinger provides new insights on the functioning of social networks in child rearing. Obesity is a major health issue in the United States today, and the paper by Katahn and McMinn illustrates the biobehavioral approach to this area. The growing use of biological information in behavioral approaches to clinical problems is demonstrated again in another socially significant area in the paper by Barowsky on the use of biofeedback to treat disorders of childhood.

We believe that these papers present important perspectives on past and present developments in the field of psychology. We enjoyed hearing them, and hope the reader will enjoy reading them.

Introduction

Historical Perspectives from Darwin to Culture to Divergence

JERI A. SECHZER

E. W. Bourne Behavioral Research Laboratory
Department of Psychiatry
The New York Hospital–Cornell Medical Center
White Plains, New York 10605

When Darwin's *Origin of the Species* appeared in 1859, the scientific community and the general public had to realize that the boundary between human and nonhuman animals was no longer unique but instead represented a gradual "evolution" of biological complexity from one-celled organisms to man that was dependent upon many complex theoretical factors. Darwin's work suggested an entirely different relationship between humans and animals within nature. Not only would Darwin's theory of evolution have a tremendous impact on science, philosophy, and religion, but of relevance here is the effect his theory had on the development of the embryonic field of psychology. A crucial part of Darwin's work was his theory of natural selection, and, according to Eugene Taylor, it was this aspect of the evolutionary hypothesis that so influenced William James's theory of consciousness. James's interpretation of Darwin and the influence it had on James's "evolutionary theory of consciousness" is the theme of the first paper in this section. Darwin's work influenced James in his search to understand the "origin of certain human faculties, of certain instincts and tastes, or of conscience, the higher reason and the religious sense." And James, in turn, through his *Principles of Psychology*, his other writings, as well as his interactions with scientists, philosphers, and religious adherents, would have an impact on every aspect of the newly developing science of psychology from physiological and experimental psychology to social psychology and psychopathology, influences that are still evident today.

In the first paper of this section, Taylor tells us that conclusions of others about Darwin's influence on James are only "half-truths" drawn from the "incomplete body of facts [and] . . . perpetuated as stereotypes that conform to the way this or that scholar would *like* to view James." Taylor goes on to analyze what he perceives to be the four major stereotypes of Darwin's influence on James. First, it is commonly assumed that James's familiarity with Darwin's theory of natural selection came through reading Darwin's published writings and the writings of others about Darwin. A second misinterpretation of James on Darwin assumes that James's published statements on Darwin's ideas began in 1868 with his review of the *Variation of Plants and Animals under Domestication.* A third common stereotype, according to Taylor, is that James's interpretation of Darwin "must have been derived from the tradition of natural theology according to William Paley." The last interpretation to which Taylor objects is that "most scholars . . . are unable to see the continuity between his earlier work as a psychologist and his later work as a philosopher." Taylor addresses in detail the reasons for such stereotypes and the assumptions upon which each is based. By filling in the gaps with James's papers and publications, with James's correspondence with the Darwin family, as well as with evidence of the pervasive influence from the field of natural theology and of that of other notable persons of the period, we can begin to understand more clearly the influences on James's theory of consciousness.

Taylor, who has probably read more of James's writings and correspondence than any other historian, takes us on a fascinating journey, increasing our knowledge of James and his response to Darwin's writings. He acquaints us with James's relationships and interactions with Charles W. Eliot, Asa Gray, Chauncey Wright, Charles E. Norton, the Social Darwinists, and the natural theologists of the period. Taylor also shows how James's early ideas on evolution were further elaborated through his increasing interest in Henri Bergson and then Gustav Theodore Fechner, whose ideas on panpsychism he incorporated into his notion of a "continuum of cosmic consciousness" and "pluralism." In his final works, James still followed Fechner and suggested the importance for psychology of studying the "fall of the threshold of normal awareness."

Taylor ends his chapter with an appropriate and still timely quote from James: "We shall not *understand* these alterations in consciousness either in this generation or the next."

The second paper in this series is a historically interesting personal account of the development of the area of social psychology. Otto Klineberg, now considered the father of social psychology, traces the growth of this field from a narrow view to the concept that "all psychology is social psychology."

Because "social psychology means different things to different people," Klineberg defines it according to his view of how this special area developed. He describes four areas of the discipline with which he has been involved throughout his career: (1) a cross-cultural approach to social psychology, (2) race differences, (3) international affairs, and (4) the social psychology of mental health and mental illness.

Although Klineberg addresses these areas separately, he sees them as products of their interrelationships. He describes his early interest and the state of knowledge at that time in each of these overlapping spheres. For example, in the section on cross-cultural approaches, Klineberg tells us that in 1923 he took his first course in social psychology at McGill University (while he attended medical school). The course, based almost exclusively on McDougall, stressed instincts and their functioning and presented only one technique as useful to social psychology—that of observation. This, Klineberg feels, is an indication of how far psychology, particularly social psychology, has moved since 1923. After graduating from medical school,

Klineberg studied for a doctorate in social psychology with Professor Woodworth at Columbia University. Klineberg describes how his attitudes toward social psychology came to involve cross-cultural concerns—that only by seeking to understand the unique qualities of a culture, which provide some of the most exciting and interesting phenomena of human behavior, can we begin to define social psychology in its broadest sense. Klineberg goes on to tell of his involvement with various cultures and how he separated experimentally cultural from intellectual qualities of different groups as well as elucidating the conditions essential to define each in its appropriate context. In doing so he brings us up to date on the current state of cross-cultural studies.

In his section on race differences, Klineberg was particularly concerned about the validity of intelligence tests, which were standardized for one culture and tested on another. Much of this work was conducted with a variety of Indian tribes in the United States. Looking back from the perspective we have today, it is difficult to imagine how hard Klineberg had to work to begin to overcome attitudes about racial superiority and to achieve some degree of acceptance of the idea that not only did educational and cultural factors play crucial roles in the "shaping of the individual," but also when evaluated properly (not with standardized tests from another culture/race) disparaties in intelligence would disappear. He describes some of the early conflicts among psychologists, sociologists, and anthropologists, arguments that Gunnar Myrdal believed had been laid to rest by 1969 because the idea of inborn racial differences was scientifically indefensible. Nevertheless, Jensen and Eysenck have resurrected the issue and are currently publishing evidence they feel support the notion of group differences. Klineberg's own doctoral thesis at Columbia, back in 1928, addressed one aspect of this problem, that of speed of reaction of different racial groups under different conditions.

The field of international affairs has been a long-term interest of Klineberg which, early on, he related to the area of national differences. He describes the changing nature of psychological research and publications in international affairs. This section also emphasizes the striking changes in perspective that have occurred in both the lay and scientific communities concerning the possibility and consequences of a nuclear holocaust.

His last section discusses the social psychology of mental health and illness. Klineberg became actively involved in the area of mental health through his work with the World Federation for Mental Health. We learn of beginning international efforts by psychologists, sociologists, and anthropologists to identify problems and seek some solutions to the increasing incidence of mental illness, particularly in the post-World War II period. The contributors to this effort were notable, including Harry Stack Sullivan, Margaret Mead, L. K. Frank, and Brock Chisholm. Klineberg, with the support of Margaret Mead, was able to achieve recognition of the need for efforts by the Federation to be cross-cultural in approaching the formidable array of issues of mental health and illness, which ranged from aging and nutrition to the role and status of women in different parts of the world to violence, crime, and peace and war.

Throughout this narrative Klineberg takes us through the stimulating, sometimes agitating, developments in social psychology, giving us his projections for its future, which he feels strongly will take place in field studies outside the laboratory. In this future world of social psychology, emphasis will be given to applications in the areas of politics and international and race relations. Klineberg also predicts, albeit regretfully, that the comparative approach in social psychology will receive little attention for the foreseeable future.

The final paper in this section addresses the state of the art of American psychology as we approach 1992 and the centennial of the founding of the American Psychological Association (APA). Because the American Psychological Association is so closely associated with the development of psychology in this country, the hundredth anniversary of the APA "stimulates reflection on our association's history and on the achievements of American psychology."

Historian Virginia Sexton describes the current crisis in American psychology both organizationally and as a discipline. To clarify the issues underlying the present crisis, which became evident in the late 1970s and early 1980s, Sexton reviews the background of the development of psychology in the United States and the earlier crises which recurred throughout the APA's first century. She describes the importation of scientific psychology from Germany, its ready acceptance into the academic curriculum in the United States, and the social and economic forces that shaped American psychology as well as those who pursued it.

Early in the twentieth century, psychology, having abandoned its philosophical and theological entanglements, established itself as a science, a natural science. Sexton tells us about the rapid growth of psychology during the first quarter of the twentieth century, the beginning of specialties within the discipline, and the applications of psychology to education, law, business, and industry. As more diverse views developed within the young science, so did dissension, particularly concerning the direction that the APA should take. (The APA was founded in 1892 with the specific purpose of advancing psychology as a science.) At this time the scientific psychologists, who outnumbered the "other" psychologists, began to oppose applications of psychology other than those favoring its advancement as a "pure" science. Dissatisfaction with the APA increased with the influx of these "nonscientific" psychologists in the organization. Other societies were formed to specifically address experimental psychology, and these eventually developed into the regional associations of today.

With the continued growth of psychology and its contributions during World Wars I and II, the professionalization of psychology increased and competition with scientific psychology intensified at the expense of some of the scientific specialties (experimental and physiological). Sexton describes the parallels between the growth of nonscientific specialties and the dissension within psychology, particularly within the American Psychological Association. Although the founding of the APA was based on scientific psychology, by the late 1970s there was a complete reversal, with the professional groups outnumbering by far the scientific groups.

With what Sexton calls "the changing face of American psychology," psychology continues to lose its traditional research base. This crisis in scientific psychology is especially evident in the field of the neurosciences, which, as they developed during the 1970s, should have been a province of scientific psychology. Unfortunately, behavioral neuroscience has essentially (although not completely) become the focus of medical research institutions, and little emphasis is placed on learning the principles and techniques of behavior essential for exploring the integrated functions of the nervous system. Experimental psychology has now become fragmented into a variety of specialties such as neuropsychology, biopsychology, and so forth. As dissatisfaction grew with the perceived lack of time and effort for scientific psychology in the APA, these subspecialties formed their own societies and brought psychologists into collaboration with scientists other than psychologists. This fragmentation has had the effect of further alienating the psychological scientists from the APA. The late 1980s also saw the formation of the American Psychological Society (APS), which attends primarily to psychological science and not to the clinical disciplines. Many of its members had left, or had never joined, the APA, although some hold memberships in both organizations.

By the late 1980s, the disunity and disorganization in psychology was widely recognized. Various explanations for the disunity and opinions about its resolutions have been proposed, including questioning whether or not psychology could ever become unified again or whether psychology should declare itself to be composed of a number of different fields with little communication between them. Sexton believes, however, that the histories of other sciences show us that psychology is still in an early stage of scientific development with respect to establishing a unified body of knowledge. In her view the more critical problem is that psychologists have not yet decided whether unification is their goal. If fragmentation continues, there will be little hope of psychology's becoming unified into a coherent discipline. In this vein, Sexton also informs us about a group of distinguished and concerned psychologists who recently established the Society of Unimonic Psychology to study the impact of the conceptual fragmentation as well as the sociopolitical implications for psychology as a science and as a profession.

In an epilogue Sexton describes the efforts of the APA to reorganize as a means of resolution. Unfortunately, this attempt was rejected by the membership. Sexton foresees a long and arduous task for this group and for psychology as a whole, a task that may take us well into the next century. She leaves us with the feeling that unity both in the APA and in our discipline must be our goal to assure a place for American psychology in the future. Whether the newly formed American Psychological Society will be able to hold the scientific psychologists and attract more is a matter of conjecture as is the question of realignment with APA.

Sexton, with her long view of psychology's historical development, leaves us with the hope that some form of unity and coherence within the discipline of the science of psychology eventually will be achieved.

William James on Darwin

An Evolutionary Theory of Consciousness

EUGENE TAYLOR[a]

Associate in Psychiatry
Harvard Medical School
Cambridge, Massachusetts 02138

William James is arguably the most important American philospher-psychologist of the late nineteenth century. He is preeminently remembered for his interpretation of C. S. Peirce's pragmatism, which, with the help of John Dewey, E. L. Thorndike, James H. Tufts, F. C. S. Schiller, and others, James retailed into the first uniquely American philosophy to have international consequences. His *Varieties of Religious Experience* (1902) is still the most widely used text in psychology of religion courses today. His *Principles of Psychology* (1890), the first major work to situate psychology within the domain of the natural sciences, is the only text of its kind still continuously in print after one hundred years. First to establish a laboratory of experimental psychology in the United States, first to teach a course in physiological psychology, and first to grant a Ph.D. in the new science at an American university, verily, James well deserves his title as father of American psychology.

In this vein, James's interpretation of Charles Darwin has long been a topic of interest, principally for two reasons. First, James was the earliest American to make psychology physiological by placing the subject matter of the discipline in the context of evolutionary theory. Sensation and perception, cognition, emotion, instinct, habit, and more, he grounded in functional adaptations of the nervous system to the environment. Second, and more problematic for later experimentalists caught in the thrall of reductionistic positivism, was James's focus on the evolutionary function of consciousness. Consciousness is the great paradoxical problem, James suggested, for science may be one of its products, but purposefulness is also its aim. In the evolution of the human species, consciousness is ever a fighter for ends.

But many scholars interested in James and Darwin tend to read a few passages out of James that specifically refer to the ideas of Darwin or his disciples and then to draw only those conclusions that seem warranted and reasonable from the most readily accessible sources. The result has been that the gist of James's interpretation is common currency, but the conclusions

[a] Address for correspondence: Rare Books, Countway Library, 10 Shattuck Street, Boston, MA 02115.

drawn from the incomplete body of facts are half-truths, perpetuated as stereotypes that conform to the way this or that scholar would *like* to view James. Meanwhile the total picture of how James saw the situation is often missed. As my small contribution to the Academy's Darwin Centennial, I would like to address four such stereotypes that, in my opinion, persistently survive in the minds of the otherwise well-educated afficianadoes of Jamesean thought.

[I]

First, it is a commonly held assumption that James knew the theory of natural selection chiefly through Darwin's published writings and through the writings of Darwin's other interpreters. We know, for instance, that James definitely read the *Origin of Species* (1859). James says as much in a veiled statement when he reviewed Darwin's *Variation of Plants and Animals under Domestication* in 1868.[1] Also, among the James papers at Harvard there is a list of book titles owned by James that contained his extensive marginal marks and annotations.[2] It is a mere list, for after it was compiled all the books cited in it were sold, probably around 1923. Item number 57 says "Charles Darwin, *The Origin & Species* (1859), *The Descent of Man* (1871), *Variation* (1863), *The Expression of the Emotions* (1873), all show use but almost wholly without markings or annotations." These entries were undoubtedly made by Ralph Barton Perry, James's first biographer.

Only two of these volumes that James owned are still extant. Among the James papers at Harvard is Darwin's *Variation of Plants and Animals under Domestication,*[3] and in private hands is *The Expression of the Emotions in Man and Animals.*[4] James received the *Variation* when it first appeared in 1868, while convalescing at the baths at Teplitz, Germany.[5] Letters between James and his brother Henry mention the arrival of the volume, and soon afterward James wrote two separate notices of it, one in *The Atlantic Monthly* and the other in the *North American Review.*[1] James's copy of *The Expression of the Emotions,* unexpectedly rediscovered, contains his signature on the front fly leaf, followed by "St. Paul, January 23, 1875".[4] It was purchased on a brief excursion to visit Wilky, one of his younger brothers, between teaching semesters at Harvard. The volume has a few interesting annotations.[6]

James also read the two-volume *Letters of Charles Darwin,* first published by Darwin's son Francis in 1888.[7] James wrote to Croom Robertson at that time saying; "I have just been reading Darwin's life . . . and, whilst his nervous system makes bad nerves respectable, the tale of it shuts the mouth of all lesser men against complaining."[8] He saw Darwin as a heroic figure, one to whom truth came in a quiet whisper while in solitude, rather than the way it comes to lesser men who try to draw attention to their half truths by proclaiming from the roof tops that they are the official expositors of the absolute.[9]

But James's acquaintance with Darwin was not through reading alone. Many of James's teachers and friends knew Darwin personally. Professor Asa Gray, the Harvard botanist, Chauncey Wright, the philosopher, and Charles Eliot Norton, editor of the *North American Review,* are all examples. Gray, in particular, was an intimate in Darwin's inner circle. He knew of Darwin's thesis on the *Origin* before it was first publicly announced, and he was the first to introduce Darwin's ideas on the transmutation of species by means of natural selection into America. The date is pinpointed exactly by Gray's biographer, December 10, 1858, when Gray addressed the Cambridge Scientific Club.[10] Gray soon became the foremost American exponent of Darwin and intellectually fought a number of pitched battles with Agassiz throughout the 1860s, until Agassiz's creationist approach to evolution—that all species were an idea in the mind of God—had been soundly routed.

During this time William James had been studying chemistry under Charles W. Eliot and biology under Jeffries Wyman at the Lawrence Scientific School. Both Eliot and Wyman stood with Gray in the contest against Agassiz, Benjamin Pierce, and Wolcott Gibbs over control of science at Harvard. James had entered the Lawrence Scientific School under Agassiz's aegis because of the James family's social connections with Emerson and the Saturday Club, but James was naturally attracted to the empiricism of Gray and Wyman, partly because of the greatness of their personalities, and partly because in their scientific orientation James found a haven from the nearly suffocating influence of his father's religious metaphysics.[11] The Grays and the Jameses were also connected socially, as Katherine Peabody Loring, Asa Gray's niece, became best friends and a close traveling companion with Alice James, William and Henry's sister. Also, the Lorings and the Jameses lived next door to each other on Ashburton Place in Boston between 1864 and 1866.

Another person whose ideas on Darwin strongly influenced James was Chauncey Wright.[10,12] Wright worked in the Harvard Observatory making gravitational measurements, but his principal interest was philosophy. Gray put him to work on the mathematics of leaf arrangements, and Wright's first paper on the subject got mixed results from Darwin's group in England because of its theological implications. Wright soon published a piece in the *North American Review* supporting Darwin's theories against the attacks of British opponents. Darwin needed just such a philosophical weapon against Mivart at the time, so he arranged at his own expense to have Wright's paper reprinted as a pamphlet and circulated throughout England. Wright's natural interest in philosophy led him to fuse Darwin's evolutionary theory with British empiricism in the tradition of John Stewart Mill, and this fusion was a singular influence on William James, C. S. Peirce, Oliver Wendell Holmes, Jr., and others who attended the informal meetings of the Cambridge Metaphysical Club in the early 1870s. Out of these philosophical exchanges came the American intellectual movement of pragmatism.

There is an interesting letter from Darwin to Wright worth quoting because it suggests that Darwin was, in fact, interested in the problem of the will and its influence in the evolutionary process. Darwin wrote to Wright on June 3, 1872:

> As your mind is so clear, and as you consider so carefully the meaning of words, I wish you would take some individual occasion to consider when a thing may properly be said to be effected by the will of man. I have been led to the wish by reading an article by your Professor Whitney *versus* Schleicher. He argues, because each step of change in languages is made by the will of man, the whole language so changes, but I do not think that this is so, as man has no intention or wish to change the language. It is a parallel case with what I have called "unconscious selection," which depends on men consciously preserving the best individuals, and thus unconsciously altering the breed.[13]

In her biography of Alice James, Jean Strause notes that brother Henry, the novelist, while traveling in 1869, met "Darwin" at the Charles Eliot Norton residence in London.[14] Circumstantial evidence suggests that this reference probably refers to Darwin's son. The Nortons had known the James family from their Newport days; and when the Jameses moved to Quincy Street in Cambridge after 1866, they had the Nortons for neighbors, as the Norton estate in Cambridge was situated off Kirkland Street just east of Harvard Yard on a tract known as Shady Hill. Charles Eliot Norton had married Susan Sedgwick, and Susan's sister, Sara, soon came to live with them at Shady Hill. Sara also became a close, lifelong friend to William and Henry's sister Alice. While Sara was traveling in England, she naturally stayed with the Nortons when they were there. On one such visit in 1867 she met one of Charles Darwin's sons, young William Erasmus Darwin, the banker. A courtship followed and in 1877 they were married. Mr. and Mrs. William Darwin came to Boston that year and the James family, William James included, met Sara's new husband.[15]

In addition, in the James Jackson Putnam Papers at Harvard Medical School, there is an interesting letter written in an unknown hand to Putnam on the back of a medical school brochure that announces the formation of a committee to study the proposal to admit women to the medical curriculum. The handwritten letter, which bore no relation to the brochure on the back, is dated only November 8 (probably 1877). After relating some local social gossip, the writer tells Putnam that Darwin's son has been to hear William James's lectures on automatism, in which Charles Darwin had been mentioned. Darwin's son asked James for permission to copy that portion of the lecture "to send to his father for use in arguments to confound Huxley."[16] Undoubtedly the son was William Darwin, on his honeymoon trip with his new wife, Sara.

After the death of Henry James, Sr. and his wife in 1882, Alice James moved to London with Katherine Loring to be near her brother Henry, the novelist. Numerous references attest to visits with the William Darwins during this time.[16] William James was still in contact with the Darwins in 1901,[17] and we may presume that his relations with them remained cordial up until James himself died in 1910.

The point is that James had direct access to all Charles Darwin's major works; he had colleagues and friends who were intimate with Darwin's inner circle, and a long-standing social relationship was maintained between the James family and the Darwin family from 1868 to at least 1910.

[II]

A second misinterpretation of James on Darwin assumes that James's published statements on Darwin's ideas begin in 1868 with his review of the *Variation of Plants and Animals under Domestication.*[18] This is reasonable, because all the definitive William James bibliographies begin with the first piece known that James ever published, a review in *The Nation* in 1867 of Herman Grimm's *Unüberwindliche Mächte.* James followed this in 1868 with several more notices; among them, a review of A. A. Liébeault's *Du Sommeil et des États analogues* in *The Nation,* the review of Charles Darwin's *Variation of Plants and Animals under Domestication* in the *Atlantic Monthly,* a review of Claude Bernard's statement on the progress of physiology in France in the *North American Review;* and also in the same issue of the *North American Review* is James's other notice of Darwin's *Variation.*[12] All major James bibliographies conform to this progression. Perry first published this sequence in 1923; it was confirmed by revisions added to the original bibliography by Perry's son in 1950 and confirmed again by John J. McDermott in 1975 when James's bibliography was again revised and republished as the most up-to-date and authoritative source available.[19] Ralph Barton Perry wrote his Pulitzer Prize winning *Thought and Character of William James* with this bibliography, and most of the James biographies recently published or currently under way derive from this same bibliographic progression.

The truth of the matter is that Perry's bibliography of James's writings is not complete. James's first publication was not in 1867, but in 1865; moreover, he followed it the same year with another piece in the same publication.[20] The first piece he ever published was a review of Thomas Huxley's *Lectures on Elements of Comparative Anatomy,* and the second was on Alfred R. Wallace's *Origin of the Human Races.*[21]

Both the Huxley and Wallace reviews were unsigned when published, and the index for 1865 of the *North American Review* does not credit them to William James.[22] However, in the Charles Eliot Norton papers in Houghton Library at Harvard, the original manuscripts for both the Huxley and Wallace pieces are in James's handwriting, and Eliot has noted their authorship by James at the top of the first page.[23] Included also in the Norton papers are James's original letters proposing the reviews. Since these materials were not in the James papers but in the Norton papers, they were overlooked by Perry, Allen, McDermott, and others. In both the Huxley and Wallace reviews, James makes a major statement on Darwin's theories, and so they are important for our story.

James first wrote to Charles Eliot Norton on September 13, 1864, from Henry James, Sr.'s residence at 13 Ashburton Place in Boston, setting forth his proposal: "As my friends and relations seem to be successful in their attempts to draw a revenue from the *North American Review,* I am emboldened to try what I can do myself."[24] He then asked "Should you like for the January number a notice of Huxley's *Lectures on Comparative Anatomy*?" James continued in a somewhat pitiful and pleading tone. He made an interesting reference to the influence of Jeffries Wyman when he asked "If you conclude to let me 'notice' it, should you wish me to go into detail of the homologies of particular bones; or are they of too special an interest?" He then pleaded for supplication. "If you find you would like the notice of a book someday which might be in my scope, I will do my best to give a fair account of it." He then concluded by saying, "I should prefer to write on some subject connected with Biology."

Norton evidently replied in the affirmative, for ten days later, on November 14, 1864, James again wrote from his father's home. He enclosed the review of Huxley, saying that he had some doubts about the pertinence of the "analytic-synthetical disquisition and the Program of the Future of Science" which he had hung on the subject. James said that Norton could omit those parts. He had only included them to lengthen the article, and "by the impossibility of doing so in any way that would fall within the scope of Mr. Huxley's book." In other words James filled in with his own ideas because he did not see much to extract from Huxley's own work, other than what he had already plainly stated. Again, in a rather pitiable tone, he signed the letter, "yours submissively, Wm. James."[25]

Norton accepted the article immediately and only excized the most technical portion on cranial bones. James wrote again on November 17, just three days after sending in the article. He lamented the omission of the cranial material on the grounds that "it was there to protect by its more solid qualities the somewhat windy remainder of the article."[26]

In its substance, James praised Huxley's vigor and activity and the vivacity of his mind, but regarding his views of science and his interpretation of Darwin, James thought that Huxley decidedly belonged to the left wing, "if naturalists were divided as politicians are." For Huxley demanded that everything be subsumed under the laws of matter, and all questions that he took up required him to pronounce on them a definite yes or no. No equivocation was allowed, or even possible. In general, however, James cited Huxley's support of Darwin's idea of the transmutation of species. The notion deserved respect, if only for the reason that it so persistently cropped up in the work of such naturalists as "Asa Gray, Lyell, Owen, Schleiden, Vogt, Van Baer, and Kolliker," many of whom primarily opposed it, but then espoused it heartily.[27]

James then launched into a division of theorists as either systematizers or analyzers. The systematizers had the grand scheme to which the facts must conform, while the analyzers had the facts out of which they tried to construct plausible theories. Huxley was apparently a systematizer but resorted to analysis, using embryology in his attempt to demonstrate the theory that the skull is an extension of the vertabrae. James concluded with the technical details of Huxley's argument.[27]

In July, 1865, just six months later, the review of Wallace appeared. Here James first took up a direct discussion of Darwin's theory. The thrust of the review lauded Wallace for his style and for his important contribution toward clearing up the great controversy between the "monogenists and the polygenists," meaning those like Darwin and Gray, who espoused the view that all species are decended from some primordial purer form, as opposed to those like Agassiz, who maintained that all present species are very old and were all formed long ago, at once, by God. James believed that Wallace used Darwin to answer the particularly perplexing question raised by their opponents as to why the causes of variation in man no longer appear active.[28]

Mr. Wallace, James said, thought that Darwin's theory of natural selection supplied an answer to the polygenists. It is true, he said, that in mankind the causes of variation *are* no longer active, but this is because of the fact that any further physical change must be checked as soon as certain conditions are fulfilled. "These conditions are given when man's emotions and intellect are sufficiently developed to make of him a truly social being, instead of a solitary, or merely gregarious, being."

James stated Wallace's argument in this manner: The individual among the brutes is self-dependent and isolated. The least deficiency in vigor eliminates him from the struggles for existence. Regardless of the superior qualities of his own kind, the solitary individual is at the mercy of his own resources solely. As a general rule, there is no mutual assistance rendered between adult brutes during sickness, nor is there any division of labor. Natural selection thus keeps up a uniform standard, for each individual must fulfill *all* the conditions of its existence. The particular race as a whole will come to change in a relatively short period of time, with the most superior passing on to their descendants the peculiarities to which *they* owe their success.

The situation is different in man, however. In that he is social and sympathetic, all members of the community profit by the gifts of any one member, and the deficiencies of any one are smothered by the wealth of the general population. Less robust health and vigor does not mean death. Entire limbs can be missing and existence goes on, as it would not in the lower animals. In this manner "the action of natural selection [on the physical man] is therefore checked."[28]

Similarly, James went on, another trait unique to man is his ability to artificially adapt to extreme changes in the environment, whereas in animals even the slow changes of physical geography or climate make it necessary to change their food, clothing, and weapons, which means a corresponding change in internal organization and bodily structure. But using his intellect alone, man cultivates food independent of the changing seasons, he domesticates animals to work and catch food for him, he has the use of fire and is thus enabled "with an unchanged body still to keep in harmony with the changing universe." James then concluded that "Natural

Selection . . . in its action upon man, singles out for preservation those communities whose social qualities are the most complete, those whose intellectual superiority enables them to be most independent of the external world. The physical part of him is left immutable, and his mental and moral advance is secured." The wonder is, James mused, why such a discovery has been so late in being articulated.[28]

We see here that James embraced Darwin's idea of natural selection and saw in it a special significance as applied to man—the consequences of individual choice in the context of social evolution. It was the seed for the development of his later ideas on the evolutionary function of great men in society, and it was the bulwark from which he launched his attack on the Social Darwinists.

The controversy between James and the Social Darwinists heated up throughout the 1870s; and as part of a series of exchanges with Grant Allen, a disciple of Spencer, James published "Great Men, Great Thoughts and the Environment" in 1880. His attack bristled with sharp thrusts at the Spencerians.[29]

James maintained that communities change from generation to generation because of the accumulated influences of individuals, of their examples, their initiations, and their decisions. The Spencerians held that the real basis for social change lies in the institutions by which organized society is held together—institutions which in their development conserve and generate an intellectual and social atmosphere without which the so-called great man could not exist.

But James was not merely adopting a polemic. He wished to redress the omissions of the Social Darwinists by placing the individual and his powers of choice into the proper scheme of the evolutionary process. He admitted these social influences but gave equal weight to the power of the individual to effect changes when he said, "Social evolution is the resultant of the interaction of two wholly distinct factors: the individual, deriving his peculiar gifts from the play of physiological and infra-social forces, but bearing all the power of initiative and origination in his hands; and second, the social environment, with its power of rejecting both him and his gifts. Both factors are essential to change. The community stagnates without the impulse of the individual. The impulse dies away without the sympathy of the community."[30]

James spent the 1880s at Harvard teaching physiological psychology and also philosophy in the tradition of the British empiricists. His additional activities in psychical research will be discussed later. He finished the decade with publication of his long-awaited *Principles of Psychology* in 1890. His references to Darwin in this work are well known. Pleasures and pains, James said, would hardly be so intense if the former were not connected with truly beneficial and the latter with truly injurious events.

As late as 1894 James was still reviewing arguments on the origin of species when he published a notice of William Bateson's *Materials for the Study of Variation.*[31] There James depicted the strict view of Darwinism "to which the word Wallaceism might perhaps better applied," as synomous with the doctrine that discrete differences between existing species are due to the summation, pursued through successive generations, of numerous small variations in the same direction. Intermediating degrees of these variations have become extinct, leaving chasms larger or smaller, between the extremes.

Bateson's view, backed with weighty empirical evidence, was that original variations have been more abrupt and discontinuous. Darwin and Wallace's view of continuous variations, or the accumulation of small steps of variation, was not denied by Bateson, only that such variation and selection cannot alone be responsible for the entire diversity found in the animal kingdom. In James's words, Bateson "mistrusts the explanation of so many of the small details of structure by survival of the fittest." Species, James points out, "are only approximately adapted to their circumstances, and live as much *in spite,* as by virtue of what they are."[32] Bateson's view was that conditions accumulate over time to produce sudden changes all at once; new segments with all their parts complete, which repeat themselves throughout the whole series. A force must therefore be admitted which may lead to the production of total organs at once. Such a view, James asserted, strengthens the hand of the "anti-associationists, and in general all of those who have continued for an autogenous origin of certain human faculties, of certain instincts and tastes, for example, or of conscience, the higher reason, and the religious sense."[33]

Just what was this view James was referring to? That insofar as man's individual capacities count for anything at all in the evolutionary process, the very act of his choosing, based as it is on incomplete evidence, colored by his subjective opinion, and heavy laden with the presuppositions of belief, *injects a teleological element.* Man forever remains the conduit through which a power larger than himself may influence the outcome of biological events. Notwithstanding the influence of Huxley's determinism, Darwin himself said as much in *The Decent of Man.* His whole discussion implied that consciousness has a salient utility in man and to some degree in animals.

[III]

A third common stereotype is that James's interpretation of Darwin, which admits that a teleological explanation is still possible, must have been derived from the tradition of natural theology according to William Paley.[34] An Anglican clergyman and teacher in Christ's College, Cambridge, during the late 18th century, Paley is best known for his textbooks *Natural Theology and Natural Philosophy* and his *Evidences of Christianity.* But Paley's influence in England and America was all out of proportion to his originality. By his own accounts, his textbooks were collations of the work of others. The singular point to recommend them was, by copious illustrations, he demonstrated that the order seen in nature was so pervasive that it could have only come about by the guiding influence of an Unseen Hand, namely the Creator. Including even botanical and anatomical material, Paley's *Natural Theology* became a standard text for generations of scholars at Cambridge and Harvard.

Alexander Bain, adding a dissertation and notes, brought out an edition of Paley's *Moral Philosophy*. Emerson's copy of Paley's *Principles of Moral and Political Philosophy* is heavily annotated; so is Henry David Thoreau's copy. The copy left by James Jackson Putnam was Paley's *Moral Philosophy, Abridged and Adapted to the Constitution, Laws, and Usages of the United States of America.*[35] We know that James himself taught Paley in his Philosophy 4 course in theistic ethics, along with Plato, Aristotle, Adam Smith, and Butler, but that was in 1888. (He alluded in a letter to his brother Henry that the work for the semester was "dull and steady," although he probably found talking to his class about these authors interesting.)[36]

What notes we have on Paley's works in James's library are scant. Only one volume is listed, the 1821 edition of Paley's *Natural Theology*. It contained flyleaf inscriptions showing that James read the work through completely and made occasional comments.[36] There can be no doubt that as a student at Harvard James breathed the Paley-laden air.

Nevertheless, I wish to plead for a more pervasive influence on James from the field of natural theology, one that was also in the air at the time but also part of the family literary legacy that James inherited from his father, Henry James, Sr. I refer to one of the most frequently overlooked sources that impinged upon William James's view of evolution, namely, the work of the eighteenth century scientist and revealed theologian, Emanuel Swedenborg.[37]

One of Swedenborg's greatest contributions to science lay in the field of his specialization as a mining engineer. He was one of the first to apply the laws of geometry and mechanics to the facts of physics and chemistry. In this he is given credit as one of the originators of the modern science of crystallography.[38]

Swedenborg's works on the mineral kingdom were well known to his younger colleague Carolus Linnaeus. Linnaeus systematized the botanic world according to the artificial grouping of plants by their sexual characteristics.[39] Although his forte was botany, Linnaeus attempted to extend his classification efforts to the animal and mineral world as well, with mixed results. Swedenborg's use of geometry brought a rigor to the study of minerals that was previously unknown, and cast him into a community of scientists whose empirical research and rational outlook anticipated the kind of evolutionary theories that came some one hundred years later. While basically propounding a Christianized science, Swedenborg drew conclusions in mathematics and astronomy that clearly stated what later came to be known as the nebular hypothesis. The speculations he made on the formation of the earth's crust, he cast into surprisingly modern geologic terms.[40]

But the primary use Swedenborg made of science was to search for the soul. Mathematics, astronomy, and minerology led him to cosmology. He then turned to anatomy and physiology, then to rational psychology, and finally to the study of religious experience itself. In 1744 he underwent a personality transformation of such proportions that his life was irrevocably changed. He experienced what he called an opening of the internal spiritual sense. Abandoning the language of mathematics, at age 56 he turned to prose metaphor, the major medium for the remaining 26 years of his life. His first major task was to begin a reinterpretation of the books of the Bible, according to what God dictated to him as the true meaning of the internal spiritual sense of the word. All his subsequent work suggests the religious interpretation of his previous scientific accomplishments.

Evolution, for Swedenborg, meant creation; and creation meant, not the original historical creation of the earth, but rather the complete regeneration of personality. To be regenerated was to be created anew—to undergo the transformation from egotistical self-love to love of God and one's neighbor. Creation meant the transformation of the merely natural man into the spiritual man. When the Bible told of the six days of creation, for instance, Swedenborg took this to mean the six states of a man's regeneration. Spiritual wisdom meant a man's capacity for understanding. Love meant the life of the heart and the power of the will. In heaven, Swedenborg said, there is continual purification and, so to speak, a new creation. Likewise with man, the progression of faith resides with those who are being created anew. This parallelism between the natural and the spiritual world he called the law of correspondences.[41]

The purpose of all creation, he further said, was revealed in terms of its use for the perfection of man's soul. So he said, "The Divine created the universe for no other reason than the existence of mankind"; "Man was no otherwise created than to be a receptacle for the Divine"; and "That which has been created by the Divine increases in perfection towards its interiors . . . for everything which is from the Divine begins from him, and progresses according to order down to the ultimate end; thus through the Heavens down into the world." The natural world, Swedenborg said, has no existence without the depth of the spiritual world; and so, for the spiritual man, no mere natural explanation of events will do.

After Swedenborg died, three great centers for the dissemination of his teachings sprang up in London, Philadelphia, and Boston.[42] Throughout the 19th century Swedenborgian ideas were directly connected with interest in phrenology, hypnotism, the utopian communities, homeopathy, and the mental healing movement. I have detailed elsewhere the impact of Swedenborgian ideas on Ralph Waldo Emerson during the period that led up to publication of his first book, *Nature,* in 1836.[43] Mostly through Emerson we see the dissemination of Swedenborgian ideas throughout the Transcendentalist circle. Emerson, you will remember, was the godfather of William James, having been a regular guest at the James family dinner table in New York before Henry James, Sr. suffered his great spiritual crisis in England in 1844. James, Sr. was then led by circumstance to Swedenborg's writings and, through Carlyle, to James John Garth Wilkinson, member of the Royal College of Physicians and translator of Swedenborg's scientific writings.[44]

A lifelong friendship sprang up between the Wilkinsons and the Jameses. Wilkinson acted as a pastoral psychiatrist to alleviate Henry James, Sr.'s spiritual suffering; Henry James, Sr. financed Wilkinson's translations of Swedenborg. Wilkinson named one of his daughters after Henry James, Sr.'s wife; James named one of his sons after Wilkinson. James convinced Wilkinson to turn to public lecturing and then coaxed him into becoming a homeopathic physician. Wilkinson dedicated his book *The Human Body and its Connection with Man* to Henry James, Sr. and acted as host to the James family when they lived in England in 1855.

Wilkinson also established an enduring relationship with the young William James. They had a mutual interest in medicine, hypnosis, and mental healing that formed the content of their later exchange, buttressed all the while by the long-standing family ties that were of a religious nature.

Both Henry James, Sr. and Wilkinson interpreted Swedenborg's theory of creation, and although he professed utter incomprehension, we know that William James was steeped in the details of their thinking. Henry James, Sr. gave a philosophical interpretation to Swedenborg that at one point he called "The Physics of Creation," meaning to unite under one cover the laws of the natural and spiritual world.[45] Wilkinson, following Swedenborg, said simply that instead of classifying the plant and animal kingdoms according to similarity of structure, modern scientists should classify these kingdoms according to their use for man.[46] Wilkinson's was the view of the empiric, as he had a more detailed knowledge of Swedenborg than Henry James, Sr., and his medical training caused him to produce, like Swedenborg, a kind of philosophic anatomy in his writings.

Emerson, of course, looked into nature and everywhere saw the oversoul. William James would later take a stand against Emerson's monism and his utter lack of emphasis on the morbid side of life. Of the once-born, Emerson's personality in James's eyes did not need to undergo the evolution from abject dispair to eternal hope; Emerson had already achieved it by being born that way. It was the pragmatic side of Emerson's theories that most attracted James; so too James gave great emphasis to Emerson's ideas on the development of individuality in nature.

Taken as a whole the Swedenborgian and Transcendentalist influence on William James was so pervasive, so powerful, and so over-riding that James himself was not able to achieve the proper distance to assess clearly the stature of these ideas until some twenty years after both Emerson and Henry James, Sr. had died. Suffice it to say here that the substance of this legacy was that in any scheme of the universe the spiritual life of the mind had to be accounted for. Moreover, mind was not a mere subsidiary to the development of the physical world, but was the very basis for all our perceptions of what is called natural. Science could legitimately be used as a tool in search of the soul; the true function of personality was so that we could evolve into something greater, and the scientific study of nature was one means to reveal Divinity within us. In the *Varieties of Religious*

Experience (1902) William James called this view one of natural supernaturalism. "Divinity lies everywhere around us," James had said, "but society remains too hide-bound to accept the fact." To awaken to the Divinity within one's self was at the heart of an evolutionary transformation of consciousness.

[IV]

We now come to my last objection; namely, that most scholars have missed the center of James's vision, and therefore are unable to see the continuity between his earlier work as a psychologist and his later work as a philosopher. A case in point is the application of James's evolutionary theory of consciousness to his philosophy of radical empiricism.[47]

It is a common fact that scientific psychologists do not read James after the publication of his *Principles of Psychology* in 1890, while religious philosophers tend not to read him before the publication of his *Varieties of Religious Experience* in 1902 (or at least they do not read him before the publication of his *Will to Believe* in 1897).[48] This means that any attempt to account for James's interpretation of Darwin as it contributes to psychological science usually draws on James's publications between 1868 and 1890. At least the job is usually thorough for this period (excluding the 1865 materials) and usually includes James on Darwin's *Variation* and James's controversy with the interpreters of Darwin, such as Huxley, Clifford, Lewes, Bateson, and the Social Darwinists, Spencer, Allen, and John Fisk. Modern interpreters, of course, always give James's references to Darwin in the *Principles,* chiefly in the chapters on instinct and emotion. The period of the 1890s remains a blank or if addressed at all is described as James's era as a popular lecturer on education for teachers and as a dabbler in abnormal psychology and psychical research. Anything after 1902 is simply considered philosophy, not science.

I would like to contradict this interpretation by referring to archival documents which show that the ideas on evolution that James developed in the early period were further elaborated with his interest in F. W. H. Myers's conception of subliminal consciousness between 1882 and 1901, an idea that, according to James, found further corroboration in the works of Henri Bergson and Gustav Theodore Fechner after the turn of the century.

WILLIAM JAMES AND F. W. H. MYERS

William James and F.W.H. Myers first met in England in 1882 at a time when the English Society for Psychical Research was just forming around Myers, Edmund Gurney, Henry Sidgwick, and others. Myers was a Cambridge scholar, known for his prose and poetry, and he had a great sense of personal attachment to the classical tradition. After Plato, he believed that the first evidence for survival after death lies in the spiritual qualities of man.[49] But Myers also believed that the contemporary church doctrine could not command the loyalty of serious thinkers, nor at the same time could any sensitive person subscribe to the mechanistic conception of biology as an answer to life's larger questions.

During the course of their relationship, both James and Myers turned to the then recent developments in French psychopathology, which were showing that ideas in the life of the mind could have a profound influence on effecting bodily changes. For Myers, as well as James, hypnosis held the key to the alleviation of mental suffering and at the same time made it possible to open the doors of the subliminal region, giving access to its furthermost reaches. This had important philosophical implications that were of interest to James, but for Myers it meant much more. He thought he had discovered the key to the greatest secret of the century—a way to prove that there was, in fact, life beyond death.[50]

James was immediately attracted to the conception of a subliminal consciousness that Myers developed in a series of long essays in the early issues of the *Proceedings of the English Society for Psychical Research.* This vast region of one's inner life, Myers maintained, was the greater portion of who we really are. Rational consciousness was but one possible state out of many; but because in the process of evolution it had become overdeveloped in order to meet the needs of the external environment, it was an easy mistake to take the waking state alone as all there is to personality. Meanwhile, within each of us there are far greater realities awaiting potential development. In addition to the collective experiences of our archaic past, Myers said, we also hold within us the seeds of what is to come. He took the appearance of such phenomena as telepathy, clairvoyance, and prevision as not mere anomalies, but as hints given us now of what mankind will evolve into in the future. Bestial, archaic, underdeveloped states, he said, we see in the physical form as animal instincts and in the psychological form as mental pathology. The worst and the best that is within us express themselves to waking consciousness through the same channels; thus, they are often confused for the same thing, such as when religious visions are classed as pathological.[51]

Myers devoted his entire life to an exploration of psychic phenomena and James joined him in this effort by founding the American Society for Psychical Research in 1884. Its founding members included, among others, Simon Newcomb, Charles Sedgwick Minot, Henry Pickering Bowditch, and none other than Professor Asa Gray. James discovered the famous Belmont medium, Mrs. Leonora Piper, who later went to England and became the first paid subject in parapsychological research, and who was the subject of much experimentation here in America. James also experimented with hypnotism and automatic writing. These were the bases for his studies in the Harvard Psychological Laboratory in the 1880s and 1980s, and he participated for many years in actively investigating the claims of the American mental healers.[52]

James supported Myer's work, hoping that Myers would produce the long-awaited magnum opus on the nature of the subconscious, but Myers died in 1901 without completing it. Relying heavily on Myers, James himself made a major statement on the nature of the subconscious in 1896, where it was the central theme of his unpublished Lowell Lectures entitled "Exceptional Mental States."[53] His titles were "Dreams and Hypnotism," "Antomation," "Hysteria," "Multiple Personality," "Demonical Possession," "Witchcraft," "Degeneration," and "Genius." The manuscript lecture notes for this series are among the James papers in Houghton Library at Harvard.[54]

I will not dwell on their content. The question that does concern us here, however, is the implicit statement James made concerning the evolutionary function of the subliminal consciousness. It was James's opinion, in agreement with Myers, that a scientific explanation of the subconscious not only held great hope for those presently judged incurably insane, but also would put us into direct contact with our greatest potential for growth. To explore the subconscious reveals both the pathological and the transcendent in each of us. Trauma puts us at risk, for we open ourselves up to actualizing the primitive and instinctual that is most easily accessible from below; while active exploration allows us the possibility of choosing to realize the good in spite of the presence of the evil in our nature. James expressed this view at varying times during his later career as the voluntary control over normally involuntary mental processes, the realization of our values, and the actualization of our beliefs. Personality is in a constant state of becoming, he said. Not perfection, but balance is the measure of health. Each person is flawed in some way, but each reacts to their shortcomings in different ways. Even the morbid have something to teach us about the meaning of life. Geniuses may have morbid traits, but true geniuses are those whose idiosyncratic capacities are turned into something socially useful, so that all in society are the benefactors. Reiterating a theme he had written upon in the 1880s, he said our solitary men and women of genius are the movers and shakers of an evolving social consciousness. So we see that by 1896 James's earlier statements now find a wider and fuller application.

That James was most interested in the practical consequences of the subconscious cannot be doubted, for his interest drew him to the early work of Pierre Janet in the 1880s. It was through Myers, then James, that Janet's work first became known in the United States. Again through Meyers and Janet, James was led to the work of Breuer and Freud, and it was James who brought the earliest communication of Breuer and Freud on hysteria to the attention of American psychologists in 1894.[53] But Myers was less interested in the general idea of the subliminal and more enamored with psychic phenomena themselves. He was less interested in the social significance of the subconscious and instead was consumed by the question of life after death. But, he died in 1901 without ever producing any evidence that he felt was conclusive.[55]

Myer's great contribution, James later wrote, was that observation of the farther reaches of the subliminal region reveals an ultimate plurality of states of consciousness. It was, James said, "a hypothesis of first-rate importance." Waking consciousness was only a small fragment of the psychic spectrum. "It is a special phase of mentality, teleologically evolved for adaptation to our natural environment, and forms only what he [Myers] calls a 'privileged case' of personality." Myers, James further said, "had an unusually daring grasp of the principles of evolution, particularly in the wonderful way in which he has worked out suggestions of mental evolution by means of biological analogies . . . his conception of mental evolution is more radical than anything possible. It is absolutely original; and being so radical, it becomes one of those hypotheses which, once propounded, can never be forgotten, but sooner or later has to be worked out and submitted in every way to criticism and verification." Myers's idea, James said, was destined to alter the course of psychology in the twentieth century.[56]

JAMES AND HENRI BERGSON

James's association with Bergson probably began through acquaintance with the latter's writings. Ralph Barton Perry concludes in his biography of James that a reference in the *Principles* shows James read Bergson's *Données immédiates de la conscience* just after its publication in 1889. Bergson's autographed *Matière et mémorie,* James read in 1896.[57] Then in 1902 James reread both works and the result was a new spark of interest. James wrote to Theodore Flournoy that now he was excited and stimulated about Bergson, while admitting that "four years ago I couldn't understand him at all."[58] The earliest correspondence between James and Bergson dates from 1902, when James wrote, heaping effusive praise upon Bergson for his "exquisite genius." James also sent with his letter a copy of his Ingersoll Lecture on immortality "in which it may amuse you," he wrote, "to see a formulation like your own that the brain is an organ of filtration for spiritual life." He also sent a copy of his recently published *Varieties.*[59]

Bergson wrote back that the *Varieties* had made a profound impression. From then on a regular correspondence ensued. They frequently exchanged publications and constantly referred to each other in their work. But it was not until 1905 that they met for the first time. Parenthetically, it was during this particular visit to Paris, Dr. Marianne Teuber hypothesizes, that James met Pablo Picasso through Gertrude Stein.[60] A minor coincidence, but of interest nonetheless, is that James stayed with Dr. Rupert Norton, the son of Charles Eliot Norton.[61]

While James and Bergson were very different kinds of philosophers, they self-consciously agreed on many points. James had written to Bergson, for instance, "I think that the indispensible hypothesis in a philosophy of pure experience is that of many kinds of other experiences than ours, that the question of co-conscious/conscious synthesis (its conditions, etc.) becomes a most urgent question."[62] Later Bergson replied:

> I believe that on many essential points I could join you, but perhaps I would not go quite so far as you do in the way of "radical empiricism." The principal differences bears probably (again I am not wholly sure) in the role of the unconscious. I cannot avoid making a very large place for the unconscious, not

only in the realm of psychology but also in the universe in general, the existence of unperceived matter seeming to me to be of the same *genre* as a psychological state which is not conscious. The existence of a reality outside of all actual consciousness is, something intimately mingled with the conscious life, "interwoven with it," and not "underlying it" as substantialism would have it. But it is possible that even on this point I am nearer to you than I imagine.[63]

In the spring of 1907 James read Bergson's newly published *L'évolution creâtrice.* Afterward he wrote: "Oh my Bergson, you are a magician, and your book is a marvel, a real wonder in the history of philosophy, making . . . . a new era in respect of matter . . . . a pure classic in point of form."[64] For James, the book "inflicts an irrevocable death-wound upon Intellectualism."[65] He further said, "I feel that at bottom we are fighting the same fight, you a commander, I in the ranks. The positions we are rescuing is Tychism (chance, freedom, spontaneity) and a really growing world."[66]

James's copy of Bergson's *L'évolution creâtrice* is an original edition.[67] It contains Bergson's signature and an inscription to James, and in addition to a hand-penciled index in the back with copious entries, the entire book is filled with James's characteristic marginal markings. These markings tell us the important story concerning which of Bergson's ideas were most attractive.

Bergson began with the idea that unorganized bodies exist in abstract time; organized bodies exist in a state of real duration. When the latter first dies, the complex mental organization becomes disaggregated, followed quickly by disintegration of the physical body. The vehicle for the expression of this organization is the unique individual, who is in a constant state of transformation (in other words, constantly involved in the process of growing old).

Bergson then reviewed the various criteria by which this change is measured in terms of physics, chemistry, biology, and philosophy. He examined Darwin's hypothesis of insensible variation, the theories of Bateson and Devries on sudden variation, the work of Eimes on orthogenesis, and finally the theory of neo-Lemarckianism and the heritability of acquired characteristics. Each theory was true in its own way. The result of Bergson's inquiry was a statement of his own theory on the vital impetus, the *elan vital.* "Consciousness is this vital element that is at the origin of life. Consciousness, which is a *need of creation,* is made manifest to itself only when creation is possible. It lies dormant when life is condemned to automatism; it wakens as soon as the possibility of choice is restored."[67] Consciousness corresponds exactly to the living being's power of choice. "It's co-extensive with the fringes of possible action that surround the real action; consciousness is synonymous with invention and freedom, the rising above the purely mechanistic and deterministic life of inorganic matter and single organic reflex . . . It is as if a vague and formless being, whom we may call, as one will, man *or* superman, had sought to realize himself, and had succeeded only by abandoning a part of himself on the way."[67] Thus, "the organized world as a whole becomes as the soil on which was to grow either man himself, or a being who morally resembles him. The animals, however distinct they may be from our species, however hostile to it, have none the less been useful travelling companions on whom consciousness has unloaded whatever encumbrances it was dragging along, and who have enabled it to rise, in man, to heights from which it sees an unlimited horizon open again before it."[67]

James took particular note in these passages in Bergson as his marginal markings attest. It is interesting to conjecture in the longer view how sympathetic these ideas are to those of Swedenborg and J. J. G. Wilkinson. In any event, Bergson's ideas found an immediate place in James's philosophy, and their relationship continued until James died in 1910.[68] A chapter appears on Bergson's critique of intellectualism in James's Hibbert Lectures on *A Pluralistic Universe* (1908),[69] and we know that James was involved with the English translation of *L'évolution creâtrice.* This English edition of Bergson's *Creative Evolution* was published in 1911 by Henry Holt, James's own publisher. The translator, Arthur Mitchell, was a first-year graduate student at Harvard the year James retired. Mitchell's opening note as translator reads:

> In the writing of this English translation of Professor Bergson's most important work, I was helped by the friendly interest of Professor William James, to whom I owe the illumination of much that was dark to me as well as the happy rendering of certain words and phrases for which an English equivalent was difficult to find. His sympathetic appreciation of Professor Bergson's thought is well known, and he has expressed his admiration for it in one of the chapters of *A Pluralistic Universe.* It was his intention, had he lived to see the completion of this translation, himself to introduce it to English readers in a prefatory note . . . Professor Bergson has himself carefully revised the whole work.[70]

Bergson later published a preface to the French translation of James's *Pragmatism* and also added an introduction to the French edition of William James's *Letters.*[71] In his preface to *Pragmatism* (1911) Bergson wrote that according to James, we bathe in an atmosphere traversed by spiritual currents. Many resist, but others open themselves wide and thus allow themselves to be influenced by these wide beneficent breezes. Evolution, for James, meant the creation of what is true for man. Reality flows; we flow with it; and we call true any affirmation which, in guiding us through moving reality, gives us a grip upon it and places us under more favorable conditions for acting. While for other more traditional doctrines a new truth is a discovery, for James it is an invention. Truth, according to pragmatism, has come little by little into being, thanks to the individual contributions of a great number of inventors. Truth, as Kant says, may depend upon the general structure of the human mind, but James adds that the structure of the human mind is the effect of the free initiative of a certain number of individual minds.

No one loved truth with a more ardent love, Bergson concluded, no one sought it with greater passion. James was stirred by an immense unrest and went from science to science, from anatomy and physiology to psychology, and from psychology to philosophy, tense over great problems. All his life he observed, experimented, meditated. And as if he had not done enough, he still dreamed, as he fell into his last slumber, of extraordinary experiments and superhuman efforts by which he could continue even beyond death to work with us for the greater good of science.[72]

JAMES AND GUSTAVE THEODORE FECHNER

James's great attraction to Gustave Theodore Fechner's work was no doubt based on Fechner's interest both in empiricism and metaphysics and in the reconciliation of science and religion. Fechner is first of all remembered as the founder of modern psychophysics. Even Wundt called him his teacher. James derived from Fechner fruitful ideas on imagination, attention, discrimination, and perception in the *Principles,* but considered Fechner's psychophysical law as the "patent whimsy" of "a dear old man."[73] The true impact came after 1890, when James incorporated Fechner's psychology and his metaphysics into the Ingersoll Lecture on Immortality. James wrote a preface to the English edition of Fechner's *Little Book on Life After Death.* He read Fechner's *Die Tagesansicht* and *Über die Seelenfrage* in 1905, Fechner's *Zend Avesta* in 1907, and in the published version of the Hibbert Lectures on *A Pluralistic Universe* (1908), James devoted a whole chapter to Fechner's ideas.[74]

In 1908 James recommended Fechner to Bergson, "He seems to me to be of the real race of prophets, and I cannot help thinking that *you* in particular, if not already acquainted . . . would find [him] very stimulating and suggestive. His day, I fancy, is yet to come."[75] James had sent a copy of *Pluralistic Universe* to Ernst Mach, his friend the physicist, who wrote back on May 6, 1909

> I have read the fourth lecture, on Fechner, who was a fatherly friend to me personally as well as in his work . . . . I came into contact with Fechner after the appearance of his *Psychophysik* in the year 1860, and was associated with him at intervals until near the time of his death. His ideas gain ground steadily in Germany, even his ideas concerning the soul-life of plants, with which the scientific botanists would have nothing to do in the years 1880–1885. People called Fechner a fool and a fanatic. He was himself in part responsible for this on account of his leaning towards spiritism . . . . And one must acknowledge that a little sobriety would have greatly furthered his always scientific thinking."[76]

There is also some anecdotal evidence that James was a patient of the Reverend Elwood Worcester in Boston after 1904, and that their relationship was based on their mutual regard for Fechner. Worcester had earned a Ph.D. in philosophy from Leipzig and had studied with both Wundt and the ailing Fechner in his last days of teaching. Worcester came to Boston from Philadelphia and as an Episcopal priest inaugurated what came to be known as the Emmanuel Movement, combining the moral teaching of religion with the most recent scientific advances in the psychotherapy of the functional neurosis. Worcester had recently published a book on Fechner's philosophy, without footnotes and based wholly on his personal interaction with Fechner. James wrote after reading the book that it was the most remarkable case of the revivification of one personality through another that he had ever known.[77]

The obvious fact recommending Fechner to James was that, like Swedenborg, Henry James, Sr., and James himself, Fechner had passed through a religious crisis that transformed his view of the world. Everywhere, Fechner saw matter imbued with spirit. James's radical empiricism asserted that reality and the field of consciousness were co-mingled and Fechner's panpsychism became particularly attractive.

Throughout James's writings in the 1900s, for instance, we see reference to the provocative idea that "there is a continuum of cosmic consciousness, against which our individuality builds but accidental fences, and into which our several minds plunge as into a mother sea or reservoir."[78,79] While Fechner was an incurable monist, James adopted the attitude of a pluralist precisely because pluralism admitted a monism like Fechner's as one of life's viable options.

For Fechner, James said, the abstract lived in the concrete, and the original sin of both popular and scientific thinking is the habit of regarding the spiritual not as the rule, but as an exception in the midst of nature. "The hidden motive of all he did," James said, "was to bring what he called the daylight view of this world into even greater evidence, that daylight view being this, that the whole universe, in its spans and wavelengths, exclusions and envelopments, is everywhere alive and conscious."[80] Fechner first speculated on the inner life of plants. The consciousness, he wrote, may be of an entirely different quality than that of humans, commensurate exclusively with the type of organization they possess.

Fechner also believed the earth had a higher, more general conscious life than the merely human. In fact, the Earth-Soul, as he called it, and all of the other planets, are God's angels, intermediaries between God and man. Passionately believing in the Earth-Soul, Fechner treated the earth as our special guardian angel of superior consciousness, because it did not need the usual arms, legs, circulatory and breathing apparatus, or brain and nervous system to function. Her moving, breathing, circulation, and her innumerable unifying and correlative functions go on nevertheless.

We as persons are sense organs of the Earth-Soul and contribute what we can from our quarter, which ceases when we die. But our *effect* lives on as the immortal contribution of each unique being, influencing all others who survive us. Vague as the system of Fechner's may seem, James said, the one definite connection is that we must first come to terms with the Earth-Soul if we are to evolve any higher. We must first, James implied, develop an "earth-consciousness."

In his final works James suggested, still following Fechner, the importance for psychology of studying the "fall of the threshold" of normal awareness. Reiterating his earlier hypothesis of the *Varieties,* James said that states of mystical intuition may be only very sudden and great extensions of the ordinary field of consciousness. Despite the fact that the ordinary psychologist disposes of such phenomena under the conveniently "scientific" title of *petite mal,* if not "bash" or "rubbish," and since we know so little of the noetic value of such states, it was James's opinion that we develop a more sympathetic attitude and patiently continue to collect the facts for a long time to come. For he said, "We shall not *understand* these alterations of consciousness either in this generation or the next."[81]

POSTSCRIPT

Given the cataclysmic pace of the revolution now underway in the neurosciences, we may look back and conclude that James's forecast was indeed prophetic.

After his death in 1910, in an era of spectacular gains in neurophysiology, the overriding influence of positivism in the nature sciences, and technological advances unprecedented in the history of modern civilization, psychology splintered into rival schools, a not entirely maladaptive example of evolutionary differentiation. The German experimental laboratory ideal came to dominate American academic departments of psychology, quickly followed by the vogue of Watsonian and then Skinnerian behaviorism. Psychologists in the workplace became associated with mental testing. The treatment of psychopathology, long dominated in America by the French experimental psychology of the subconscious, psychical research, and the so-called Boston School of Psychotherapy, was displaced by Freudian psychoanalysis, the only form of depth-psychology able to withstand the positivist onslaught, at least within clinical psychiatry and the social sciences. Gestalt psychology, the laboratory-based heresy from Germany, appeared in the 1920s, but never fully succeeded in penetrating the epistemological barriers of experimental psychology. For all intents and purposes, from 1910 to the mid-1970s, the study of consciousness was a dead issue in psychology.

True, psychoanalysis, with its focus on unconscious processes, helped to spawn the psychosomatic movement from the 1920s to the 1940s and finally came to control clinical teaching in psychology and psychiatry during the 1950s, but its status as a legitimate science has never been a foregone conclusion. Thus, it has had no influence on the methodology of laboratory empiricism. Its progeny, object relations theory, enjoyed a brief period of notoriety because it focused more on the adaptive functioning of the ego, but this too failed to have any impact on the study of consciousness by normative science. Meanwhile, existential psychiatry and psychology, which focus directly on the dynamic processes of inner experience, have been kept at bay by being subsumed under clinical practice, or else relegated to the subcatagory of philosophical psychology or the psychology of religion, endeavors seen as more in the domain of the humanities than the sciences. At the same time, altered states of consciousness became a focus of humanistic and transpersonal psychology from the 1960s onward, but these movements have been discounted by most academic psychologists and historians of science as experiential folk-psychology.

The scientific study of consciousness is only a recent phenomenon in American psychology, made possible largely by advances in other disciplines. The so-called cognitive revolution had to be fueled first by developments within the neurosciences, in turn driven by advances in computer technology. Sperry's theory of the emergent properties of consciousness in the evolutionary process, which won him the Nobel Prize, was based on neurophysiological evidence for hemispheric lateralization. The computer modeling of brain states led eventually to the holistic implications of artificial intelligence. The new information hypothesis in molecular biology and the discovery of the endogenous opiates have lead to spectacular advances in understanding the neuropeptide network, which may unlock the key to the biochemistry of the emotions and to understanding the conscious alteration of mood states. Modern interest in behavioral medicine, which includes such formally neglected areas as the study of yoga, meditation, hypnosis, biofeedback, and the emerging field of psychoneuroimmunology, presage new developments in the relationship between consciousness and immune competence in health and disease.[82]

These developments suggest that we may be only now on the verge of understanding what James envisioned more than a century ago as an evolutionary theory of consciousness.

ACKNOWLEDGMENTS

Acknowledgments are gratefully extended to Houghton Library for permission to consult the James material in their collections, to Mrs. Stanley Smith Stevens for access to James's marked copy of Darwin's *The Expression of the Emotions in Man and Animals,* and to Richard Wolfe, Curator of Rare Books and Manuscripts at the Harvard Medical School, for access to the James Jackson Putnam papers. A great debt is owed to Robert J. Richards and William Woodward for sharing their interpretations of James on Darwin and to Robert Reiber and Jeri Sechzer of the New York Academy of Sciences who created the forum for the presentation of this work.

NOTES AND REFERENCES

1. James, W. 1868. Review (unsigned) of Charles Darwin's *The Variation of Animals and Plants under Domestication.* Atlantic Monthly **22:** 122–124. North Am. Rev. **107:** 362–368.
2. William James's Sources. James Papers, Houghton Library, Harvard. bMS Am 1092.9 (4578).
3. Darwin, Charles. 1863. Variation of Plants and Animals under Domestication. WJ 516.78. Houghton Library, Harvard.

4. Courtesy of Mrs. Stanley Smith Stevens, Cambridge, Massachusetts.
5. PERRY, RALPH BARTON. 1935. The Thought and Character of William James, Vol. **1:** 262–265. Little, Brown. Boston.
6. James purchased the volume for $3.50 from the Merrill Book and Stationery Company, located on 35 East 3rd St. in St. Paul, Minnesota. There is only one entry in the hand-penciled index on one of the last blank pages of the book: "Echolalie in Bateman on aphasia, 1870, p. 110." A bookmark is inserted between pages 282 and 283 on which is scribbled the note "225 frown[s] open mouth w/ surprise, 283." Page 225 refers to the natural progression of frowning, then crying in young babies who have been exposed to some noxious event. Page 283 concerns the probable biological significance of unconsciously opening one's mouth during moments of wonder, surprise, or astonishment. No other marks were made in the book, not even on those pages later referred to in James's *Principles of Psychology* (1890, Holt, New York). This volume came from the 95 Irving Street library and was given to Mrs. Stanley Smith Stevens by John S. R. James in 1965.
7. PERRY,[5] vol. I, p. 803.
8. PERRY,[5] vol. II, p. 277.
9. PERRY,[5] vol. II, p. 700.
10. DUPREE, A. HUNTER. 1959. Asa Gray: 1810–1888. Harvard University Press/Belknap. Cambridge, MA. pp. 252–253.
11. TAYLOR, E. I. 1989. William James and C. S. Peirce: A reappraisal. Paper presented at the Charles S. Peirce Sesquicentennial Congress, Sever Hall, Harvard University, September 12, Cambridge, MA.
12. See also Francis Darwin *In* Life and Letters of Charles Darwin. 2 volumes. New York. 1925 edition (first pub. 1888). **II:** 323–324, 342–343; John Fiske *In* Darwinism and other Essays. 1888. New York. Madden, E. H. 1954, Wright, James, and radical empiricism. J. Phil. **1:** 868–874; and Madden, E. H. 1952. Chauncey Wright. Forgotten American philosopher. Am. Q. **4:** 25–34. Also Weiner, Phillip. 1945. Chauncey Wright's defense of Darwin and the neutrality of science. J. History Ideas **6:** 19–45.
13. DARWIN, FRANCIS. 1925. Letters of Charles Darwin. New York. pp. 342–343.
14. STRAUSE, JEAN. 1980. Alice James: A Biography. Houghton Mifflin. Boston. p. 137.
15. STRAUSE,[14] pp. 178–179.
16. James Jackson Putnam Papers, Rare Books, Countway Library of Medicine, Harvard, dated November 8, (1877?). See also William James's manuscript lectures on automatism, originally delivered for the Lowell Institute as part of a series entitled "The Brain and the Mind," 1877–78 season. James Papers, Houghton Library, Harvard. There is also a reference to Darwin's comments on automatism in *The Life and Letters of Thomas Henry Huxley*, by Leonard Huxley, New York, 1901.
17. JAMES, HENRY JR., Ed. 1920. W. James to Charles Eliot Norton, June 26, 1901. *In* The Letters of William James. Vol. **2:** 151–152. Atlantic Monthly Press. Boston.
18. See, for instance, Richards, Robert J. 1982. The personal equation in science: William James's psychological and moral uses of darwinian theory. Harvard Library Bull. **30(4):** 387–425. And more recently, see Richards, R. J., 1987, Darwin and the emergence of evolutionary theories of mind and behavior. University of Chicago Press. Chicago.

19. JAMES, W. 1867. Review of Grimm. The Nation (Nov. 20): 432–433; 1868. Review of Liébeault. The Nation **7** (July 16): 50–52; 1868. Review of Bernard. North Am. Rev. **107:** 322–328. For the Darwin reviews, see James[1] above.
20. The editors of the William James Critical Edition Collected Works project had been aware of the 1865 James reviews before my independent discovery of them in 1982. I pointed them out to Professor Gerald Myers in 1982, who subsequently noted them without comment in his *William James: His Life and Thought.* (New Haven: Yale University Press) in 1986. The reviews have since been reprinted in Burkhardt, F., Bowers, F., and Skrupskelis, I., Eds. 1987. The Works of William James: Essays, Comments and Reviews. Cambridge: Harvard University Press. pp. 197–208.
21. JAMES, WILLIAM. 1865. Review (unsigned) of Huxley's "Lectures on Elements of Comparative Anatomy.' North Am. Rev. **100** (January): 290–298; 1865. Review (unsigned) of Wallace, E. R. 1865. Origin of the human races and the antiquity of man, deduced from the theory of natural selection. North Am. Rev. **101:** 261–263.
22. Index for the *North American Review.*
23. JAMES, W. Review of Huxley, handwritten ms. attributed to James by C. E. Norton; Review of Wallace, handwritten ms. by James, confirmed by C. E. Norton, Charles Eliot Norton Papers, Houghton Library, Harvard. There can be no doubt of the authorship of these reviews, as they are in James's unmistakable handwriting.
24. JAMES, W. to C. E. Norton, Sept. 13, 1864. Norton Papers. Houghton Library, Harvard.
25. JAMES, W. to C. E. Norton, Nov. 14, 1864. Norton Papers. Houghton Library, Harvard.
26. JAMES, W. to C. E. Norton, Nov. 17, 1864. Norton Papers. Houghton Library, Harvard.
27. JAMES, W.[20] Review of Huxley.
28. JAMES.[20] Review of Wallace.
29. For a discussion of James's controversy with the Social Darwinists, see Richards, Robert J.[18]; see also James, W. 1880. Great men, great thoughts, and the environment. Atlantic Monthly **46:** 441–459.
30. JAMES,[29] p. 448; also Clark, John Spencer 1917. The Life and Letters of John Fiske, Vol. **2:** 192–193. Houghton Mifflin. Boston. I have freely appropriated Fiske's comments on James and Spencer.
31. JAMES, W. 1894. Review of W. Bateson's *Materials for the Study of Variation,* treated with especial regard to discontinuity in the origin of species. Psycho. Rev. **1:** 627–630.
32. JAMES,[31] p. 628.
33. JAMES,[31] p. 630.
34. See, for instance, Dupree.[10]
35. PALEY, WILLIAM. 1859. Moral Philosophy, with additional dissertations and notes by Alexander Bain. W. R. Chambers. London. Paley, W. 1785. Principles of Moral and Political Philosophy. R. Foulder. London. Emerson's copy is *Ac85/EM345/Zy788p; Thoreau's copy is *Ac85/A1191/Zz791p. See also, Judd, B. 1828. Paley's Moral Philosophy, Abridged and Adapted to the Constitution, Laws, and Usages of the United States of America. Collins and Haay. New York. James Jackson Putnam's copy, PHIL 205.40.13. All in Houghton Library, Harvard.

36. PALEY, WILLIAM. 1821. Natural Theology. Miscellaneous Works, vol. 4. Annotated, #272 on the list of William James's Sources.[2]
37. See Taylor, E. I. 1982. Some historic implications of Swedenborg's spiritual psychology. Invited address for Division 36 of the American Psychological Association, 90th annual meeting, Washington D.C., August 26, 1982, reprinted with additions in *Studia Swedenborgiana,* January, 1983, **4(4):** 5–38.
38. WILKINSON, J. J. G. 1849. Swedenborg: A Biography. Otis Clapp. Boston. p. 25. See also, Transactions of the International Swedenborg Congress, 1910, Swedenborg Society. London, for statements on Swedenborg's scientific contributions.
39. GOERKE, HEINZ. 1973. Linnaeus, trans. Denver Lindley. Scribner. New York.
40. See, for instance, Arrhenius, G. 1988. Swedenborg as cosmologist. *In* Swedenborg and His Influence. E. J. Brock *et al.,* Eds.: 179–186. Academy of the New Church. Bryn Athyn, PA.
41. Adapted from Potts, J. F. 1888. The Swedenborg Concordance, vol. 1. 862–869. (Swedenborg Society, London); and Swedenborg, E. 1906. Angelic Wisdom Concerning the Divine Love and Concerning the Divine Wisdom, Rotch edition. New Church Union. Boston, MA (original edit. 1763).
42. BLOCK, MARGUERITE. 1968. The New Church in the New World. Octagon. New York.
43. TAYLOR, E. I. 1983. Ralph Waldo Emerson and the Swedenborgian Tradition at Harvard. Emerson Centennial Lecture, Swedenborg Chapel, Cambridge MA. April 27, 1983. Expanded in Taylor, E. I. 1988. Emerson: The Swedenborgian and Transcendentalist Connection. *In* Emanuel Swedenborg: A Continuing Vision. R. Larsen *et al.,* Eds.: 127–136. The Swedenborg Foundation. New York. See also, Hallengran, A. 1988. The Importance of Swedenborg to Emerson's Ethics. *In* Brock,[40] pp. 229–250.
44. TAYLOR, E. I. James John Garth Wilkinson: Homeopathic-Swedenborgian physician. The Swedenborgian and transcendentalist roots of American pragmatism. In preparation.
45. TAYLOR, I. E. The religious philosophy of Henry James, Sr. The Swedenborgian and transcendentalist roots of American pragmatism. In preparation. Until then, see Croce, P. J., 1988, A scientific spiritualism: The elder James's adaptation of Emanuel Swedenborg. *In* Brock,[40] pp. 251–262.
46. See Wilkinson, J. J. G. 1847. A popular sketch of the life and work of Emanuel Swedenborg. Tracts for the New Times. New York.
47. Radical empiricism, the name given by James to his entire philosophic endeavor, recognizes the world as a pluralism and all unitary theories about the world as merely provisional attempts at synthesis. Here is James's "ever not quite," that an "absolute unity, in spite of brilliant dashes in its direction, still remains undiscovered." Radical empiricism in psychology admits raw experience before the differentiation of subject and object as the basic data of the discipline. This is to say that no phenomenon of experience can be excluded from legitimate study simply because we lack the tools to measure it. Rather, radical empiricism admits fate, chance, freedom, and spontaneity into every equation. See, J. J. McDermott, Ed. 1977. The Writings of William James: A Comprehensive Edition.: 134–136. University of Chicago Press. Chicago.

48. See, for instance; Boring, Edwin G. 1950. A History of Experimental Psychology, 2nd ed. Appleton, Century, Crofts. New York. *versus* Bixler, Julius Seelye 1926. Religion in the Philosophy of William James. Boston. Marshall Jones.
49. See Murphy, Gardner. 1971. Frederick Myers and the subliminal self. J. Am. Soc. Psychical Res. **65(2):** 130–143.
50. Myers says to James, for instance, "Remember that in spite of our individual inferiority to Darwin, our collective work is far more important than Darwin's: more important insofar as the evolution of a boundless spiritual future is more important than the evolution of a finite terrene past." Quoted in Perry,[5] vol. II, p. 163.
51. See, for instance, James's review of Frederick W. H. Myers's *Human Personality and its Survival of Bodily Death,* 2 vols. (Longmans Green & Co., London, 1903) *In* Proceedings of the Society for Psychical Research, June, 1903.
52. See Murphy, Gardner & Robert O. Ballou. 1960. William James on Psychical Research. Viking. New York.
53. See Taylor, E. I. 1982. William James on psychopathology: The 1896 Lowell lectures on "exceptional mental states". Harvard Library Bull. **30(4):** 455–479.
54. Taylor, E. I. 1983. William James on Exceptional Mental States. The 1986 Lowell Lectures. Scribner. New York.
55. Munthe, Axel. 1929. The Story of San Michele. Dutton. New York. pp. 372–373.
56. James, W. 1901. Frederick Myers's services to psychology. Proceedings of the Society for Psychical Research. **17:** 13023. Reprinted in James, W. 1911. Memories and Studies. Longmans Green. New York.
57. Perry,[5] vol. II, p. 603.
58. Perry,[5] vol. II, p. 604.
59. Perry,[5] vol. II, p. 606.
60. Teuber, Marianne. 1982. New sources for cubism: William James and Pablo Picasso. Paper delivered at the Meeting of Cheiron, International Society for History in the Behavioral and Social Sciences, Salva Regina College, Newport, RI.
61. Perry,[5] vol. II, p. 613.
62. Perry,[5] vol. II, p. 610.
63. Perry,[5] vol. II, p. 612.
64. Perry,[5] vol. II, p. 618.
65. Perry,[5] vol. II, p. 619.
66. Perry,[5] vol. II, p. 73.
67. Bergson, Henri. 1907. *L évolution créatrice.* Alcan. Paris. James's copy is WJ607.75.2, Houghton Library, Harvard.
68. Perry,[5] vol. II, p. 603+.
69. James, W. 1977. A Pluralistic Universe. Harvard University Press. Cambridge, MA. (orig. pub. 1908).
70. Mitchell, Arthur, trans. 1911. Bergson's Creative Evolution. Henry Holt. New York.
71. For one assessment of James and Bergson, see: Kallen, Horace M. 1914. William James and Henri Bergson; A Study in Contrasting Theories of Life. University of Chicago Press. Chicago.

72. BERGSON, HENRI. Preface to the French edition of James's *Pragmatism.* English translation: On the pragmatism of William James. Truth and reality. *In* Bergson, H. 1946. The Creative Mind. Translated by M. L. Andison. Philosophical Library. New York. pp. 248–260.
73. PERRY,[5] vol. II, p. 586.
74. PERRY,[5] vol. II, p. 587.
75. PERRY,[5] vol. II, p. 627.
76. PERRY,[5] vol. II, p. 594.
77. Letters between James and Elwood Worcester, 1904–1908, in possession of the estate of the late Miss Constance R. Worcester, Boston, MA.
78. PERRY,[5] vol. II, p. 172.
79. JAMES, W. 1911. Memories and Studies. Longmans Green. New York. pp. 196–20, 201–202, 204.
80. JAMES, W. 1909. The doctrine of the earth-soul and of beings intermediate between God and man. An account of the philosophy of G. T. Fechner. Hibbert **7:** 280.
81. These quotations adapted from Taylor, E. I. 1981. The evolution of William James's definition of consciousness. Revision (Fall/Winter) **4(2):** 40–47.
82. See, for instance, TAYLOR, E. I. 1987. Prospectus for a person-centered science: The unrealized potential of psychology and psychical research. J. Am. Soc. Psychical Res. **81:** 313–337; TAYLOR, E. I. 1988. Cyberphysiology: The Science of Self-Regulation. Minneapolis: The Archaeus Project; TAYLOR, E. I. 1988. The new medicine and the new science: Do they have a history? Advances: J. Institute Adv. Health **5;3:** 50–56; TAYLOR, E. I. 1990. The current status of William James's psychology of the emotions. Paper presented at the 22nd annual meeting of the Cheiron Society. Westfield State College, Westfield, MA. June 24.

A Personal Perspective on the Development of Social Psychology

OTTO KLINEBERG

Department of Psychology
Columbia University
New York, New York 10027

In this paper I will address certain aspects, not only of my own work, but of the experiences and contacts with some areas in social psychology that I have had since the early days of the field and which seem to me to have some importance. On these I can write with more certainty than if I tried to encompass the whole area of social psychology and its development.

In preparing this paper, I experienced a mild shock. I was reading the December 1983 issue of *Contemporary Psychology,* which included a review by Dr. Bem Allen of Western Illinois University of three recent textbooks in social psychology.[1] He states his approach to the review thus: "I will consider each book separately here first enumerating materials unique to the book, then discussing its treatment of the following five topics which have generated much current data and about which there is a great deal of excitement among social psychologists as well as among students: Physical Attractiveness, De-Individuation, Rape, Applied Social Psychology and Androgyny."

I am not quite sure what he means by de-individuation; I think I understand the other terms. I am overwhelmed by the distance between what I know about social psychology and the areas that this reviewer regards as essential to a good contemporary social psychology text. Because social psychology does mean different things to different people, although perhaps not quite to the same extent as the Rorschach test, I hope that what I have to say will be acceptable as at least one view of what has happened of interest in social psychology as I have experienced it. I will deal with four interrelated areas of social psychology that have been of particular importance to me; a cross-cultural approach to social psychology, race differences, international affairs, and the social psychology of mental health and mental illness.

These four areas cut across one another and have to be seen in their interrelationships rather than as separate and individual areas.

A CROSS-CULTURAL APPROACH TO SOCIAL PSYCHOLOGY

I took my first course in social psychology while I was studying medicine at McGill. It was given by a young instructor, listed as a visiting assistant professor from Harvard, and I was able to attend, since fortunately it was given during hours when I did not have to be at courses in anatomy or physiology or clinical medicine. His course, given in 1923 (I received my medical degree from McGill in 1925), was based entirely on McDougall, whom we now remember mostly for historical reasons. The lectures dealt with one instinct after the other, with indications of how the instincts operated. I'm not sure whether there were more instincts than classes, but it worked out fairly well in that we finished the list of instincts by the end of the year. I remember his saying only one research technique was applicable in the area of social psychology and that was observation. This is an indication of how far psychology has moved since that day.

My next course was with Professor Woodworth at Columbia University in 1925–26. I learned a good deal from Woodworth, as all of us who had the honor and pleasure of knowing him would testify. But the one statement that has stayed with me ever since was a remark he made after discussing many different areas of investigation, including F. Allport's early research; "I think, perhaps, it may be true that all psychology is social psychology." When some years later I wrote my own text in social psychology, I found myself dealing with problems that now are largely relegated to other areas of psychology but which then seemed to me absolutely essential to include if we wanted to cover the area of social psychology. The whole area of differential psychology—perception and memory, motivation and emotional behavior, social pathology—all of these are based to such a large extent on social interrelationships that I thought Woodworth might be right in saying all psychology was social psychology.

When I came in contact with Harry Stack Sullivan, I found that he defined psychiatry as the study of interpersonal relations. This comes close to the area of social psychology and shows the interrelationship and the interpenetration of social psychology with the other social sciences.

Some years ago, I ran into the following quotation from a psychologist for whom I had very great respect and warm affection, namely, the great E. L. Thorndike. Thorndike wrote, as far back as 1913, "The original nature of man is roughly what is common to all men, minus all adaptations to tools, houses, clothes, furniture, words, beliefs, religions, laws, science, and the arts." He went on to say, "From human nature as we find it, take away first all that is in the European, but not in the Chinaman, all that is in the Fiji Islander, but not in the Eskimo, all that is local and temporary." My reaction was twofold: First, how can we take away what is in the Chinese or the Eskimo but not in other groups unless and until we know a great deal more about what is in them? The second part of my reaction was that if you take away those qualities that are unique to a culture, you're taking away some of the most exciting and interesting phenomena of human behavior that you might otherwise get to know and enjoy. Certainly knowledge of the Chinese means more than simply eliminating the ways in which they differ from Eskimos—it also means getting to know in what ways each culture is unique. Surely, that is social psychology in the broad sense if anything ever was.

I certainly was not the only proponent in psychology, even at that early time, to propose that we social psychologists learn more about the rest of the world. Sherif[2] in his textbook and Sherif and Sherif[3] in their later work, were among those who had been influenced by sociological and anthropological concepts and research, and they urged that we look at other societies besides our own. As many of you know, Sherif himself wrote a little book very early on called *The Psychology of Social Norms* (1936),[4] which showed the considerable influence of the work that he had done in cultural anthropology.

Does this mean cultural relativity? That everything that is human is based entirely upon what we learn as members of a particular society? Is there nothing common-human? Is there nothing biological that unites humanity? I would say that many of us who work in this area did adopt a position of cultural relativity, but within limits. Even though in some critiques of my own papers and books, I have been labeled an environmentalist, as if I saw nothing in biology that was at all important, my actual position has always been much closer to that of my dear friend and teacher, Gardner Murphy, who wrote a book called *Personality: A Biosocial Approach to Origins and Structure.*[5] The biosocial always seemed to me to be of the greatest importance, and we had to keep that constantly in mind as we were addressing these problems.

One of the earliest proponents of a more-or-less full-fledged cultural relativity was the sociologist Sumner, who in 1906 in his book on this general area, wrote that the mores can make anything right.[6] This has sometimes been used as a shorthand slogan for cultural relativity in general. Another American sociologist at the University of Chicago, Robert Parks, agreed but added, "That's a very important idea, but they (that is, the mores) have a harder time making some things right than others." I would strongly subscribe to the idea that the mores can make anything right. Yes, they can, but they have a harder time making some things right than others. If we look at the anthropological material dealing with one of the most fundamental of all human relationships, namely, the mother-child relationship, we may be struck by the fact that in certain societies, relatively simple in other respects but complicated in their social relationships, adoption has been practiced to such an extent that it is rare to find children with their own biological parents. Children are exchanged, are sent from one family to live with another, and if one tries to build genealogical trees of relationships of the family, one fails, because in some cases people simply do not know who are their biological parents and who are their adoptive parents. If, however, we look at all societies in the world, we find this a rarity, compared with the frequency with which parents live together with their own children, and mothers keep their own children rather than exchange them for others. This suggests that it is easier to find certain behaviors which apparently do have a biosocial origin, than it is to find other behaviors. It is also wrong to go the whole length with cultural relativity, as some people have done. We certainly need to know something about the rest of humanity if we want to speak about social psychology. We need to know how motives work in other societies besides our own. We need to know how emotions are expressed by other people, and the ways in which they communicate in the expression of emotions. We need to know a great many things that we can never learn if we stay within our own society.

Woodworth was responsible for my writing a textbook in social psychology. He, at that time, was the white-haired boy at Holt's because his textbook in general psychology was a great success. He was asked if anyone at Columbia would write a textbook in social psychology, and he was kind enough to mention my name. The last thing in the world I thought of at that time was to write a textbook; however, this invitation came shortly after I had undergone a kind of conversion, which was similar to a religious conversion. That conversion occurred when I first had contact, during the period when I was studying for my doctorate in psychology, with the anthropologists: people like Boas, Benedict, Sapir, and later on, Margaret Mead, and still later on, Malinowski, Lowie and Kroeber, and many others. The result was that it seemed to me impossible to speak about general psychology if we knew only our own students and others like ourselves. Only if we knew the rest of the world could we develop a social psychology worthy of the name. Because of this feeling, I decided that I would write the textbook, and it appeared first in 1940 with the second edition in 1954.[7]

In writing this textbook, I made an attempt to indicate what seemed to me the major trends that were operating in the area of social psychology. I identified three such trends: The first was that it was growing increasingly comparative, not only in the sense of comparison with animal behavior, but comparative in the sense of being related to the behavior of other communities, other cultures, other societies, and not based only on the work being done in our own community. Second, it was growing increasingly experimental and statistical. Third, it was growing increasingly applied.

I, therefore, in this textbook moved from McDougall's instincts to what I called dependable motives, which differed in the degree of dependability and which seemed to me to give us some information as to how sure we could be that certain forms of behavior could be predicted to occur with any regularity, with any certainty, in the societies of the world.

If I were asked what I believe to be the most important contribution that I have made to social psychology, I would probably place in the first rank my insistence on the importance of a cross-cultural approach to all social psychology problems. Nevertheless as I look at contemporary textbooks in social psychology, I find very few of them paying any attention to the cross-cultural approach—very few indeed. It is a rarity to find anything in a textbook in social psychology which takes into account the cross-cultural approach that I have been preaching. On the other hand, a whole area of cross-cultural psychology has now developed and is flourishing. In 1979 and

1980, Triandis and his colleagues published a six-volume handbook on cross-cultural psychology.[8] Even a look at the table of contents will indicate the tremendous range and number of different problems that have been studied from this point of view. It could be argued that, if this problem is so important and if it is not being dealt with by social psychologists, at least it is being dealt with by cross-cultural psychologists. Still, I think that it is a pity that this point of view has lost ground to such an extent in social psychology texts, and I can just repeat my conviction that we can only build a social psychology if we know how people behave in all varieties of society and not just in our own.

RACE DIFFERENCES

Another area, race differences, is one that has concerned me as long as I have been a psychologist. I conducted my first investigation in the area of race differences in the summer of 1926, when I went to the West Coast to work with Indian and white children near the town of Toppenish, Washington. I went more or less by accident, because friends who were working toward doctorates in anthropology asked if I wanted to come along and test the children. This work became the basis of my doctoral dissertation, to which I will refer later. My own work, then, began with American Indians (Amerindians) and then later extended to Negroes (blacks) and also to certain European groups. The general situation in psychology at that time was that the idea of innate racial differences was very widely accepted, although dissenting opinions were sometimes heard. The generally held opinion was influenced by the results of the application of intelligence tests to groups of different ethnic backgrounds. For the most part, psychologists expressed the opinion that, because after all the tests could not tell lies and since the tests measured "native intelligence" without any interference by anything else, then obviously if the differences that emerged were so striking, this must mean fundamental, inborn race differences existed. Sociologists and anthropologists, more aware of and more concerned with the way in which the individual was shaped in society by cultural and educational factors, were much less ready to accept that notion. I was not the first psychologist to question the results of these tests. But, I would say as objectively as possible that my early work on Negro intelligence and selective migration and then later my book *Race Differences* were quoted frequently at one time and gave rise to a number of public lectures on my part.[9] (Incidentally, this book was requested by Gardner Murphy, who at that time was the editor of a series in psychology for Harper's. It was Woodworth who later asked me to write a social psychology text.) Anastasi, in her books on differential psychology, made many references to my research.[10] One reviewer even used the phrase "hidden dynamite" to refer to the content of my book *Negro Intelligence and Selective Migration,*[11] because there was then this widespread view that blacks were, on the average, inferior; and my results were fairly definitive in the opposite direction, indicating, for example, to what extent the level of measured intelligence varied, depending on where and how long the children went to school, in what part of the country, to what kinds of schools, and so forth. I was able to demonstrate that there were marked changes in this level of "intelligence" obtained by the intelligence test, depending upon the varieties of background of the children who were tested.

I suppose I was, without knowing it, playing with dynamite; one of my friends and colleagues, Marshall Segall of the University of Syracuse wrote in a recent volume that I showed courage "in daring to study inter-group relations at a time when academic respectability demanded obeisance to pure science." I was pleased that he thought I showed courage, but I must admit that I never thought of it as requiring any particular courage at all. I was interested in this area; I thought it was important; and the fact that it was different in nature from that which so many of my colleagues studied, especially at Columbia at the time, did not lead me to feel that I was doing anything dramatic or dangerous or daring by working in a different area. On the contrary, I did this because I found it fascinating, and I thought it was important. My colleagues, who have sometimes been portrayed as unified in opposing the work that I did, were not, by any means, unanimous in that respect. Gardner Murphy was a great support, and Woodworth was understanding even when he was not at all sure that I was right when I started on this research. He was sympathetic to my interests and supported me as much as anyone would need in connection with the preparation of my doctor's dissertation. It was Woodworth who brought to my attention the results of his own reading of a study that I had missed up to that time: It was a study by R. P. Rohner in Oklahoma on the intelligence test performance level of Osage Indians.

This tribe had lived originally in what became North Carolina and were relocated in Oklahoma. At that time, test results showed that American Indian children were below all other groups of children in the United States in their mental test level. Their average IQ, if we can still use a term that is beginning to be outdated, was inferior to that of all other ethnic groups studied in the United States with the exception of these Osage Indian children. (I remind you that it was Woodworth who brought this to my attention.) These Osage children showed an IQ somewhat higher than 100, a little higher than that of white children with whom they were being compared. The reason Rohner gave for this was that after the Osage Indians had been settled in Oklahoma, oil was found on their land. This oil did not make them millionaires, because the royalties had to be divided among a lot of families. But it did mean that they could have better schools and have automobiles; they hired good teachers, and their IQs went up to a level slightly beyond that of the white children with whom they were compared. In lecturing on this subject, I always tell this story which I got from Woodworth and which I later checked on myself; and I usually add that all you need to do if you want the minority groups to reach a level at least equal if not superior to that of the comparison group is to find oil on their lands.

This is one of the studies I wish I had done myself, but the next best thing was to let other people know about it.

In this area of race differences, or innate versus culturally determined group differences, my position has caused me to be put into the environmentalist category. My position and the position that many others have followed is that a negative attitude toward group differences as based on innate intellectual differences is not the same as saying that heredity plays no part. I happen to believe that heredity is required to help explain the variations that one finds within the very same community—within a community where all the members are equal in the opportunities for learning, equal in their acceptance by the society, and which, in all probability, must be explained by the presence of hereditary factors. Here I follow the example and the statement made by my friend at McGill, Donald Hebb, who many years ago said, "All our behavior is due 100% to our heredity and 100% to our environment." I think that is a very important comment and a very true one. Certainly what any of us *can* do requires a certain biological heritage to start with, but what we *do* with that heritage depends so much upon the opportunities we have had to develop it.

Some years ago, I attended a meeting in Stockholm under the auspices of the Nobel committee at which one of the speakers was Gunnar Myrdal. Any of you who have read anything in the field of race know about his classic contribution in this field. Myrdal in the year 1969 said that the notion of inborn racial differences in intelligence has now disappeared, which is a very good thing because it is not possible to defend it scientifically in any way. This was just about the same time that A. R. Jensen published his first monograph in the Harvard Educational Review in which he reopened an issue that had, by this time, apparently faded away. So much has been said and written about Jensen, and so many people have commented on him that my remarks shall only be in terms of the recent work that Jensen and his colleague in London, H. J. Eysenck, have been doing. They have published work on the measurement of reaction time as a rather simple form of measurable behavior—reaction to variable stimuli—in which the subject makes a distinction between stimuli and reacts to them as quickly as possible. They have found substantial positive correlations between the results on IQ as measured on a general intelligence test and the results obtained by this research on reaction time. They have argued that because reaction time is based upon fundamental, innate psychological phenomena and is not susceptible to learning or culture, it becomes all the more important to measure these simpler activities, hence the significance of the substantial correlation between speed in these reaction-time experiments and the general measurement of intelligence. They build on this positive relationship an additional story to their edifice in favor of the likelihood of fundamental, inborn group differences by saying, "You see, even in an area where culture is at a minimum, you still get this fundamental phenomenon of group differences."

My own research for my doctorate at Columbia (published in 1928) was based upon this very phenomenon of speed of reaction.[12] When I went to the

Yakima Indians in the State of Washington, I took along a group of performance tests and very quickly made a discovery that was entirely unexpected. (It is not true that we psychologists always find what we set out to find.) Using performance tests, I asked all the children to put the pieces in their proper places as quickly as possible. The white children scrambled around to do this as quickly as they could, whereas the Indian children, in general, would look at these pieces, and very slowly and deliberately, or so it seemed to me, pick up one piece and put it, usually, in the right place. They made relatively few errors as compared with the whites, but they used a great deal more time. This was the unexpected discovery. I had no idea that that would occur. I was just trying out the test on these two groups of children, and to my surprise, it was the substantial variation in speed which struck me as the real difference in their behavior. I don't have to add that since so many intelligence tests and performance tests are based upon speed, in part, this seemed to me to be a fundamentally important factor. I tried to explore, as much as possible, how speed of reaction worked in this case. One of the things I did was to compare the speed of reaction of these children with the speed of reaction of Indian school children going to Haskell Institute in Kansas, which was not on a reservation but in an environment that was open to Indian children from a great many areas and many different tribal groups. I found that these children at Haskell Institute, a more or less Westernized (or "whitened") kind of school, reacted much more quickly than the Indians living on the reservation. I also found that the black children in New York City reacted more quickly to a series of tasks than black children in a West Virginia rural community.

The theme of my Ph.D. thesis was the importance of speed as a factor affecting group differences in abilities. I point this out now because, as in so many cases, early research may be neglected in favor of what is new; Jensen and particularly, Eysenck, seem to be proceeding on the assumption that speed is so little contaminated by culture that it can be used as a measure of native abilities, because speed of reaction is so highly positively correlated with the measures of intelligence in general. My own work on speed suggests that the assumption that speed is a culturally uncontaminated quality is incorrect.

It was an easy move from the material dealing with race differences to the general problem of prejudice, discrimination, and relations among various groups. One study I like to cite that is as striking as the study by Rohner was done by a former student of mine, Eugene Hartley, and reported in his little book, *Problems in Prejudice.*[13] In this book he reports, among other things, the results of his measurement of degree of social distance or friendly or unfriendly reactions toward various groups—some real groups, but also three imaginary groups. The imaginary groups were the Wallonians, the Pirenians, and the Danerians. He found, on the average, just as much social distance shown against these three wholly imaginary groups as was shown against the real groups that were included in this study. The reason that that has always seemed to me to be so significant (another study I wish I had thought of) is that even if you had never been assaulted by a Pirenian or insulted by a Danerian, you may still, if you have generally negative attitudes toward other ethnic groups, extend this attitude even to groups of whom you have never heard anything and with whom you have never had any contact whatsoever. Meanwhile, the interest in Jensen and his colleagues continues; their publications appear rapidly. Eysenck has edited a new book with a chapter by Jensen on their recent research. Unfortunately, Myrdal, who was right on so many things, was not right in his belief that this idea has disappeared completely. We can only wait and see.

I want to include one more thing: As I work in this area, I have been struck by the number of people who have changed their minds from a position in which they promoted the idea of superior and inferior groups in intelligence, due to their heredity, to one of skepticism or even complete reversal of this position. After I had worked on European groups I ran into Brigham, the author of the book *A Study of American Intelligence,* sometimes regarded as one of the influences resulting in the reflection in our immigration laws of negative attitudes toward certain groups.[15] In this book he concludes that whites are superior to blacks, Northern Europeans to Central Europeans, and they, in turn, to Southern Europeans. When I told him about some of the work that I had been doing in Europe and said I would like to discuss it with him, he replied, "I don't stand by a word in that book." He had changed his mind completely, and for good statistical reasons, because he had found so much independence of the various items that were used to make up the tests. He is not the only one. Some of you who have worked in sociology may remember the name of Howard Odum, a former president of the American Sociological Society, who wrote as his doctoral thesis a book called *The Social and Mental Traits of the Negro,* in which he developed the notion of fundamental differences in the innate capacities of the two racial groups. Some years later, he wrote an article that he called "The Errors of Sociology." The leading error to which he draws attention is the former belief in innate psychological difference between whites and blacks as contrasted with the notion of the importance of social, cultural, and educational factors in determining such differences. Florence Goodenough[17] applied her draw-a-man test to children of various ethnic backgrounds; she decided that there were fundamental differences, and then discovered that cultural factors played such a part in determining how one draws a man, that her whole study fell completely to the ground, and she said so honestly and courageously. Garth, in his earlier work among the American Indians, took the position that there were almost certainly fundamental psychological differences, but changed his mind before he wrote the textbook *Race Psychology.*[18] Other examples can be given; I am awaiting the opportunity to give a lecture perhaps a few years from now, in which I can add the name of Jensen to this list.

INTERNATIONAL AFFAIRS

The third area to which I would like to draw your attention is that of international affairs. As with race, this has been a long-term interest of mine; when I was president of the Society for the Psychological Study of Social Issues some years ago I wrote my presidential address on the topic "A Science of National Character." It was not based on any of my own research; it was a library study. I give it as an indication of an early interest in this area of national differences and international relationships. A great impetus came to me from my appointment at UNESCO in 1948–1949, and again in 1953–1955. At the time that I first went to UNESCO, I was asked by the Carnegie Endowment and the Social Science Research Council to prepare a monograph on tensions affecting international understanding that appeared in 1950.[19] In Paris, I joined with Hadley Cantril, my predecessor in the post that I occupied, in conducting a seminar in which people like Gordon Allport and Harry Stack Sullivan and others participated. That was when Gordon Allport wrote his important paper on the psychology of expectations, in which he developed a position very similar to that which Merton took almost at the same time on "the self-fulfilling prophesy." When I went to UNESCO in 1953–1955, the head of the department was Alva Myrdal, with whom I worked for two years after having worked earlier in New York with her husband, Gunnar Myrdal. Among the activities that we encouraged at UNESCO were studies such as Gardner Murphy's in India, published in the book *In the Minds of Men* in which he and colleagues studied group tensions, particularly between caste groups and untouchables in India, as well as between Hindus and Muslims.[20] He encouraged a number of colleagues in that country to continue with this research on their own. We also helped to send Jean Stoetzel, my friend and colleague in Paris, to Japan; he wrote a book called *Without the Chrysanthemum and the Sword.*[21] Stoetzel's book was not so much a critique of Ruth Benedict's *The Chrysanthemum and the Sword*[22] as it was an indication that things had changed in Japan to such an extent that one could no longer use the symbols of the chrysanthemum and the sword to describe Japan. At UNESCO we worked with scholars from other countries on national stereotypes and national characteristics. A little later, I published with Wallace Lambert of McGill University a little book on the development of ethnic stereotypes in children.[23]

More recently, I have conducted a series of studies with students going to foreign countries, in order to determine the effectiveness of this as a possible contribution to the reduction of tensions between peoples.[24] It is still occasionally stated in public meetings that if only we knew each other better, if only we had more contact with others, our relations would be so much friendlier. This work that my colleagues and I did in eleven different countries included an attempt to discover whether the students going to other countries would really leave with a friendlier attitude or whether it made very much difference. There was one finding that I present, not as a discovery but as a hypothesis, which I think could be verified in further research. We were struck by the fact that in some studies of these international exchanges, the results indicated that there had been a great number of friendly relationships developed, whereas other studies indicate no change or even, in some cases, a slight change in the negative direction. I had the thought that maybe one of the reasons different people were getting different results was that they were doing the study at different stages in the experience.

Many of the studies were conducted during the year of the sojourn abroad. In a more recent study published in 1979 under the title, "At a Foreign University," with Frank Hull as my co-author, we studied not only students during their year abroad, but ten to fifteen years after they had returned home. We found that when we did that we got the idea pretty definitely that if one waited awhile, the results looked very much more friendly and favorable than if the study were conducted at the time of the sojourn abroad. For the foreign student, there are all kinds of problems that may develop. You may find that the university is not run in the same way as the one that you left. You have trouble figuring out what a French professor wants from you inasmuch as it differs from the expectations of an American professor. You may have difficulty making friends, and you feel lonesome and adrift. Later on, you find out that this whole experience was so valuable and had such a favorable influence on your whole career that even though you don't really forget all the unpleasantness, you reduce it to a lower level of awareness. This is a hypothesis which I think is correct, but I hope someone will carry out further research on a larger sample to make sure whether or not it is valid.

I want to conclude this section with a comment on the changing nature of psychological research and publications in the area of international affairs. I have recently read a paper, "Psychology and Nuclear War: A Chapter in Our Legacy of Social Responsibility," written by Jill Morowski and Sharon Goldstein.[25] Morowski is at Weslyan University, Goldstein is in New York. This paper struck me as being of very great interest. The authors point out first that the interest of psychologists in doing something about human affairs goes back almost to the beginnings of scientific psychology. The presidential address to the American Psychological Association in 1894 by Ladd urged psychologists to do what they could to solve the problems of humanity. In the following year, James McKeen Catell said something very similar, also as president of the APA. In Europe at about the same time, Claparède spoke to the Internation Psychological Congress more specifically about the fact that psychologists should be able to do something to reduce the likelihood of war. In the United States, however, the early research conducted was on issues such as: If we're going to have a nuclear war, how do we prepare people to handle the accompanying problems? What do we do to reduce the impact of all the death and destruction around us? How do we build morale among the soldiers in the army so that they will withstand the burdens placed upon them in a nuclear war? There seemed thus to be a tendency at that time, suggested by the authors of this paper as being frequent in the late forties and early fifties, to feel that some day we may be in a nuclear war, so the real issue is, How do we prepare for it?

A very great change in perspective has come about, with the emphasis on the horrors that nuclear war would bring, and raising the question whether psychologists could help to avoid nuclear war. In a paper I gave at Anaheim at the APA meetings that dealt with public opinion and nuclear war, I tried to make three points. The first was that this was a good moment for psychologists to try to do more than they have in the past; I found reference to psychological ideas and even research in the writings of so many nonpsychologists. For example, there have been many references to the work on the mirror image, the idea that we see in the Russians the same thing that they see in us, but in reverse; this is the kind of thing that Bronfenbrenner, Ralph White, and others have been working on. The idea of dehumanization, which means looking upon the "enemy" as less than human and treating them accordingly, is an idea that has been developed by psychiatrists and psychologists and that is now beginning to be used by others. My second point is that there has been a great increase in the relevant material being accumulated by people from a number of different disciplines, including psychologists. Third, the fact that so many people are becoming personally involved through demonstrations, participation in study groups, and so forth, means that maybe we now are in a position where psychologists can be more effective than has been possible in the past. I also tried at the International Congress in Acapulco in September of 1983 to raise some of these questions with psychologists from other countries. I felt that if psychologists are to do something, that "something" can be greatly multiplied if it can be done in collaboration with psychologists who are outside the United States, but who could come to an agreement with us on what psychologists could contribute in this area. Whether it is a nuclear freeze, or no first use of nuclear weapons, or the psychological effects of nuclear war on children, areas exist where the minds of psychologists from different countries can meet. We did try to do something like this about fifteen years ago, but we didn't carry it far enough.

MENTAL HEALTH AND MENTAL ILLNESS

My next and last area is the social psychology of mental health and mental illness, or social pathology in general. I had thought when I decided, in spite of my medical degree, to go on to a Ph.D. in psychology in order to become a professor of psychology, that I would be specializing in physiological or biological psychology, or some aspect of abnormal psychology, in order to make use of my medical training. Then, I got led astray by the anthropologists and social psychologists. It was through work with the World Federation for Mental Health that I moved back, at least partially, into the area of mental health, and joined with others to try to build an international, nongovernmental, nonpolitical association in the area of mental health. We started this activity by meeting in Roffey Park, which is outside of London. The meeting included Harry Stack Sullivan; anthropologists, including Margaret Mead; a number of sociologists and psychologists; and others, such as L. K. Frank, the man who introduced projective techniques into this country and was the chairman of that meeting. Brock Chisholm, the Canadian psychiatrist who was Director General of the World Health Organization, came frequently to visit us, as did Jack Rees, who was a leading psychiatrist in the British army during the war and was the founder and father of this organization. Our contribution, particularly Margaret Mead's and mine, was to emphasize the need for the federation to be cross-cultural in its philosophy and its activities. In this connection, we studied a number of different areas: old age; the search for positive identity, group as well as individual identity; problems of violence and crime; the relation of mental illness and mental health to rapid social change, particularly in Third World countries; problems of cultural factors determining food habits; ethnic relations; the role and status of women in various parts of the world; mental health issues relating to peace and war; and so forth. In the first publication of this organization, which was called "Mental Health and World Citizenship," we ended one section with this phrase which has been quoted many times: "The goal of mental health is to enable people to live together in one world." As you see, we have come full circle from the work I described in the beginning on a cross-cultural social psychology to the similarly cross-cultural mental health concerns presented at the end.

THE FUTURE OF SOCIAL PSYCHOLOGY

As to the future, although prediction is very difficult, I would like to try to indicate where I think social psychology is going. I will begin with the story of a man who, relatively late in life, decided that he wanted to be a musician. He brought home a cello and began to play. He apparently had a very patient wife, because after listening to him for a long time, she said, "You know, my dear, I love to hear you play the cello, but I have noticed that other cellists move their hands up and down, and they move the bow around. You keep playing in the same position all the time." He said, "You don't understand, my dear: They're looking for the right note; I've found it." I am tempted to state that social psychology has found the right note and let it go at that, but that would not be the whole truth. I recently attended a meeting of the Experimental Social Psychologists in Pittsburgh, and I'm happy to say that I understood about 50% of it, but I regret to say that I didn't understand the other 50%. I think this was mainly because my knowledge of statistics has great limitations which I have not been able to compensate for in recent years. The statistical area will continue and grow, and play a very important part in the future. We will also be doing a lot of field studies, that is, outside of the laboratory, but from the same scientific, objective point of view, at least as far as possible. This, of course, is in turn related to survey research, or attitude research, and I think that in social psychology this research will continue to be important. Another prediction I feel fairly safe in making is that there will be an extension of practical applications in the future, some of which will be in the direction of what might be called the social conscience of psychologists. The Society for the Psychological Study of Social Issues (SPSSI) started out a good many years ago as a kind of gadfly, or conscience, of the American Psychological Association, pushing it to be a little more concerned with affairs of politics and international and race relations, and so on. We now find, I think it is fair to say, that the American Psychological Association is just as far advanced in this respect as SPSSI is, to the point where the present role of SPSSI is under question now that the gospel has spread to the whole association. It was, as you know, the whole association that came out strongly in favor, just last year, of establishing a nuclear freeze as a first step in the direction of peace. My own guess is that the applied area will continue to develop, particularly the area of concern with important social issues, and more and more experimental and objective research will occur. The one thing that I think will not develop within social psychology in the immediate future is what I have called the comparative approach, because I see no evidence that current textbooks by social psychologists show great concern with the study of other cultures besides our own. I have already expressed my regret at that development. I also would *like* to see, and this I'm not so sure I can predict, more concern with the history of social psychologists' approach to the problems that we are dealing with and will be dealing with in the future. Publications these days show great attention to recent work and very little to publications that date more than four or five years back. It was Ben Jonson who said something like: "Confound these ancients. They have stolen all our best ideas." That may be an exaggeration; I'm not so sure we would always find that all our best ideas are in history, but I think we ought to have a look once in a while.

CONCLUSION

I have probably focused too much on myself, although I have tried to show my own activities only in relationship to what was happening in these areas. As I look back and try to judge my own work, I have probably spread my wings a little too far and wide, in at least four different areas. You cannot become a specialist in too many fields, and maybe I should have stuck to one, in which I might have done something a little more worthwhile. Nevertheless, my life has been much more interesting because I moved in a number of different directions. I owe a genuine debt to my teachers, my colleagues, and my students. Nearly everything that I have written was tried out on my students, and I profited from their comments and criticisms before I ventured to commit my texts to publication.

ACKNOWLEDGMENTS

A lot of people express appreciation to their wives, but I want to do so in a more than usually sincere fashion, because so much that I have done depended to such a large extent on her. When we wrote *Race Differences,* I wrote at the end of the page of acknowledgments that I would express my thanks to my wife if this book had not been hers as well as mine. Well, at the time she felt that was a nice, generous remark, and I thought myself it was reasonably generous, as well as honest, of course. A little later when the first edition of the social psychology text came out, I ended the preface to that by saying that my wife had helped me so much once again that her name should really appear as co-author of this book. I think we were both happy with that until my daughter happened recently to be reading at least the preface to my book and commented that if that was the case, why wasn't her name on the cover as co-author? Well, *we* wrote that book but *I* wrote my name on it at a time when, shall we say, the rights of women were not quite so widely or fully recognized. The fact that her training was in French history and not in psychology made me feel a little uncertain about the appropriate action, but if I had it to do over again, she would be co-author, so it is entirely appropriate that I publicly express my thanks to her once more.

REFERENCES

1. ALLEN, BEM P. 1983. Contemp. Psychol. **28(12):** 931–934.
2. SHERIF, M. 1947. The Psychology of Ego Involvements, Social Attitudes and Identifications. Wiley. New York.
3. SHERIF, M. & C. W. SHERIF. 1956. An Outline of Social Psychology. Harper & Row. New York.
4. SHERIF, M. 1936. The Psychology of Social Norms.
5. MURPHY, GARDNER. 1947. Personality: A Biosocial Approach to Origins and Structure. Harper & Row. New York.
6. SUMNER, W. G. 1906. Folkways: A Study of the Sociological Importance of Usages, Manners, Customs, Mores and Morals. Ginn. Boston.
7. KLINEBERG, OTTO. 1940. Social Psychology. Holt. New York.
8. TRIANDIS, H. C. 1979–1980. Handbook of Cross-Cultural Psychology. Allyn & Bacon. Boston.
9. KLINEBERG, OTTO. 1935. Race Differences. Harper. New York.
10. ANASTASI, A. 1937. Psychology: Individual and Group Differences in Behavior. Macmillan. New York.
11. KLINEBERG, OTTO. 1935. Negro Intelligence and Selective Migration. Columbia University Press. New York.
12. KLINEBERG, OTTO. 1928. Ph.D. thesis, Columbia University, New York.
13. HARTLEY, EUGENE L. 1946. Problems in Prejudice. Columbia University Press. New York.
14. EYSENCK, H. J., Ed. 1988. Individual Differences in Children and Adolescents. Hodder & Stoughton. London.

.15. BRIGHAM, C. C. 1923. A Study of American Intelligence. Princeton University Press. Princeton, NJ.
16. ODUM, HOWARD W. 1910. The Social and Mental Traits of the Negro. Columbia University Press. New York.
17. GOODENOUGH, FLORENCE. 1949. Mental Testing: Its History, Principles, and Applications. Rinehart. New York.
18. GARTH, T. R. 1931. Race Psychology: A Study of Racial Mental Differences. McGraw Hill. New York.
19. KLINEBERG, OTTO. 1950. Tensions affecting international understanding. Soc. Sci. Res. Council Bull. **62:**
20. MURPHY, GARDNER. 1953. In the Minds of Men. Basic Books. New York.
21. STOETZEL, JEAN. 1955. Without the Chrysanthemum and the Sword: A Study of the Attitudes of Youth in Post-War Japan. Columbia University Press. New York.
22. BENEDICT, RUTH. 1946. The Chrysanthemum and the Sword: Patterns of Japanese Culture. Houghton Mifflin. Boston.
23. LAMBERT, WALLACE & OTTO KLINEBERG. 1967. Children's Views of Foreign People. Appleton-Century Crofts. New York.
24. KLINEBERG, OTTO, MARIA ZEVALLONE, CHRISTIANE LOUIS-GUERIN & JEANNE BENBRICKA. 1979. Students, Values and Politics. Free Press. New York.
25. MOROWSKI, J. T. & SHARON E. GOLDSTEIN. 1985. Psychology and nuclear war: A chapter in our legacy of social responsibility. Am. Psychol. **40:** 276–284.

[*Editor's note*: This paper has been adapted from a talk given at a Psychology Section meeting of the New York Academy of Sciences in January of 1984. The list of references was generated from the transcript and is intended only to serve as a guide to writing and research that address the issues Dr. Klineberg has discussed here.]

American Psychology at the Crossroads

Science or Profession?

VIRGINIA STAUDT SEXTON

Department of Psychology
St. John's University
Jamaica, New York 11439

In two years (1992) we shall commemorate the founding of the American Psychological Association in 1892. Planning for the APA's celebration of this Centennial has already been started by the APA Task Force on Centennial Celebrations. All members are invited to unite in the association's celebration of a century of American psychology. Its hundredth anniversary stimulates reflection on our association's history and on the achievements of American psychology. While we reminisce about the past, our anniversary also inspires contemplation and planning for the future. What directions do we want our discipline, as science and profession, to pursue in the next century? What kind of psychology do we want, and does society need, if we are to promote human welfare? The future of American psychology and of the APA is ours to make.

But first, what about the present? American psychology today is in a twofold crisis—organizationally and as a discipline. The current reorganizational crisis in the APA reflects indirectly, I believe, a disunity crisis in psychology itself. The buzz word for American psychology in the 1980s has become *unity*—organizational unity in the APA and unity in the discipline of psychology. The crisis was most evident in the heated debates going on within the American Psychological Association about needed reorganization in 1987; in many ways the debates were reminiscent of the bitter, unyielding rhetoric of the pre-Civil War era in United States history. The APA crisis, however, is not new. It has, in fact, been perennial and has arisen because psychology is unique. It has a bifurcated character. It has tried to be at once a "pure" science and a profession. Relating the profession to the science of psychology has been, and as former APA president Donald Campbell observed in 1973 will continue to be, an organizational problem for the APA. Our national organization, APA, is the arena where the battles have historically been waged and is where they are again being waged in 1987. The basic issues are the science, politics, and the practice of psychology. As a historian of psychology, I would like to review the background of these issues in American psychology's development that underlies the present organizational crisis. This review will demonstrate that there have been several recurrent crises during the APA's first century.

BEGINNINGS OF AMERICAN PSYCHOLOGY

At the end of the 19th century, scientific psychology was imported from Germany. Its ready acceptance was concomitant with reforms in higher education. The traditional classics curriculum in colleges and universities yielded its place to science. Psychology as a new science readily won support. Recently, historian John O'Donnell[1] has pointed out, however, that psychology's early rise and popularity as an academic discipline cannot be attributed simply to an emphasis on science and an increase of scientific knowledge. He attributes it to the social processes, economic adaptation, and economic competition that molded American psychology and careers of those who pursued it.

Quite early in American psychology, dissension arose among the scientific psychologists themselves concerning the direction American psychology should take and the kind of organization the APA (originally founded in 1892 to advance psychology as a science) should be. British-born E. B. Titchener, professor of psychology at Cornell University—an important figure in American academic psychology and a strong protagonist of psychology as pure science—opposed the applications of psychology introduced by his academic research colleagues Hugo Münsterberg, Walter Dill Scott, and James McKeen Cattell, to name a few. He dealt with applied psychology by proposing that the name psychology be reserved for the science of psychology and that its applications should be designated as psychotechnology. Titchener became increasingly dissatisfied with the APA and, after failing to gain support for an organization to compete with the APA, formed his own group in 1904, The Experimentalists, who met independently from the APA, although most members retained membership in the APA. Following Titchener's death (1927) they continued under the name Society of Experimental Psychologists, as a small organization of about 50 self-selected members who were principally interested in experimental and physiological psychology. Subsequently, regional associations—Western (1921), Midwestern (1926), Eastern (1930), and Rocky Mountain (1931)—emerged as protagonists for experimental psychology, offering faculty and students increased opportunities to present their research papers.

Having abandoned its philosophical and theological entanglements, and vigorously insisting that it was a science, a natural science, American psychology made rapid strides in the first quarter of the 20th century. A phenomenal growth in laboratories, journals, and specialties ensued. Applications of psychology to education, law, business, and industry also progressed, but these by no means received the universal endorsement of experimental psychologists. For example, Lightner Witmer, Wundt's student and a professor of psychology who founded clinical psychology and the first clinic at the University of Pennsylvania in 1896, was ignored, as was clinical psychology, by academic experimental psychologists. To them, Witmer, as a scientist, appeared too loose and too speculative. Witmer's failure to gain their recognition seems to have heralded the beginnings of a mutual disdain between academic experimentalists and applied psychologists.

From about 1902 to 1911 the schools of psychology arose. American scientific psychologists, as structuralists, functionalists, and behaviorists, debated their diverse views concerning the content and method of their science. Out of that battle, behaviorism with its mechanistic emphasis emerged as a dominant force. Stimulation for various experimental studies was furnished by the rival schools whose violent controversy was temporarily interrupted by World War I when psychologists united to support the war effort.

Between World Wars I and II, academic psychology established a strong laboratory tradition. Within the laboratory the behavioristic psychology of learning of Thorndike and Watson prevailed. This psychology seemed to augur an exciting future for psychological science. As psychology's academic status improved, applied psychology also gained prominence because of its World War I contributions. For instance, group intelligence tests—Army Alpha and Army Beta—were developed. Classification of servicemen for various jobs was so successful that the methods used became the foundation for personnel classification in industry. Also, studies of morale in the armed services were produced that stimulated studies of morale among workers in industry. In addition, World War I inaugurated the use of personality testing of recruits. This was much expanded in World War II when psychologists began treating "troubled" servicemen with psychotherapy. At the end of the war, 44,000 mentally ill patients were in VA hospitals, and psychologists began to be trained in VA programs. Free training programs were provided, and they attracted large numbers of students. As psychologists moved into nonacademic occupations, conflicts arose between them and their academic colleagues who dominated the American Psychological Association. During the 1920s and 1930s applied psychologists struggled for status and recognition. Their minority status within APA led to the creation of such separate organizations as the Association of Clinical Psychologists (1917) and the American Association of Applied Psychology (1937). The latter made a strong impact. For a while it seemed as if the academics and professionals would go their separate ways in the APA and AAAP, respectively. It appeared as though there would be, on the one hand, a professional group comparable to that of physicians and, on the other hand, a scientific group comparable to psychologists. A major difficulty was that both the professionals and the scientists wanted to call themselves psychologists.

Compared to the applied areas, the number of persons interested in pure experimental areas that were formerly popular, such as sensation, perception, and language, decreased. In 1979, the historian O'Donnell described this period of American psychology as one of crisis for experimentation and suggested that Boring's principal motive in writing his famous *A History of Experimental Psychology* (1929) was to stem the rising tide of pressure by applied psychologists to achieve professional status before World War II.[2] Despite the progress of applied psychology before 1941, psychology remained a predominantly academic discipline. In 1941, when the United States entered World War II, the numbers of faculty and students in the universities decreased, and academic research was severely curtailed. However, the war created new service and research opportunities in the military, clinical, and industrial areas.

World War II played an important role in elevating the status of psychology. In their wartime service at home and in the military, American psychologists won distinction for their contributions to the successful selection and classification of both defense workers and armed services recruits and to the treatment of mentally disordered servicemen. Many of the 1500 psychologists in the armed services were ill-prepared for their tasks because formal professional training beyond that of assessor–diagnostician had not been available to them in most universities before 1940. They had to acquire their therapeutic skills on the job. However, war service firmly established an additional role beyond assessor–diagnostician for the professional in the clinical area—that of psychotherapist.

POST–WORLD WAR II PROFESSIONALIZATION

In the post–World War II period, psychological services were in enormous demand, and the supply of professional psychologists was meager. The federal government needed clinicians to attend the 44,000 neuropsychiatric patients in the VA hospitals. It then became imperative for psychologists, academic and professional, to unite and to institute long-needed and long-overdue changes of attitude, curricula, training, and professional standards. The first step was in the direction of organizational unity, an objective essential in creating and maintaining a proper public image of psychology. Accordingly, the American Association of Applied Psychology was dissolved and its objectives incorporated into a reorganized APA with newly stated objectives "to advance psychology as a science, as a profession, and as a means of promoting human welfare" (1945). To implement these objectives, the APA was transformed into a multidivisional structure. (Originally there were 18 divisions; in 1987, 45.) In their divisions the various specialties had autonomous units through which to pursue their goals. Professional psychologists, too, at last had a platform from which to launch a larger public campaign for acceptance and recognition.

The post-war Zeitgeist in the United States clearly supported behavioral science. Many benefits accrued to psychological science, not the least of which was generous government and foundation support for research and training. Government grants became available to help students finance their education, to enable the universities and colleges to develop and expand their psychological laboratories and research facilities, and to enable faculty to be released from heavy teaching schedules and to conduct research. At the same time, considerable support was provided for training clinical psychologists through VA and USPHS traineeships. In fact, as early as 1947,

Samuel Fernberger, a professor at the University of Pennsylvania, expressed his concern about the impact of these government programs on academic preparation and employment, noting that no academic institution could compete with government salaries, especially at that time.[3] He predicted dire effects on psychology as science because he felt that the best men and women would go into applied work for some years to come, motivated not only by the contribution they could make to human welfare, but also by the assurance of the excellent jobs and salaries promised. This situation, Fernberger maintained, would result in a reduction in the amount of strictly experimental research conducted and in the lack of availability of first-rate professors. Pure science, he insisted, must come before application. How right he was forty years ago!

During the 1950s and 1960s, academic psychologists had every reason to feel secure. Psychology was the most popular undergraduate major. Students in great numbers applied to graduate schools, attracted by generous fellowships, assistantships, and by excellent employment prospects in academe and in the community. Graduate departments of psychology flourished. College students aspired primarily to Ph.D. programs—the doctorate had become the standard for practice. Gradually, the universities began training more students for professional work than for careers in research and teaching. A determined campaign was soon instituted, too, to mold the character of the rapidly developing profession. Numerous training conferences were held. The first training model, originally developed in 1947, was that of scientist/practitioner, familiarly known as the Boulder model. By 1958, however, there was no agreement as to how well the Boulder model worked. Many professionals argued that they were not interested in research and that they were not getting adequate professional training. The dissatisfaction later led to the development of new training programs, professional schools, and to the Psy.D. But professionals are still not in agreement on these models.

Because of the excessive amount of time and APA resources going into professional concerns like licensing and legislation—urgent as they were for professionals—Division 3 (experimental psychology) members in the 1950s began to talk about withdrawing from the APA. While such a move was supported by only a minority, feelings on the matter were intense. This group preferred to pursue scientific work and to maintain APA dues at a minimum. At this point, however, psychologists in clinical, industrial, human engineering, and personnel significantly outnumbered those in nonapplied areas such as developmental, experimental, social, and personality.

Accordingly, Clifford Morgan (1915–1976), distinguished researcher in physiological psychology, a writer of textbooks and editor of *Psychological Abstracts,* in 1959 organized a group of more than 800 Ph.D. psychologists who were invited to join on the basis of their proven competence in psychological research. The new Psychonomic Society, as Morgan's group was called, sought to conduct annual meetings and disseminate recent research results in scientific psychology, especially through their *Bulletin of the Psychonomic Society.* They claimed that they did not want to fragment the APA and that Division 3 should remain part of the APA. The society aimed to preserve and foster high scientific standards for research and traditional academic values. They were uninterested in the rising professional concerns regarding licensing and practice issues. Hilgard has noted that, in spite of their good intentions, the Psychonomic Society was the first to generate a defection of members from the APA, although it did not threaten the APA.[4] Several other organizations like the Society for Research in Child Development (1934) also began attracting more APA scientist members to their organizations.

During the 1970s, and especially during the 1980s, academic dissatisfaction with the APA's preoccupation with pressing professional concerns such as licensing, advocacy, litigation, legislation, peer review, and insurance problems, and the concomitant escalation of membership dues that they necessitated, sharply intensified. Some academics resigned. Some never joined, many of them new Ph.D.s who had been advised by their mentors and graduate school professors not to join the APA. Consequently, in recent years the balance of power within the APA has shifted dramatically, with practitioners far outnumbering the academic psychologists, a situation very much resembling the situation in the state associations. The political and power structure of the APA has now become the reverse of what it was in the first half of the 20th century—and therein lies the current organizational crisis.

CRITICAL CONCERNS OF THE 1980s

Today both academics and professionals have legitimate concerns that continue to compete for APA attention and funds. What has added to the general disruption is the note of alarm that has been sounded by the recent report of the Committee on Employment and Human Resources entitled "The Changing Face of American Psychology," which points out that psychology is increasingly losing its traditional research base and its representation by persons trained in high quality research-oriented departments.[5,6] The report also warns that there is a marked decline in traditional research membership in the APA, as we have already noted. And yet society today is making increasing demands on psychology, as it struggles with problems on which psychology's help is desperately needed: surrogate motherhood, teen suicide, AIDS, child abuse, abortion, cults, crime and violence, drug and substance abuse, terrorism and ethnic and racial bias, women's issues, and gay and lesbian issues. Researchers and practitioners together must intensify research and develop strategies to cope with these problems if we are to promote human welfare. As in the past, we can surely unite and work together today in an APA, restructured by whatever plan, if we sincerely want to cooperate. In its history, psychology has had to face a tension common to all scientific groups, a tension between basic science and applied or technological interests, as, for example, between physics and engineering. As Isidor Chein observed in 1966, "The enterprises of science, technology, and welfare—individually, in paired combination, and collectively—are all big enough to have a place even for extremists, provided the latter are not endowed with the power to control or exclude others."[7]

From the foregoing review of psychology's organizational development, it is clear that clashes of interests and methods have generated disruptive tendencies in various forms in the past. At times the scientists have been disruptive, and at times the professionals have been disruptive. In spite of the disruption, psychology's national organization has been able to survive the controversies and storms and to resist dismemberment. Hilgard[4] has aptly summarized the situation pointing out that thus far American psychologists, in spite of their individual preferences and grievances, have been willing to recognize each other as sharing a common heritage to which the name *psychology* applies. In the United States up to now that common heritage has been formally represented by the American Psychological Association. In spite of intervals of tensions and struggles that have threatened the organization, it has continued to represent that common heritage of American psychologists. Indeed we must make it continue to do so. I firmly believe that the 95-year history of our national organization proves that we can master our present organizational crisis and preserve our organizational unity.

And now let us examine our second crisis situation, a crisis in psychology itself.

CRISIS IN THE SCIENCE OF PSYCHOLOGY

To further reduce diviseness among psychologists, we need more than unity of action in a reorganized APA. We need unity and coherence in the discipline of psychology. This goal will be far more difficult to achieve than organizational unity and will demand more time and energy of all of us well into our next century. To begin, we need to look at how our science has fared in the last decade or so while we have been distracted by internecine battles and by various restructuring plans.

American psychology has been changing rapidly in directions that are not completely appreciated by many psychologists. We have been responding to varied internal and external pressures challenging our science. Humanistic psychologists in the 1970s, disenchanted by behaviorism and psychoanalysis, attacked psychological science for failing to fashion psychology more directly as a human science. As Third Force protagonists, they chastised their experimental colleagues for avoiding the study of human behavior. On the other hand, animal rights groups have vehemently attacked psychological research using animals and denounced what they have perceived as undue cruelty to animals. Comparative and physiological psychologists have taken much of that pressure. Added complications and difficulties for the pursuit of both human and animal research have been occasioned by government legislation and regulation and decreased government support for research. Moreover, as job opportunities in academe and in research have declined, fewer and fewer students have been seeking Ph.D.s in experimental psychology. In the light of these serious challenges to psychological scientists, it is little wonder that their numbers have dwindled.

Moreover, experimental psychology—once a single field—is now split into numerous subspecialties such as neuropsychology, biopsychology, psychopharmacology, and psychoendocrinology. These hybrid sciences have led to a fragmentation of psychology and have in many cases brought psychologists in closer contact with scientists of other disciplines than with psychologist colleagues. As a result these specialists, finding that they have little in common with their psychologist colleagues, join interdisciplinary societies. This development, too, has contributed heavily to psychology's lack of unity.

As early as 1974 Koch called attention to psychology's fragmentation[8] and a little later Giorgi underscored psychology's disunity.[9] In the July/August 1980 issue of the *APA Monitor* Stephan Chorover, professor of neuropsychology at M.I.T., described the continuing division between American scientists and applied psychologists as a reflection of the division of labor in science.[10]

> Psychology students are socialized into progressively narrower and narrower channels, they are trained to become as different as possible. Training in psychology produces large numbers of highly specialized but uneducated people who find it harder to understand what others are doing. The division within APA is due to psychologists' inability to see the connection between what they do and what anybody else does. The field is in a terrible state of fragmentation.

In a similarly critical vein two professors of psychology at Bishop's University in Quebec, Lionel Standing and Stuart McKelvie,[11] reported in a recent issue of the *Bulletin of the British Psychological Society* that "overspecialization is damaging our discipline." They cite that there are too many "absurdly specialized" journals of psychology which draw off the better papers from the wider readership of general interest journals. In fact, they claim that only about 70 of the approximately 200 English-language psychology journals now in existence deserve to survive. They also note that 70% of the APA members do not subscribe to journals at all. Standing and McKelvie conclude that there is an incredible lack of interest in the whole publication enterprise. The amount of material published since the computer revolution is overwhelming. As one psychologist recently observed "even the best Evelyn Wood reader could go 24 hours each day for every day and, at the end of the year, have fallen behind all the information produced."

Fortunately, there is a growing realization and concern that psychology is chaotically divided and that the condition is progressively worsening. This realization has been recognized and expressed directly by a number of American psychologists such as Albert Gilgen, Amedeo Giorgi, Arthur Staats, and David Bakan and also abroad by psychologists such as Ruben

Ardila. Those psychologists who have addressed the problem of the disunity of psychology have identified some possible causes for its fragmentation. It has been suggested that they lie in psychology's emphasis on empiricism (Bevan); on novelty (Bevan, Maher, Staats); on pressure to publish experimental studies (Wachtel); as well as on methodological and organizational factors (Staats, Wachtel) and social factors (Bevan); computer revolution and the explosion of knowledge (Wittig). As Staats has observed there is yet another type of expression—a little less direct—that bemoans the lack of general meaning in our science and profession, the lack of direction, the subordination to aimless fads in research that later are abandoned, the overspecialization of psychology that makes things trivial, the parochiality of view, the ubiquitous contentiousness and lack of agreement, the plethora of experiments combined with the paucity of theory, and so on. In recent years it has been variously said that each particular field of psychology and the science of psychology itself are in a state of crisis because of these features of disorganization.

Different explanations of psychology's disorganization have been offered, as well as different opinions as to what should be done. Some believe that the problems of disorganization are the natural result of psychology's domain of study and that there is no remedy. These thinkers maintain that, unlike the natural sciences, scientific psychology is doomed to perpetual disorganization. In 1981 Koch argued that psychology should simply recognize that fact, and declare itself a number of different fields of study across which there will be no communication.[12]

It may indeed be that unification will be hard to achieve, but the history of science seems to demonstrate that the natural sciences were once just as disorganized as psychology, but that they are today unified in a manner that the behavioral sciences have not yet begun to approximate. Fortunately for physics and chemistry their task of developing from the disunified to the unified state was not so difficult as it will be for psychology. They achieved unification at a former time when there were few scientists and few scientific works so that the magnitude of the conflicting elements of knowledge did not reach the vast proportions of the modern disorganized science.

The history of science gives us assurance for concluding that psychology is still in the early stage of scientific development with respect to establishing consensual, unified knowledge. Psychologists today have the ability to derive empirical, theoretical, and methodological knowledge but have not yet learned how to make sense out of its seemingly conflicting elements. But the more critical problem—and the real crisis issue for psychology today—is that psychologists have not yet decided that putting the pieces together, that is, unification, is their goal. On the contrary, it appears that coming up with something different is the central goal. Consequently, there is progressive differentiation. If left in this condition there seems little hope that psychology can ever become a coherent discipline.

Fortunately, there is already a group of distinguished and concerned psychologists who established the Society of Uninomic Psychology (SUNI) in 1985 in an effort to study the critical issues of diversity and to examine the possibilities of unification. Among its concerns are the impact of conceptual fragmentation of American psychology on research, curricula, and applied fields, as well as the sociopolitical implications of psychology's present disunity for both the science and profession. The group's efforts and enthusiasm offer promise for developing a framework to accomplish unification of our discipline. The task will be long and arduous and may be an agenda item for psychology well into its next century, but unity in APA and unity in our discipline should be our objectives now and henceforth, until they are attained. American psychology's future as science and profession will be much better for our efforts.

SUMMARY

American psychology today is in a twofold crisis, organizationally and as a discipline. This crisis stems from psychology's bifurcated character as both a science and a profession. That the situation is perceived as critical is evident in the heated debates going on within the American Psychological Association about needed reorganization. But, more importantly, there is also a pressing need for unity and coherence within the discipline of the science of psychology. Current attempts at achieving unity in the American Psychological Association as well as minimizing psychology's disunity and lack of coherence are reviewed.

[*Note added in proof*: Since this paper was written, an APA reorganization plan was developed to try to solve the crisis. It was submitted to the membership for a vote, but was defeated. However, it did stimulate several changes that have healed some of the wounds of APA members. Some of the latter have left the APA and have started a new organization, the American Psychological Society. Many now retain APA membership as well as belonging to the APS, which focuses principally on science.]

REFERENCES

1. O'DONNELL, J. M. 1985. The origins of behaviorism. *In* American Psychology, 1870–1920. New York University Press. New York.
2. O'DONNELL, J. M. 1979. The crisis in experimentation: E. G. Boring and his uses of history. Am. Psychol. **34:** 289–295.
3. FERNBERGER, S. 1947. The future of psychology, or the goose that laid the golden eggs. Am. Psychol. **2:** 209–210.
4. HILGARD, E. R. 1987. Psychology in America: A historical survey. Harcourt Brace Jovanovich. New York.

5. GOTTFREDSON, G. D. *et al.* 1985. The changing face of American psychology. Report of the Committee on Employment and Human Resources, American Psychological Association.
6. HOWARD, A., G. Pion, G. Gottfredson, P. Flattau, S. Oskamps, S. Pfafflin, D. Bray & A. Burstein. 1986. The changing face of American psychology: A report from the Committee on Employment and Human Resources. Am. Psychol. **41:** 1311–1327.
7. CHEIN, I. 1966. Some sources of diviseness among psychologists. Am. Psychol. **21:** 333–342.
8. KOCH, S. 1974. Psychology as an integral discipline: The history of an illusion, and, conceptual sweep vs. knowledge. Thoughts towards a feasible future for psychology. Papers presented at the Annual Convention of the American Psychological Association, New Orleans, Louisiana, August 30 and September 2, 1974.
9. GIORGI, A. 1979. Toward the articulation of psychology as a coherent discipline. Paper presented at Centennial Symposium: Is Psychology a Science? The Disciplinary Status of Psychology. 87th Annual Convention of the American Psychological Association, September 4, 1979. New York, NY.
10. CHOROVER, S. 1980. An interview. APA Monitor. July/August.
11. STANDING, LIONEL & STUART MCKELVIE. Bull. Br. Psych. Soc. Reported in "Footnotes," The Chronicle of Higher Education, February 18, 1987, p. 6.
12. KOCH, S. 1981.

Introduction

A Sampling of Physiological, Comparative, and Social Psychology

ROBERT L. THOMPSON

Hunter College and the Graduate School
The City University of New York
New York, New York 10021

This selection of papers from the monthly Monday evenings at the New York Academy of Sciences is a very small sample of those having relevance to basic experimental psychology and implications for the amelioration of some human problems and the better understanding of others. Like a many-armed radial maze, contemporary experimental psychology has methodology at its center and numerous alleys of empirical content running off in separate directions. Five years before the time (1980) of the last *Annal* compiling selected papers from the Psychology Section, the *Journal of Experimental Psychology* had divided into four independent sections and the *Journal of Comparative and Physiological Psychology* followed, becoming two—*Behavioral Neuroscience* and the *Journal of Comparative Psychology*. The 1980s saw a proliferation of highly specialized journals and books as new techniques and new understandings from neuroscience, cognitive science, and behavior analysis were applied to new and old problem areas and the reservoirs of data filled to overflowing. The *Annual Review of Psychology* remained nearly the same in size only because more and more psychologists found more and more articles of interest in the *Annual Reviews* of other sciences. New handbooks summarized the state of the art in many areas and set the stage for a new decade of progress.

Biofeedback techniques and their applications are a special amalgam of behavior analysis and traditional medical concerns. Robert Fried, here in collaboration with Mary Fox and Richard Carlton, presented a breath-taking (pun intended) case for the relevance of hyperventilation to brain function and seizure disorder. Biofeedback was devised in which exhaled carbon dioxide was measured and transduced to a visual display on a video monitor. Subjects were trained to maintain normal respiratory rate, depth, and topography. Seizure-prone subjects often showed a salutary effect on seizure frequency. Fried's work is described in greater detail in his book, *The Hyperventilation Syndrome: Research and Clinical Treatment* (Johns Hopkins University Press, 1987) and at a popular level in *The Breath*

Connection: How to Reduce Psychosomatic and Stress-Related Disorders with Easy-to-Do Breathing Exercises (Insight Books, 1990).

Ellis Barowsky, Joanne Moskowitz, and Joseph Zweig report another type of biofeedback treatment, thermal (dependent upon peripheral vasodilation) and electromyographic (frontalis muscle tension), which, along with relaxation training, had a beneficial effect on sleep disorders in their three young patients.

While the ABAB design now often used in research with behavior modification procedures applied to individual subjects would add strength to the claims in both papers, the clinical efficacy suggested in these papers illustrates how often pragmatic and ethical issues must take precedence.

Karyl Swartz writes on mind as a concept in comparative psychology; that is, can we speak meaningfully of mind in relation to animal behavior. The topic has assumed enormous importance, not only for an understanding of the evolutionary processes giving rise to both the unique and the shared properties of human mental functions, but also with respect to positions for and against the relevance of research on animal behavior to knowledge of human behavior. She emphasizes work with primates, species with which we identify readily, and further, seems sympathetic to the identification of mind with conscious experience while cautioning us that the utility of the concepts of mind and consciousness for animal behavior has yet to be fully demonstrated. However immediate, the problem is not a new one. The question, "Does the animal possess consciousness and is it like human consciousness?" appears at the beginning of Chapter 1 of Oskar Pfungst's 1911 classic, *Clever Hans: The Horse of Mr. von Osten*, with which the Adlers have some concern.

The Adlers, Leonore and Helmut, report on their training and testing of two bottlenose dolphins in zero delay symbolic matching. In test sessions, one of a pair of objects (e.g., a fish or a ball; a pole or a ring) was displayed between two targets (response locations for the dolphins) bearing English words or Chinese characters. (That the words and characters corresponded to the actual objects was, of course, irrelevant. Further, there was no claim for equivalence among the stimulus classes object/word/character for which tests of reflexiveness, symmetry, and transitivity are usually prescribed.) The dolphins were perfect or nearly so in choosing the pattern (word or character) initially associated individually with the objects. The first two of the three studies they report might be challenged on methodological grounds since the animals could have responded to cues from the experimenters rather than in conditional discriminations of the patterns in combination with the preceding (and accompanying) sample stimulus. Their third study was intended to be of the double-blind type, eliminating the possible "Clever Hans" effect. They describe near-perfect performance of the one dolphin tested three years after the earlier tests. It is not easy to do controlled experimentation with large aquatic animals. The Adlers are to be commended on their diligence in obtaining these data which provide an essential replication and extension of work on the learning capacity of dolphins.

Brian Morgan addresses a problem of great social immediacy: the dependence of the development of brain structure and behavior upon proper nutrition. His data are from rats, and while implications for human problems of malnutrition are strong, a great deal of experimental work must precede human trials. This research is a good example of the importance of animal models for the understanding, detection, and treatment of human deficits due to malnutrition, particularly those characterized by marginal retardation.

Hong-Jen Chen and Brian Yates provide an interesting and useful review and analysis of attribution theory applied in a multivariate experiment assessing the role of observer involvement/noninvolvement in the success or failure of videotaped "actors" on a test of social intelligence. The observers subsequently were asked to attribute the actor's success or failure to factors of ability, effort, test difficulty, or luck. The implications for applied settings are many: How jurors attribute the reasons for a defendent's conduct and how employers assess the performance of employees in consideration of promotion are examples. The next paper takes up issues related to the evaluation of career/job performance in half of our population.

Michele Paludi's contribution to this volume represents an important topic in women's studies. As she points out, the investigation of women's vocational interests, aspirations, and achievements in the new sociopsychological perspective of interdisciplinary women's studies is also a relatively new aspect of vocational psychology, and one that has gathered considerable momentum in recent years. She cites and integrates recent research of her own and others on work role dynamics with special attention on role models and mentoring, and to prevailing attitudes and attributions concerning women's career achievements. Of much value are her criticisms of research methods and her indications for new directions of research on women, work, and careers. While much of this work is not experimental in the strict sense, it is an essential step toward the formulation of questions that can be examined in the laboratory and then tested for validity in the field.

Effect of Diaphragmatic Respiration with End-Tidal CO_2 Biofeedback on Respiration, EEG, and Seizure Frequency in Idiopathic Epilepsy[a,b]

ROBERT FRIED[c,d] AND MARY CLAIRE FOX[c]

[c]Hunter College
City University of New York
New York, New York 10021

[d]Institute for Rational Emotive Therapy
New York, New York

RICHARD M. CARLTON

333 West 57th Street
New York, New York 10019

INTRODUCTION

It is variously estimated that seizure sufferers constitute between 0.5 and 1.5% of the U.S. population.[1] The subpopulation of concern in this study consists of persons classified as having idiopathic epilepsy. This subpopulation constitutes between 75 and 80% of seizure sufferers—an estimated 16 million persons in the United States. It is generally believed that this group grows at an annual rate of about 100,000.

In this subpopulation, idiopathic epilepsies, seizures typically begin around the age of 22 to 25. And, while it appears that there is a genetic predisposition to idiopathic seizures, the evidence is not overwhelming. However, it seems to be the case that these seizures fit into a cluster of apparently related disorders, including migraine, identified as early as 1907 by Gowers.[2]

[a] We wish to thank the following foundations for their generous support of this research project: the J. M. Foundation, the Clark Foundation, the Leon Lowenstein Foundation, the Gilder Foundation, and the Alcoa Foundation.

[b] This research was done at ICD-International Center for the Disabled (New York, NY) while the first author was on leave from CUNY.

Idiopathic epilepsy is generally treated medically with anticonvulsants. The effectiveness of these medications varies with the type of seizure condition. Total control ranges between 0 and 58% of treated cases.[3] Psychomotor epilepsy is the most difficult to manage.[4] Remission for two years is observed in about 30% of cases.[5] Mortality rate is relatively low, 1.3 per 100,000 (less than that for appendicitis), but it is twice as high in women than in men, and twice as high in nonwhite populations.[6]

Seizures are classified in a number of different ways. Commonly, cause, manifestations, and physiological correlates dominate the category labels. Seizures of determinable origin are labeled "symptomatic" and may take a variety of different forms: petit mal (absence), grand mal, psychomotor, and so forth. They may or may not be preceded by so-called premonitory sensations or auras which may, themselves, have different forms, such as auditory or visual.[7]

The history of the study of seizure disorders is the history of epilepsy. In antiquity, epileptics were variously admired or reviled, praised or persecuted. "Epilepsy," the "falling disease," the "sacred illness" was often attributed to demonic possession (hence the word *seizure*) and to winds—*aura* means wind. It was described in considerable detail by Hippocrates (460–357 B.C.) and by Galen (130–200 A.D.) and has a number of references in the *New Testament.*[8]

Traditionally, epilepsy has fallen into the purview of medicine (neurology), which has given its study and treatment its present characteristics. Definitions and models of seizures and their suspected cause are predicated on the concept of *spontaneously dysfunctioning cerebral neurons* acting in aggregate:

> Convulsive activity may now be conceived, not as an enhancement of the normal excitation of neurones, but as the partial or complete block of normal inhibition. A biochemical abnormality of some neurones is thought by many investigators to underline the initiation of gradually increasing depolarization in their dendritic fields so that minimal stimuli may initiate a seizure discharge. The spread to adjacent neurones and the propagation axonally to other areas of the nervous system of the discharge results in the striking manifestation of the convulsion (p. 694).

So write Wolfe and Elliott.[9] However, many investigators speculate that neuronal discharge in epilepsy may result from a biochemical abnormality. Yet the two fundamental questions about a seizure, how does it begin and how does it stop, are left unanswered.

The idea that seizures are essentially cerebral neuronal events is not new. In 1859, Samuel Wilks[10] distinguished between functional (idiopathic) and focal seizures. Hughlings Jackson[11] followed Fritsch and Hitzig,[12] in objecting to the concept of *functional epilepsy.* Jackson simply could not accept the idea that one could have seizures without a cerebral neuronal cause. Gowers,[13] on the other hand, opposed Jackson's view and held, with Wilks, that it is quite possible to observe seizures in persons who have absolutely no discernible alteration of the brain. Wilks, parenthetically, introduced the use of *bromides* in the United States. They were the first effective anticonvulsant medications.

Glaser[1] defines epilepsy as ". . . a paroxysmal disorder of the nervous system characterized by recurrent attacks usually with alterations of consciousness, with or without convulsive movement."

Brain[14] (1962) writes,

> There seems no doubt, however, that whatever its immediate or remote cause, an epileptic attack is the manifestation of a paroxysmal discharge of abnormal electrical rhythms in some parts of the brain. If one adds that such discharges are likely to be repetitive, one has defined the cardinal features of epilepsy. It will be noted that loss of consciousness is not an essential feature of the epileptic attack (p. 129).

The cause is ascribed to disordered neurons. According to Barolin,[15] "in epilepsies, we postulate an initial pathological activity in the nervous cells." And Mostofsky[16] writes that seizures are ". . . excessive repetitive firing of single or small groups of neurons in the brain . . . (with) recruitment of adjacent neurons spreading to the entire system until it is out of control." These are, essentially, theories of brain neurons run amuk. One wonders if Hughlings Jackson, an avid Darwinian, would have supported a hypothesis of the brain as an organ readily rendered useless by the wayward activity of, perhaps at most, one-multimillionth of its components. This is hardly an adaptive and functional structure.

There seems to have been a choice point in the history of epilepsy etiology and one alternative explanation was chosen over another. The choices were *neuronal* or *metabolic* etiology of seizures. On the metabolic side, Gibbs, Lennox, and Gibbs[17] state that

> Considering all those links between carbon dioxide and epilepsy, namely that (1) the influence of carbon dioxide on the EEG, (2) the abnormal values for carbon dioxide in arterial and jugular blood of patients with petit mal and grand mal, and (3) the abnormal variation of carbon dioxide preceding grand mal seizures in such a way as to indicate a causal relationship, we may conclude that carbon dioxide plays a significant role in the etiology of epileptic convulsions (p. 109).

This is certainly a notable departure from neuronal theories of cause. Only a few years before, parenthetically, Gibbs, Davis, and Lennox[18] had written that "It seems more reasonable to suppose that in epilepsy there is a defective central nervous system mechanism . . . ."

Thus, there is the beginning of another view of seizure etiology, to wit, that cerebral and/or systemic variables other than individual neuronal activity are at the root of the paroxysmal cerebral activity. On the metabolic side, also, Himwich[19] writes, "In addition to exerting physiological effects, carbon dioxide may also be involved in pathological conditions, for instance, epilepsy." He supports this belief with evidence for the following mechanism:

> Cerebral vasomotor reaction to CO_2 is probably direct, by exerting influence on the walls of the vessels . . . . They are not mediated by nervous impulses, as are the systemic changes by receptors in the carotid sinus and body under the influence of the vasomotor centers of the medulla (p. 104).

Thus, since the early days of Lennox and Gibbs, in the 1920s and early 1930s, evidence for a metabolic seizure etiology mounted. Nevertheless, the neuro-electrical theory, modeled after the telephone switchboard seems to have prevailed.

BIOCHEMICAL CORRELATES OF EPILEPSY

Numerous reports compare the biochemistry of seizure sufferers to that of persons who do not suffer seizures. These reports indicate that there are some detectable differences. However, a causal relationship between various metabolic and biochemical abnormalities and epilepsy has been pretty well ruled out. A review of the major findings follows.

Batt, Siest, *et al.*[20] report the comparison of plasma levels of various substances in adult epileptics and nonepileptic controls. For both men and women, the following showed significant differences: calcium, sodium, urea, creatinine, protein, albumin, and phosphate.

But Glaser[1] reports that with the exception of slight pleocytosis in CSF. and increased protein and water pressure, "Laboratory findings are within normal limits in the majority of the patients with seizures of unknown causes." This conclusion would not be supported by Laidlaw and Richens[21] who summarize the findings of numerous investigators and add arterial PO_2, arterial PCO_2, glucose, magnesium, and ammonia to the list. With reference to plasma pH, they write, "Activation of epilepsy by respiratory alkalosis and inhibition by acidosis is probably related to changes in intracellular pH." This is a curious conclusion for, in a preceding page, they state ". . . seizure susceptibility is often unchanged during severe changes in plasma pH occurring during metabolic acidosis or alkalosis" (p. 318).

Other investigators have pointed out the role of alkalosis in the cause of seizures. Groen[22] induced it with the injection of sodium lactate and Himwich[19] concludes that it relates to the enhancement of the production of cholinesterase. Latham[23] fails to observe alkalosis in the urine in epileptics. He cites numerous studies and finally focuses on the retention of sodium and water in seizure sufferers.

Madsen[24] is not impressed with the pH changes in the blood and suggests a number of other factors. Among these are hyperammoniuria, which has been previously reported—in fact, as early as 1918 (Bisgaard & Bisgaard[25]). Hyperammoniuria has a number of proponents, including Altenberger and Stern[26] who ascribe it to pituitary hormone imbalance: They hypothesize that the deficiency in pituitary hormone accounts for a change in tonus of capillaries and somehow relates this to ammonia metabolism which is central to neuronal function. Subsequent studies have shown the relationship between anterior pituitary hormone and capillary tonus and may possibly account for the fluctuation in seizure frequency that accompanies the menstrual cycle in women seizure sufferers.

In an extensive review of the literature, Meyer and Waltz[27] support the contention of Davis and Wallace[28] that metabolic acidosis has no particular effect on the EEG. The latter produced it by ingestion of ammonium chloride and sodium bicarbonate. Thus, the picture that emerges is that while alkalosis is commonly observed in connection with seizures, it may not be a precipitating factor. Likewise, Lubin and Price[29] concluded on the basis of their work and that of Davis and Wallace[28,30] that it is CO_2 alteration in the arterial blood and not the pH that is the critical factor. This conclusion is supported by Swanson, Stavney, and Plum.[31]

A comprehensive study by Faurbye[32] simultaneously addresses ammonium metabolism, alkalosis, and CO_2 content of the blood. He concludes that there are marked ammonia irregularities in epileptics but that these irregularities are not specific to epileptics; there is no relation between blood pH and convulsive attacks but that there seems to be a relation to attacks of *change* in pH. Finally, there are *types* of responders to the effects of hyperventilation: those who are, and those who are not, susceptible to ictus as a consequence of CO_2 changes.

Mostofsky[16] adds corticosteroids and glucose to the list of implicated factors. The role of blood sugar has been elaborated in some detail. In fact, there is evidence for hypoglycemia in connection with idiopathic epilepsy. Findings in this connection lead to the conclusion that hypoglycemia *potentiates* the effects of hyperventilation—rather than being a factor per se.[33]

The observation of many other excretion abnormalities, including aminoaciduria have been reported by Millichap and Ulrich.[34] Clinically significant quantities of glycine have been noted in connection with aminoaciduria in a study of the effects of dipropylacetate on convulsions.[35] Wolfe and Elliott[9] summarize studies that implicate ACh and cholinesterase mechanisms, hepatocerebral dysfunction involving ammonia and glutamine, and γ-amino-butyric acid (GABA) and vitamin B_6 (pyridoxine). The latter is a well known, though little considered, anticonvulsant. It acts, most likely, by potentiating vasodilation.

EEG FEEDBACK TRAINING

In 1935, Gibbs, Davis, and Lennox examined the EEG of a number of their patients in connection with epilepsy and other conditions of impaired consciousness.[18] They described the normal EEG as consisting, in part, of various dominant frequencies including *alpha* (Berger' rhythm), an 8- to 12-Hz waveform at 10 to 50 UV. And, they reported that as their patients sank into a state of drowsiness, the EEG frequency decreased and the amplitude increased to about 60 UV. In addition, they reported that petit mal epilepsy accompanied a particular EEG waveform consisting of a low-frequency sinusoidal wave and sharp negative spikes in the 3- to 4-Hz range, at 100 to 300 UV.

They also observed grand mal seizures and the EEG pattern that accompanied them: dominant waves, 5 to 18 Hz, becoming larger and faster just before the patient's "cry." Then, as the seizure subsided, slower rhythms began to appear among the fast ones and the electrical activity decreased along with the muscle activity. Following this phase, an abnormal flat EEG prevailed during the stupor, returning to normal about 20 minutes later.

It is the alpha rhythm that was among the earliest of the cortical rhythms to be studied in connection with biofeedback and "operant conditioning."[36] It was held that the self-control of brain waves would effectively enhance a number of "altered states of consciousness" benefitting mood and increasing "self-awareness" while helping some to cope with their anxiety and even their drug dependence. A number of these prophesies did not come to fruition, but the technology required to study the phenomenon grew, increasing in complexity and usefulness. Attempts to condition other cortical rhythms were reported in the literature with varying degrees of success and accompanying equivocation.[37]

In 1967, Sterman and Wyrwicka[38] reported the observation of a discrete EEG rhythm in cats, consisting of 12- to 20-Hz bursts localized to the coronal gyrus of the cat. They called this rhythm the sensorimotor rhythm (SMR) and described it in connection with various behavior strategies of the cat, whose common feature was withholding somatomotor responses. Sterman and Wyrwicka concluded that the SMR is observed in response to a "*negative conditioned stimulus.*"

In 1968, Wyrwicka and Sterman[39] followed with an elaboration of the SMR: Production of the SMR by the cat was rewarded with milk for a number of sessions of 50 reinforcements each. Episodes of production of the SMR became more frequent; it was evidently conditionable. It became increasingly clear that the behavioral correlates of this rhythm were stereotyped posture and complete cessation of spontaneous activity. To these investigators, it seemed that they were observing the conditioning of a "central state related to inhibition of phasic motor behavior." In 1971, Chase and Harper[40] performed a similar study. They reiterated the conditionability of the SMR, which they confined to the 12- to 14-Hz segment of the rhythm and likewise observed the accompanying cessation of movement and depression of somatic activity. In connection with their analysis of the respiratory correlates of the SMR they state that "visual observation of the animals gave us the impression that they were regulating closely their pattern of respiration during epochs of conditioned EEG activity" (p. 87). If that is accurate, and there is no reason to doubt it, then some question exists about whether, as later investigators claim, it is *operant* conditioning. But the interesting point here is that either they need to control their breathing to produce SMR, or producing SMR controls their breathing. In a subsequent study, Harper and Sterman[41] also report that conditioned SMR shows a functional relationship to "regulation of respiration."

Chase and Harper further state, in the above-cited study,

> Onset of each epoch [of SMR] was correlated positively with the inspiration phase . . . . Termination of 12 to 14 c/sec activity tended to occur during expiration in all cats ($P < 0.005$) . . . . *Short bursts were time-locked to the respiratory pattern described above*" (p. 87) [italics mine].

Then, in 1972, Sterman and Friar[42] published for the first time the suppression of seizures in an epileptic by training the patient to increase her production of SMR. They had observed the same SMR in their human subjects that they had reported in connection with their feline studies. The procedure was a relatively simple one. The subject's production of frequencies in that rhythm bandwidth triggered a visual stimulus that served as a biofeedback indicator. In a series of subsequent communications,[43] further reports on SMR conditioning with epileptics yielded these conclusions: (a) a 12- to 14-Hz rhythm can be recorded in human subjects over the Rolandic region; (b) its operant level is low (as is also its amplitude—3 to 4 UV); (c) it shows an increase after about two weeks of training; and (d) nonepileptics show no reduction in *alpha* during training. Six epileptics were studied over a period ranging between 6 and 20 months. Each training session began with three to five minutes of operant-level recording, followed by 20 to 40 minutes of SMR biofeedback, after which there was again three to five minutes of noncontingent recording. There were three such sessions each week for each client.

Sterman reports a number of associated phenomena. Epileptics showed a decreasing spontaneous production of low-frequency discharges accompanied by a reduction in petit and grand mal seizures and, surprisingly, an improvement in the quality of sleep.

Kaplan[44] reports a replication of the Sterman *et al.* SMR conditioning studies from which she concludes that biofeedback had no effect on seizure reductions in her subjects. She basically discounted Sterman's findings and attributed seizure reduction to "relaxation training" or placebo.

The publication of Kaplan's critique was immediately followed by a supporting statement by Gastaut[45] who essentially stated that SMR conditioning was exploitation of the alpha-type, altered state of consciousness. The Kaplan study was not, in fact, a replication and neither was the study by Upton and Longmire[46] which likewise failed to conclude that SMR conditioning accounted for their observed seizure reductions.

Lubar and Bahler[47] followed Sterman *et al.* with a report of their observation of the effect of SMR conditioning on eight severely epileptic patients. Following the reported procedure and recording from the C3–T3, C4–T4 (International 10/20 System) sites, they confirmed previous findings. This study was followed rapidly by the work of Finley[48]; Sterman, McDonald, and Bernstein[49]; Sterman[50,51]; and Kuhlman and Allison.[52]

It was now becoming evident that psychobiological control of seizures was feasible and that there were a number of different ways of observing it.

Mostofsky and Balaschack[53] summarized the known methods under the general topics of (a) reward management, (b) self-control, and (c) psychobiological. These categories include programs for

- denial of reward
- penalty
- relief (avoidance)
- punishment
- overt and covert reward for *free* period
- relaxation
- desensitization
- hypnosis
- dynamic and other psychotherapy
- self-control (including patient's idiosyncratic methods)
- habituation
- extinction
- biofeedback

Despite mounting evidence that "behavioral" methods for seizure control were beginning to be a realistic research avenue that promised new insights and methods, especially where traditional medication failed to be effective, these reports did not result in a stampede to the brain-conditioning laboratories. Though Reynolds[54] writes, "Even in the best of hands, existing drugs are not sufficient for the task (of controlling seizures), and hence *an urgent need exists for the development of new drugs.*" [Italics are mine.]

Kuhlman's report[55] essentially corroborates previous findings, but he seemed reluctant to state categorically that SMR conditioning is responsible for the observed change. In fact, he concludes that the procedure is "non-specific" despite his observation that the power spectral analysis showed a shift toward the higher frequencies. He concludes that a process of EEG "normalization" is taking place. That is the same conclusion drawn by Lubar and colleagues and of course by investigators in the 1920s and 1930s who observed it in connection with CO_2 inhalation.

Kuhlman's position was supported by Quy, Hutt, and Forrest,[56] who likewise reported consistent improvement of their epileptic subjects with the use of SMR biofeedback. They concluded that evidence for the existence of SMR is slender, but the procedure works anyway.

In 1979, also, Sterman and Kovaleski report the elaboration of the role of physical restraint on seizure threshold.[57] In a study of the anticonvulsant effects of restraint and pyridoxine on hydrazine seizures (in monkeys), they report that physical restraint has an effect at least equal to that of pyridoxine (vitamin B_6). As was indicated earlier, B_6 is a well-known anticonvulsant that appears in the epilepsy literature with astounding infrequency. Soulayrol[58] gives it a thorough treatment in connection with his description of avitaminosis. And, Bower, who alleges that one-third of young epileptics suffer B_6 deficiency or lack of utilization suggests the

Wachstein-Guadaitis test to determine xanthurenic acid in urine in connection with B_6 utilization. The principal action of pyridoxine is on the vascular system, further strengthening the theory that seizures are a metabolic vasculogenic phenomenon.[a]

Sterman's previous observation of the effects of restraint on the production of SMR was replicated. He showed that chair-restraint immobilization is accompanied by an increase in the spectral density of the 12- to 15-Hz component of the SMR observed at the lateral and mid-Rolandic region.[59] He concludes that the observation of the SMR corresponds to the operation of a motor inhibition center, as he previously stipulated. This contention is reinforced by the work of Bowersox and Sterman[60] who analyzed the effects of dorsal column transsection on hydrazine (MMH) induced seizures. They noted a decrease in seizure susceptibility as well as an enhancement of sleep spindles. Similar findings have been reported in persons who have suffered severing of the spine and who had, previously, been subject to seizures (personal communication, 1982).

Alteration of the power spectrum, contingent on SMR conditioning, is reported by Lubar *et al.*[61] with eight epileptics refractory to medical control. In a double-blind, cross-over design study of EEG conditioning as an anticonvulsant, the following conditions prevailed:

- baseline measure of seizure frequency for four months,
- false (noncontingent) feedback for two months,
- SMR training for ten months.

The groups were required to suppress 3–8 Hz; enhance 12–15 Hz, or suppress 3–8 Hz; and enhance 11–19 Hz. Spectral analysis indicated that where seizures decreased, an increase in the frequency band of 16–23 Hz was noted as well as a decrease in the low-frequency band, 0–7 Hz. The latter encompasses the 4–7-Hz component typically associated with seizures. The investigators also report that they noted no neuropsychological changes in their subjects.

In 1981, Sterman modified his experimental design, incorporating baseline data collection on his epileptic patients and installing "home practice" procedures and follow-up.[62] This procedure again resulted in a significant shift in power spectra.

These EEG conditioning studies may be summarized as follows: The pre-Rolandic cortex emits a detectable rhythm, ranging between 13 and 15 Hz, at a very low amplitude, which is associated with the inhibition of phasic motion. Biofeedback training somehow enhances either that rhythm or the covert behavior that gives rise to it. In the process, it seems to inhibit seizure activity by altering the threshold to the effect of known and suspected precipitants. In the process of doing so, it "normalizes" the EEG

[a] There are also numerous reports of the role of nutrition in epilepsy. Many of these center on food allergy as a seizure trigger.[97–105]

by reducing the low frequency and increasing the beta-frequency components and, in addition, regulates sleeps.

The studies that have resulted in the observation of the reduction of seizures by the SMR conditioning means have typically been carried out in refractory epileptics—those who did not show evidence of control with medication. Thus, though the evidence for the success of the procedure has not been universally upheld, and the process tends to be lengthy, it has typically been observed in connection with the most difficult cases—those that defied every other known treatment. It is hardly sensible to say, as some critics have, that these cases responded to the placebo component of the procedure. Clearly they have had ample opportunity to respond to the placebo component of the many medications they took: The medical treatment that they received had considerably more placebo power than an experimental procedure about which little is known.

It is possible that the covert behavior that is evidenced by the appearance of the SMR, or the SMR itself, is functionally related to respiratory mechanisms as has been intimated. Some evidence for such a connection has been demonstrated. Or, it is possible that cortical events are controlled by a breathing-related mechanism that both inhibits motor behavior and enhances SMR.

BREATHING, HYPERVENTILATION, EEG, AND SEIZURES

Hyperventilation is a respiratory behavior marked by an abnormal increase in the rate and depth of inspiration and expiration resulting in an abnormal exchange of gases in the lungs, particularly CO_2. Normal respiration rate is about 14–16 per minute (with about 5% end-tidal CO_2)[63–65]; chronic hyperventilators may have a respiratory rate in excess of 20. This behavior may result in varying degrees of hypocapnia and respiratory alkalosis, which can profoundly affect cerebral and peripheral vasotonus and caliber, blood flow, oxyhemoglobin dissociation, and metabolism.[66,67]

A link exists between the EEG, breathing changes, and the early reports of the role of hyperventilation in epilepsy. Hyperventilation has been shown to lead to EEG dysrhythmia and seizures.

Clinical and research evidence suggests a strong link between epilepsy and overbreathing. Rosett,[68] one of the earliest investigators to show its relationship to seizures, described the objective and subjective experiences accompanying low blood CO_2 (hypocapnia), concluding that "there are few drugs the effects of which upon the neuromuscular system are so rapid and so striking as the effect of voluntary hyperpnoea."

Previously, Lennox, Gibbs, and Gibbs[69] published their observations that electroencephalogram changes accompany various conditions and drugs that also influence seizures. They showed that anticonvulsants, such as bromide and phenobarbital, have a normalizing effect on the EEG. They also pointed out the EEG dysregulation and seizure-enhancing effect of hyperventilation which, as they put it, "blows off" carbon dioxide.

Because inhalation of oxygen had no apparent influence on seizure frequency, they further concluded that inhalation of CO_2 should wipe out the observed slow waves preceding seizures. It did in fact prove to do that. While they do not actually say so, one can reasonably interpret their conclusion to imply that the seizure sufferers they observed could be said to have an unusually low tolerance to changes within a fairly narrow range of CO_2 blood concentration values.

Although these investigators quite clearly identified the role of CO_2 in brain circulation, they felt that ultimately the *cause* of the seizures was neurological, and they stipulated that changes in CO_2 concentration that altered the acid–base balance of the blood created an unstable environment for brain neurons. From that point on, the literature reflects an effort to "dope out" the mechanism by which blood alkalosis results in neuronal dysfunction.

For instance, Tarlan,[70] in a study of the EEG changes in "neurogenic chronic respiratory acidosis" states that CO_2 tension is directly involved in production of slow EEG waves and that this is the most important factor influencing the EEG spectrum. To support his position, he cites a study by Lennox[71] concluding that many epileptics show a marked irregularity in respiratory rate and depth. But not unlike his predecessors, he also selects the acid–base route to study the cause of seizures. Spectrum analysis had been previously done by Gibbs, Williams, and Gibbs[72] who reported the modification of the cortical frequency power spectrum by the changes in CO_2, blood sugar, and O_2. This introduction of the use of power spectrum analysis is an early antecedent of the technique that is currently gaining popularity in EEG training laboratories. Power spectrum analysis displays a function of the voltage level, on a cathode ray tube graphically or on paper, of each sinusoidal component of a complex waveform sequence during a given time "epoch."

Madsen, in 1943, in a study of the biochemistry of epileptics,[24] cites Bisgaard, Jarlov, and Norvig (1918) who demonstrate pH abnormality in urine and blood. He showed that the blood pH falls within normal limits between ictal episodes but rose markedly during paroxysmal periods. Reporting on the effects of hyperventilation on Na and Cl content of serum, he concludes that the electrolyte content does not change but that ammonia output is significantly increased. Ross and Loeser[33] examined the relationship between hypoglycemia and hyperventilation. They concluded that blood sugar decline results in an acid–base instability which tended to promote over-breathing. Holmberg[73] focuses entirely on CO_2 and states that "hypocapnia is probably the essential factor which produces slow waves in the EEG during hyperventilation." Schneider[74] also supports the alkalosis hypothesis: During the active phase of the seizure, they noted a marked decrease in sodium. They postulate a mechanism, in connection with centrencephalic epilepsy, related to an excess of intracellular sodium.

Barolin,[15] like Gowers,[2] held that epilepsy and migraine are related. This position is also supported by Ikonomoff[75] and Babb and Eckman[76] in connection with abdominal migraine and abdominal ictus. Barolin attributes both to hypoxemic damage resulting in "tetanic" spasm after hyperventilation: He reports that half of his migraine patients show moderate to strong EEG abnormalities, including dysrhythmia, spikes, and focal abnormality. His observations are reportedly contingent on hyperpnia and photic stimulation. This is a very impressive argument. But, even more impressive is the discourse by Brain in *Diseases of the Nervous System*[14] on migraine and its treatment, who suggests that patients may benefit from diuretics. In fact, *epileptics* are known to benefit from diuretics because they tend to store excessive amounts of water.[74,77] He recommends, further, phenobarbital, phenytoin sodium (dilantin), and nitroglycerin. Phenobarbital and phenytoin are, of course, anticonvulsants, while nitroglycerin is a vasodilator. However, most remarkably, he suggests, "The mixture recommended by Gowers . . . ."—which includes *sodium bromide*—for the treatment of migraine! Thus, while Brain specifically distinguished between migraine and epilepsy and clearly views them as separate entities, the treatment he suggests for both is virtually identical.

Mattson, Heninger, Gallagher, and Glaser[78] propose that there is a mechanism through which "anxiety" leads to hyperventilation, which, in turn, lowers CO_2 level, thus triggering seizures. They conclude this on the basis of their polygraphic studies of hyperventilation and EEG. In their patients who showed a marked tendency to hyperventilate "unconsciously" when anxious, there was no obvious overbreathing. Yet, there was a 50% fall in CO_2 (based on end-tidal analysis) and EEG and clinical seizure activity increased. They conclude that *involuntary overbreathing* (chronic hyperventilation) increases EEG epileptiform activity.

Swanson, Stavney, and Plum[31] describe their results in connection with studies on the effects of blood pH and CO_2 on cerebral electrical activity. They address two theories equally likely on the basis of previous evidence: (a) that CO_2 has a specific effect on neural activity, and (b) that the CO_2-related change in the acid–base balance is the relevant variable in seizure etiology.

They state that when CO_2 tension and arterial blood pH are manipulated independently, change in the EEG follows the direction of change in CO_2 and bears no relationship to arterial blood pH. That statement put the alkalosis theory to rest for them. They further state that "carbon dioxide possesses unique properties that influence nerve cell function and cerebral electrical activity" (p. 792). The conclusion that the cause of seizures must vest in neurons once again takes precedence over the obvious, data-based conclusion that the cause is vascular.

Lennox,[70] Gibbs *et al.*,[17] and Robinson[79] elaborated the inverse relationship between cerebral arterial concentration (PCO_2) and seizure activity, and Gibbs, *et al.*[18] first showed a connection between cerebral PCO_2, EEG, and seizures.

These studies suggested, at first, that respiratory alkalosis is the precipitating factor in hypocapnia.[21] This premise, disputed as early as 1932 by Brody and Dusser de Barenne,[80] is no longer acceptable. Increased pH is just one link in a complex physiological chain.[31,67]

Studies of brain metabolism and blood flow in epileptics also focused on CO_2 as a vasodilator (by its direct action on arterial muscle wall), and on its role in oxyhemoglobin dissociation (Bohr effect)[19]: Wolff and Lennox[81] demonstrated vasodilation, Meduna[82] applied it clinically, and Penfield and Jasper[8] showed it during seizures.

There have also been strong suggestions that seizures are caused by cerebral vasoconstriction when PCO_2 is low and the attending neuronal discharges are due to ischemic hypoxia.[8,15,27,67,83]

The connection between seizures and hyperventilation is so strong that it led investigators to conclude that it is etiological. Cobb, *et al.*[84] were among the first to note spontaneous hyperventilation in seizure sufferers. These observations have been replicated.[1,17,33,72,73,78,85–87]

Riley[88] in fact concludes that organically based psychogenic hyperventilation causes seizures frequently "mistaken for epileptic attacks." He differentiates between chronic hyperventilators and epileptics on the basis that the first show "chest breathing while the latter do not." This has no corroboration in the literature. Robinson[79] confirms the Rosett report by provoking seizures in known epileptics by hyperpnea. But he failed to note the incidence of spontaneous hyperventilation in his subjects.

Increased $PaCO_2$ by CO_2 inhalation (7% to 10%) has been shown to have a dramatic effect on the EEG[89] and a similar effect has been obtained by setting limits to respiration rate.[90] However, it has never been shown that it can be controlled by self-regulation. The continuous self-regulation of $PaCO_2$ would have broad clinical application in all cases where control of the body acid–base balance would contribute to the restoration of physiological equilibrium either by shifting the oxyhemoglobin curve, thereby increasing O_2 delivery to tissue, or by its increase of arterial caliber and thus blood flow and metabolism.

A summary of these diverse studies points, unequivocally, to a metabolic and vascular cause of seizures. The relationship between epilepsy and migraine, the observations that the EEG follows circulatory events, and the observation that seizures, in fact, are characterized by observable arterial spasms in the focus or in connection with lesions, and finally, that the symptoms that alleviate migraine do so because of the use of anticonvulsants (and vasodilators), all point strongly in that direction.

In this study, we examine two clinical populations typically presenting with hyperventilation and test the feasibility, in one of them, of learned self-regulation of $PaCO_2$, postulating that its control will modify the EEG and seizure frequency and severity.

TABLE 1. Subjects Admitted to the Study[a]

Subject			Age of	Seizure		Entered
No.	Sex	Age	Onset	Type	Disposition	Program
102	F	24	13	GM, PM, Pm, blkouts	Active: 1×/week	Jun. 82
103	F	27	14	GM, Pm	Active: 1×/week	Jun. 82
104	F	31	10	GM, muscle fascicul.	Active: 1×/week	July 82
105	M	36	13	GM, Pm	Withdrew Apr. 83	Aug. 82
106	F	27	13	Akinetic (Syncopeo)	Active: 2×/week	Aug. 82
107	M	39	21	GM, PM, Pm, blkts	Withdrew Jan. 83	July 82
108	M	10	5	PM	Withdrew Sept. 83	Aug. 82
109	F	36	26	GM, PM, falls	Active: 1×/week	Aug. 82
110	F	30	28	GM	Withdrew after 3 weeks	Aug. 82
111	F	35		Migraine, EEG dysr.	Withdrew	Aug. 82
112	M	42	7	GM, auras	Active: 1×/week	Sep. 82
113	F	31	5	PM, Pm	Suspended: med. problem	Sep. 82
114	F	35	17	GM, PM, auras, paresth.	Active: 2×/week	Sep. 82
115	M	31	13	GM	Active: 1×/week	Sep. 82
116	F	24	4	GM, Pm, auras	Withdrew Jan. 83	Dec. 82
117	M	37	17	GM	Active: 2×/week	Feb. 83
118	(unassigned)					
119	(unassigned)					
120	F	38	18	GM	Active: 1×/week	Jan. 83
121	F	34	5	GM, PM, Pm	Dismissed: unmanageable	Jan. 83
122	M	34	19	GM, PM, Pm	Active: 2×/week	Jan. 83
123	M	28	12	GM	Dismissed: aggressive	Jan. 83
124	F	34	16	PM, Pm, amnesia	Active: 2×/week	Feb. 83
125	M	40	18	GM, PM	Active: 2×/week	Mar. 83

[a] GM: grand mal; PM: petit mal; Pm: psychomotor; blkts: blackouts.

METHOD

Subjects

Nine men and 13 women, ranging in age between 10 and 42 years, were selected for participation in the study (TABLE 1).

Procedure

Establishing seizure type, frequency, and severity in the subjects was occasionally complicated by memory loss: Seizure sufferers may give relatively inaccurate reports. Thus, pretreatment history was based in some cases on medical records and the corroborative testimony of friends and relatives. The majority of the subjects had reasonably accurate records.

Seizure logs and detailed instructions in their use were issued to each subject upon entry into the study.

Medical Evaluation

Each subject was given a thorough medical examination including an evaluation of all pertinent previous medical records. Subjects were admitted to the study only if there was no organic cause for their seizures and if they were intractable to therapeutic serum levels of anticonvulsant medication.

The subjects were required to remain on the medication in effect at the time of their entry into the program.

Respiration Rate and Percent End-Tidal CO_2

A slender tube, one end inserted about one-quarter inch into the subject's right nostril, was taped to the face, to sample end-tidal air for CO_2 analysis by a P. K. Morgan infrared gas analyzer. The analogue output of the gas analyzer was transmitted to an analogue-to-digital (A/D) converter to condition the signal for use by an Apple II+ computer. The computer determined the mean and peak percent end-tidal CO_2 for any preselected number of 15-second epochs (3 to 5 usually). The electrical analogue trace was also transmitted to an E & M Physiograph (polygraph). The respiration rate (RR) was obtained from the polygraphic tracing of percent end-tidal CO_2 by counting respiratory cycles during a one-minute span. This is equivalent to 6 cm on the chart at a transport speed of 0.10 cm/sec.

EEG Power Spectral Analysis

Grass gold-plated electrodes were attached to the scalp of the subject midway between F_3–C_3 and C_3–P_3 (International 10/20 System). The signal was transmitted to two WPI (DAV) Preamplifiers, recorded on a Vetter (Model A) FM tape recorder for subsequent fast-Fourier analysis by the Apple II+ computer, and also monitored online by a Hewlett-Packard Spectrum Analyzer (Model 3582A).

The power values are based on 10 three-second samples, 27 seconds apart. The computer was programmed to produce a power-per-frequency distribution, with either a histogram or polygon based on it.

EEG Power Spectral Composition

The EEG has a complex frequency composition that varies continuously and rapidly. A dominant fundamental frequency and numerous components of lesser amplitude are imbedded in it. All this is in addition to a "floating" dc voltage.

Fast-Fourier analysis permits the identification of the components of the complex waveform. The composition of the EEG is specified in terms of the frequency components present during a given sampling period, and their *power:* Power is voltage multiplied by current. Typically, current is now known, but because it may be assumed to be constant, an arbitrary ratio scale may be used. This permits the comparison of activity at different frequencies. The power units in spectra are a function of characteristics of the A/D converter. They are linearly related to (micro) voltage.

Diaphragmatic Respiration Training with Percent End-Tidal CO_2 Biofeedback

Percent end-tidal CO_2 was displayed to the subject as a blue pattern on a video monitor, rising and falling with increase and decrease in CO_2 sampled in end-tidal breath.

Diaphragmatic respiration was taught by a "trainer" who worked with the subject instructing him/her in the proper chest and abdomen configurations and movement. Hands-on techniques were used and, occasionally, objects such as a book were placed on the abdomen to help the subject focus on correct movement.

During the training, the subject was asked to produce a specific respiratory pattern: a more or less *sinusoidal* waveform on the video monitor with three or four peaks per screen update, rising to a gray line representing a criterion of 5% end-tidal CO_2. The respiration producing this pattern on the video monitor is approximately equivalent to normal respiration, that is, 12 to 14 breaths per minute (RR) at about 5% end-tidal CO_2.[65,66]

RESULTS

The end-tidal CO_2 and EEG measures summarized here are based on data obtained during a 10-minute observation and recording session preceding each biofeedback training session. During training and post-training, observations were also made but the use of these data was considered limited to interpretation as short-term effects and is not included here.

The Effect of Respiration Training on Respiration

TABLE 2 summarizes the statistics for respiratory measures obtained from the biofeedback treatment group ($n = 18$) and a control group of nine women and four men, asymptomatic office workers and health service professionals, ranging in age between the middle 20s and 40s.

There was a significant difference between the first pretraining respiratory rate (RR) and that of the controls: $p(F = 7.59) < 0.05$. There was also a significant difference between the first and last pretreatment RR: $p(t = 4.16) < 0.05$. A significant difference was also found between the controls and the last pretreatment RR: $p(F = 3.80) < 0.05$.

No significant difference was found between any combination of groups when comparing mean percent end-tidal CO_2 measures only.

Because of the compensatory relationship between end-tidal CO_2 and RR changes in chronic hyperventilators, a respiration product index, RR/CO_2, was calculated. It reflects the relationship between RR and percent end-tidal CO_2 in terms of output per breath.

TABLE 2. Means and Standard Deviation for Respiration Data for Controls and Treatment Group Subjects

Group		First Pretraining BPM	First Pretraining $\overline{X}CO_2$	First Pretraining BPM/CO_2	Last Pretraining BPM	Last Pretraining $\overline{X}CO_2$	Last Pretraining BPM
Treatment	$\overline{X}$ =	17.06	4.28	4.00	12.61	4.39	2.90
	S =	2.62	0.41	0.64	3.70	0.61	0.81
Control	$\overline{X}$ =	14.54	4.55	3.29			
	S =	7.22	0.56	1.76			

A statistically significant difference was found between the first pretraining and the control RR/CO_2 [$p(F = 7.56) < 0.05$]; and between the control and the last pretraining RR/CO_2 [$p(F = 3.82) < 0.05$].

FIGURE 1 shows the change in RR/CO_2 index between the first and last pretraining session in the biofeedback treatment group.

The Effect of Normalization of Respiration on the EEG Power Spectrum

FIGURE 2 compares the average EEG power spectral composition "curve" of the asymptomatic control subjects to that of 10 biofeedback treatment group subjects who have been in the program at least seven

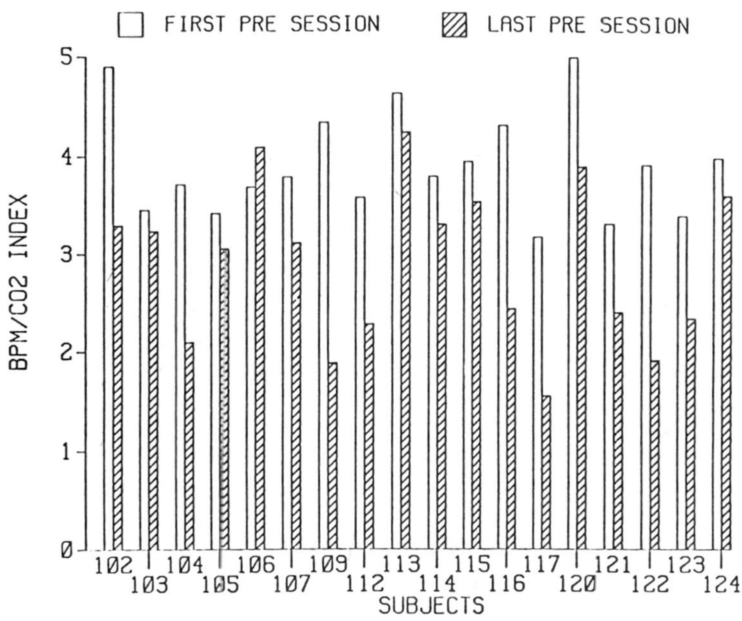

FIGURE 1. Comparison of output index in the first (or earliest available) pretraining session and on the last pretraining session on record.

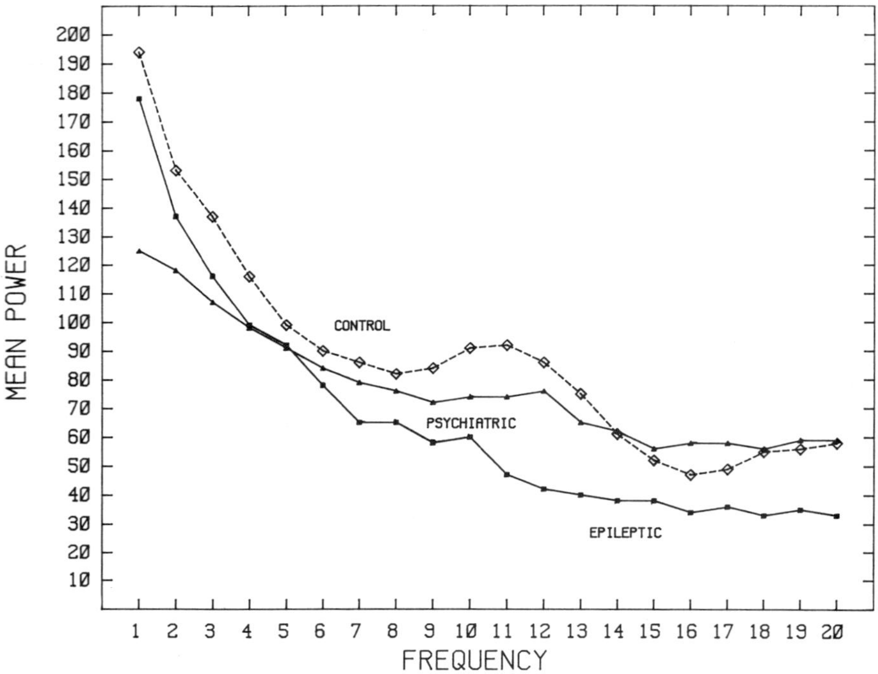

FIGURE 2. Frequency/power spectra in control and epileptic and psychiatric subject groups.

months (four men and six women ranging in age between 23 and 43 years) and the psychiatric group.

For the control group, the spectral distribution is typical, showing a deceleration from dc to *alpha*. There is, then, a slight rise to *beta*. Spectral composition on the first pretraining and last pretraining sessions are shown in FIGURE 3.

The treatment-group "curves" show the following: The curves have the same origin and are more or less parallel between 2 and 5 Hz. Between 4 and 9 Hz, they show elevation above the controls. There is a depression of *alpha* in the first pretreatment curve. This is typical in persons with seizure disorders. The curve for the last pretraining EEGs shows a more or less constant difference from that of the earlier one, beginning at about 5 Hz. It is significantly elevated above both the first-pretreatment and the control curves. This indicates that the effect of the treatment is, among other things, an elevation in power in the EEG. This may be interpreted to reflect an increase in blood flow and metabolism and, consequently, a reduction in hypoxia.

A test for the parallelity of the three "curves" was found to be significant [$p(F = 9.62) < 0.05$]. This indicates that the observed power differences, at each frequency, are not constant along the spectrum.

Normalization of Respiration and Seizure Frequency

The following seizure frequency data were obtained from the 10 subjects who have been in the study at least seven months. The best account of the pretreatment seizure frequency is that, all types combined, they averaged 56 per month. This is the mean of a somewhat skewed distribution (S = 69.88).

At the end of the first month of biofeedback training, the average seizure frequency dropped to seven per month (S = 7.89). This is also a skewed distribution. The data are summarized in TABLE 3.

Because of the obvious departure of these distributions from criteria for parametric analysis, a χ^2 test was used to compare them. This test, against chance occurrence, indicates that the observed seizure frequency differences are not likely to be due to random variation [$p(\chi^2 = 38.0) < 0.05$].

Seizure frequency decreases initially to an average of seven, followed by a decrease to about three and then a stabilization at about four per month. This pattern is shown in FIGURE 4.

Grand mal seizure frequency, examined separately, shows the following pattern: The pretreatment estimated and actual frequency of these seizures averaged about six per month. After the first month in the program, average frequency dropped to about two per month and, subsequently, to an average

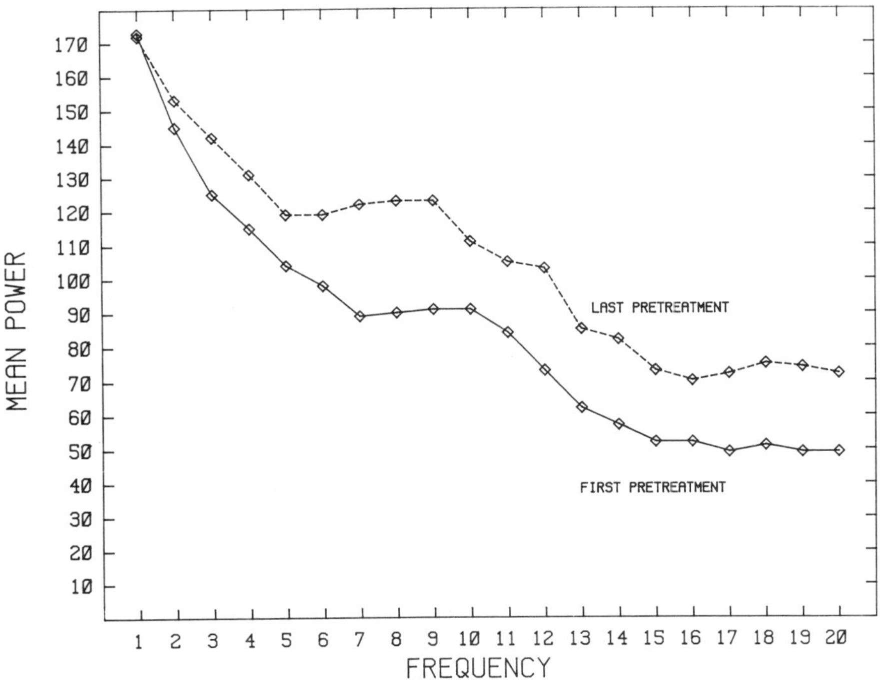

FIGURE 3. Change in frequency/power spectra in the epileptic subject group between the first and last pretreatment recording session.

TABLE 3. Mean Number of Seizures[a] Experienced by the Subjects in the First Seven Months in the Treatment Program and Percent Improvement in Respiratory Index (BPM/CO_2) from the First to the Last Pretraining Recording Session

	Month of Treatment								
Subject No.	1	2	3	4	5	6	7	Percent Improved BPM/CO_2 Index	Average Seizure Frequency
F102	3	4	5	5	10	0	9	33	5.14/month
F103	4	1	3	8	3	9	9	6	5.29
F104	10	5	2	2	9	17	8	44	7.71
M105	0	3	0	0	6	0	0	11	1.29
F109	22	7	6	6	6	7	6	67	8.57
M112	2	4	3	0	0	3	–	67	1.71
F114	16	0	1	1	1	1	1	28	3.00
M115	0	0	0	0	1	0	0	7	0.14
F116	14	8	8	7	–	–	–	38	7.40
M117	0	1	1	0	–	–	–	64	0.50
$\bar{X}$:	7.1	3.3	2.9	2.9	4.5	4.6	4.0	36.5	4.10

[a] All seizures combined.

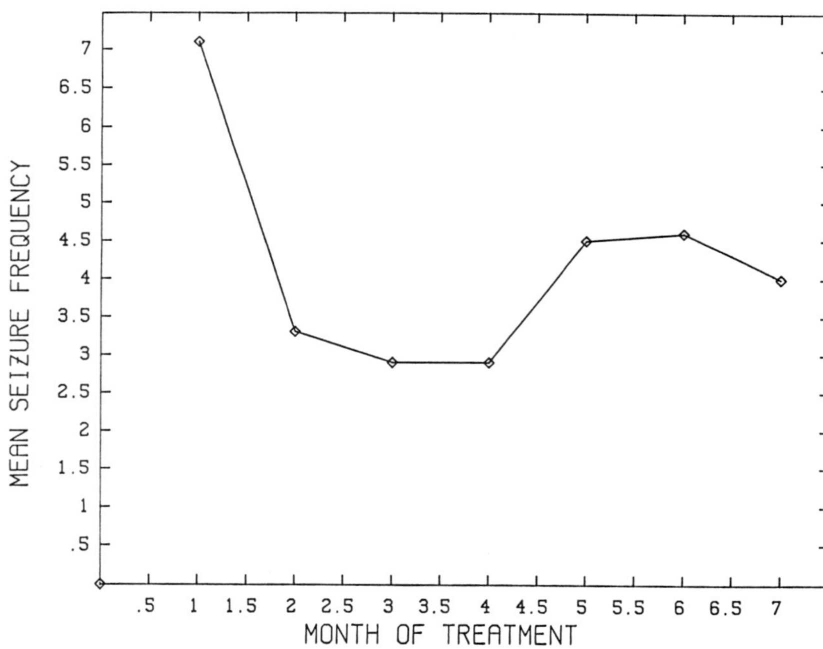

FIGURE 4: Mean number of seizure (all types combined) during the first seven months in the study.

of less than one per month for the next six months. This distribution is also skewed, but it is worth noting that in 8 of the 10 subjects who experienced

TABLE 4. Number of Grand Mal Seizures Experienced by the Subjects During the First Seven Months in the Study

	Month of Treatment							
Subject No.	1	2	3	4	5	6	7	Six Months Seizure Free
F102	0	1	1	2	0	0	2	
F103	1	0	0	0	0	0	0	+
F104	1	1	0	0	1	1	0	
M105	0	2	0	0	2	0	0	
F109	12	0	0	0	0	0	0	+
M112	1	0	0	0	0	0	0	+
F114	1	0	0	0	0	0	0	+
M115	0	0	0	0	1	0	0	
Total:	14	4	1	2	4	1	2	

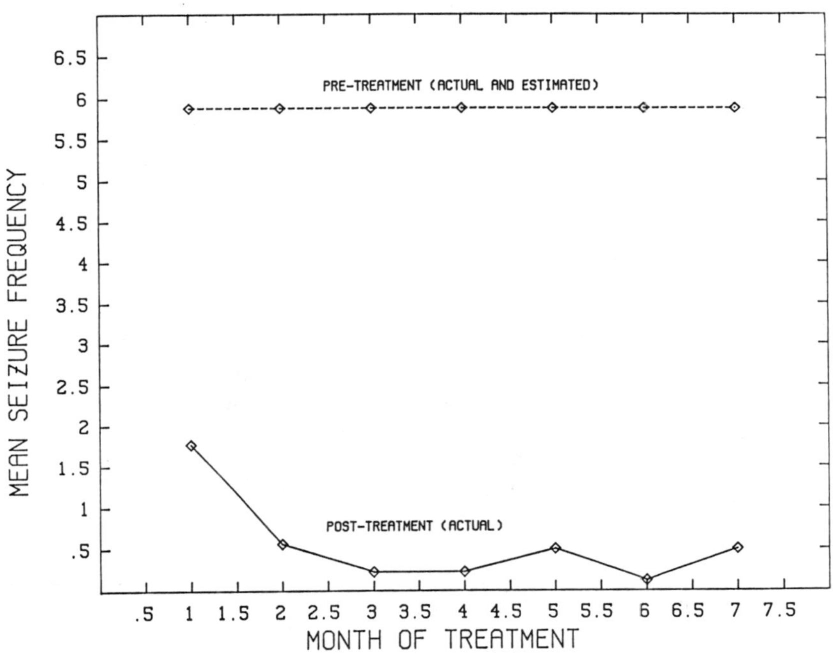

FIGURE 5. Mean number of grand mal seizures during the first seven months in the study.

such seizures, four had none at all for at least six months. These data are summarized in TABLE 4 and FIGURE 5.

The difference between the pre- and posttreatment seizure frequency is assessed on the basis of the distribution of seizures during the seven months observed: There is a statistically significant difference in the distribution of the seizures during the seven months [$p(\chi^2 = 27.7) < 0.05$, df = 6].

DISCUSSION

The present study focuses on two related observations: chronic hyperventilation and seizure activity. There appears to be little doubt that these behaviors overlap. We did not observe a single instance in which persons presenting with idiopathic epilepsy did not also show moderate to severe chronic hyperventilation. The reverse, of course, is not the case, the control group contained a number of subjects who had moderate to severe hyperventilation but did not have seizures.

There is considerable evidence, in this study, to support the contention that end-tidal CO_2 biofeedback is an essential element in the therapeutic correction of abnormal respiration. Contrary to common belief, simply adjusting rate of respiration is inadequate. In the previously cited study,[90] there was no indication that self-regulation produced a lasting outcome. Furthermore, in the numerous previous studies of the effects of hyperventilation and its treatment, no data have been presented on the outcome of training subjects in diaphragmatic respiration. We have found, empirically, in pilot studies prior to the present report, that awareness of the need for diaphragmatic respiration does not come until the subject can "see" the difference in "output" resulting from this type of respiration in comparison to thoracic breathing.

Thus, the lasting benefits of our respiration training are believed to be related to the kind of "knowledge of results" that percent end-tidal CO_2 biofeedback provides.

The Effect of Respiration Training on Respiration

The respiration training procedure appears to have had a considerable effect on respiration behavior. The data in this study represent observations on subjects who have had a different number of training sessions. They did not enter the study at the same time. In some instances, we report the earliest record available when the first record was unavailable for technical reasons. This causes a minor error, but it is in the direction of making statistical significance more difficult to attain. When later data are used, a modification in behavior will already have occurred. This would, if anything, make us underrate the effectiveness of the treatment, from a purely statistical point of view.

There was a significant RR reduction attending treatment. The reason for this is that when diaphragmatic respiration prevails, this in itself has a moderating effect on rate. Second, it is important to note that there was no significant change in end-tidal CO_2. Other factors equal, change in RR must alter percent end-tidal CO_2: If metabolic rate is constant, the proportion of CO_2 dissipated will be a function of the number of breaths per unit time because CO_2 build-up will be constant. Thus, the fact that no dramatic change in end-tidal CO_2 was noted over wide changes in RR indicates that there is an adjustment of CO_2 dissipation that occurs automatically with rate change. If that were not what the subjects were experiencing, they would be increasing their CO_2 dissipation as rate decreased. That is precisely what happens if rate is controlled in thoracic breathers.

The clearest indication of the therapeutic change is seen in the comparison of the output index RR/CO_2. While this index leaves something to be desired, it combines the observation of percent end-tidal CO_2 with rate to give a better picture of the ventilatory pattern. This index shows a dramatic change in all but one subject (106F).

The Effect of Respiration Training on the EEG

The EEG power spectrum in seizure sufferers is categorically different from that of non-seizure sufferers. Seizure sufferers typically show an elevation in the 4- to 8-Hz segment of the EEG. This pattern is observed in the subjects in this study. The analysis, unlike that for respiratory data, includes only those of the seizure subjects who have been in the study, and have received treatment, for at least seven months.

Lubar[47] refers to the changes in the EEG that he observed as "normalization." This means that the slope of the power spectral curve is greater in subjects before his EEG biofeedback training. In the present study, we corroborate this finding. The mean power spectrum curve for the last pretraining EEG definitely has a lesser slope than that for the first observed pretraining session.

In addition, there appears to be a more or less constant elevation of the curve beginning at about 7 Hz, for the last pretraining session. We contend that this elevation in power at the frequencies above 7 Hz represents an increase in the total energy in the system: This increase in power may be associated with an increase in blood flow and metabolism in the brain postulated, in previously cited research, to accompany reduction in respiratory alkalosis.

There are at least two ways in which control of respiratory alkalosis may improve brain metabolism. First, alkalosis affects O_2 delivery to the brain because it affects O_2–hemoglobin dissociation: It shifts the O_2–Hb dissociation curve to the right (Bohr effect). Second, it stimulates the synthesis of organic phosphates (2, 3-diphosphoglycerate, in particular) which compete with O_2 for binding on Hb.[91] This altered O_2–Hb affinity is at first an adaptive homeostatic mechanism, but it ultimately depletes the supply in circulating blood. Second, hypocapnia (low blood CO_2) has a vasoconstrictive effect in cerebral arteries and arterioles. Thus, the net effect would be chronic hypoxia. It is not surprising that abnormal EEGs are observed in persons who have chronic hypoxia.

Second, it has been repeatedly demonstrated that CO_2 blood tension is the only effective control of cerebral caliber and thus blood flow and metabolism.[92] Consequently, in combination, the effects of hypocapnia and the resultant alkalosis would be presumed to potentiate so as to further jeopardize an already impaired brain tissue O_2 delivery system.

The finding of abnormal EEG in moderate and severe chronic hyperventilators is consistent with our present understanding of the relationship between epileptiform EEG activity and seizure activity evoked routinely in EEG examination by hyperventilation. Such findings are also consistent with the report that abnormal EEGs are not uncommon in migraine,[91-94] likewise associated with cerebral arterial vasoconstriction and hypoxia.[94-96]

The Effect of Respiration Training on Seizure Activity

The correction of hyperventilation was accompanied by a significant diminution in seizure activity in our subjects. The reduction was not uniform, nor was the distribution of seizure types, frequency, and severity. Because of the relatively small number of subjects in the study at least seven months, it is not possible to speculate with any degree of accuracy about what variables predict seizure reduction.

None of the subjects had no seizure at all after seven months of training. However, the frequency and severity of the seizures as well as seizure type, for any subject, underwent considerable modification. It should be noted that all the subjects were intractable to therapeutic serum levels of a multitude of anticonvulsant medications. It is especially interesting to note that four of the eight subjects, out of the ten, who experienced grand mal seizures had none during the seven-month observation period. Undoubtedly, the stress-reducing value of the respiration retraining also played a significant role in the seizure reduction.[76]

It may be concluded from the findings of this study that at least some forms of idiopathic epilepsy manifest a considerable degree of autonomic nervous system dysharmony. For whatever reason it ensues, chronic hyperventilation seems to produce cerebral vasoconstriction: This may lead to an ischemic reduction in cerebral arteriolar blood flow and brain metabolism. This condition may predispose some persons to vasospasms which, we contend, supports previous conclusions of an etiological connection to seizure disorders. Secondly, respiratory alkalosis seems to reduce O_2 delivery to the brain as well as to systemic tissues, thus disrupting the reflexive relationship between the heart and the lungs.

This study also supports the contention that correcting hyperventilation in idiopathic seizure sufferers reduces, through the multiple channels described, the tendency to convulsions by reducing the chronic hypoxia and raising the seizure threshold.

SUMMARY

Breathing rate (RR), end-tidal percent CO_2, and EEG were obtained in three groups: psychiatric referral subjects presenting with anxiety, panic, phobia, depression and migraine; a group of idiopathic seizure sufferers; and a group of asymptomatic controls. Virtually all the noncontrol subjects were found to show moderate to severe hyperventilation and the accompanying EEG dysrhythmia. The seizure group subjects were taught diaphragmatic respiration with end-tidal percent CO_2 biofeedback. The training normalized their respiration and altered their EEGs and seizure frequency.

REFERENCES

1. GLASER, G. H. 1979. Convulsive Disorders (Epilepsy). *In* A Textbook of Neurology. 6th edit. H. H. Merritt, Ed. Lea and Febiger. Philadelphia.
2. GOWERS, W. G. 1907. The Borderland of Epilepsy. Churchill. London.
3. COATSWORTH, J. J. & J. K. PENRY. 1972. Clinical Efficacy and Use. *In* Antiepileptic Drugs. D. M. Woodbury, J. K. Penry & R. P. Schmidt, Eds. Raven Press. New York.
4. RENNIE, L. E. 1969. Management of epilepsy. G.P. (Kansas) **39:** 17–123.
5. RODIN, E. A. 1968. The Prognosis of Patients with Epilepsy. C. C. Thomas. Springfield, IL.
6. KURTZKE, J. F., L. T. KURLAND, I. D. GOLDBERG, N. W. CHOI & F. A. REEDER. 1973. Convulsive disorders. *In* Epidemiology of Neurologic and Sense Organ Disorders (APHA Monograph on Vital and Health Statistics). L. T. Kurland, J. F. Kurtzke & I. D. Goldberg, Eds.: 15–40. Harvard Press. Cambridge, MA.
7. GASTAUT, H. 1970. Clinical and electroencephic: Classification of epileptic seizures. Epilepsia **11:** 102–113.
8. PENFIELD, W. & H. JASPER. 1954. Epilepsy and the Functional Anatomy of the Brain. Little Brown & Co. Boston.
9. WOLFE, L. S. & K. A. C. ELLIOTT. 1962. Chemical studies in relation to convulsive conditions. *In* Neurochemistry, 2nd edit. K. A. C. Elliott, I. H. Page & J. H. Quastel, Eds. C. C. Thomas. Springfield, IL.
10. WILKS, SAMUEL. 1859. Cited in Ref. 8.
11. JACKSON, J. H. 1931. Selected Writings on John Hughlings Jackson, Vol. I. On Epilepsy and Epileptiform Convulsions. J. Taylor, Ed. Hodder & Stoughton. London.
12. FRITSCH, G. & E. HITZIG. 1870. Ueber die electrische Erregbarkeit des Gehirns. Arch. Anat. Physiol. **3:** 300–332.
13. GOWERS, W. G. 1881. Epilepsy and Other Chronic Convulsive Diseases. J. A. Churchill. London.
14. BRAIN, L. 1962. Diseases of the Nervous System. Oxford University Press. London.
15. BAROLIN, G. S. 1966. Migraines and epilepsies—a relationship. Epilepsia **7:** 53–66.
16. MOSTOFSKY, D. I. 1981. Recurrent Paroxysmal Disorders of the Central Nervous System. *In* Handbook of Clinical Behavior Therapy. S. M. Turner, K. S. Calhoun & H. E. Adams, Eds.: 447–474. John Wiley. New York.
17. GIBBS, E. L., W. G. LENNOX & F. A. GIBBS. 1940. Variations in carbon dioxide content of blood in epilepsy. Arch. Neurol. Psychiat. **43:** 223–239.
18. GIBBS, F. A., H. DAVIS & W. G. LENNOX. 1935. The electroencephalogram in epilepsy and in conditions of impaired consciousness. Arch. Neurol. Psychiat. **43:** 1133–1148.

19. HIMWICH, H. E. 1951. Brain Metabolism and Cerebral Disorders. Williams and Wilkins. Baltimore, MD.
20. BATT, A. M., G. SIEST, R. KHODJET EL KHIL, B. LE PERRON, M. WEBER & P. TRIDON. 1975. Drugs and references values in clinical chemistry. III. Effects of anticonvulsant drugs on plasma enzymes and metabolites: Correlation studies. *In* Drug Interference and Drug Measurement in Clinical Chemistry, Proceedings of the 3rd International Colloquium on Prospects in Biology. Point-a-Mousson.: 33–41. Karger. Basel.
21. LAIDLAW, J. & A. RICHENS. 1976. A Textbook of Epilepsy. Churchill Livingstone. Edinburgh.
22. GROEN, J. J. 1975. The measurement of emotion and arousal in the clinical physiology laboratory. *In* Emotion—Their Parameters and Measurement. L. Levi, Ed.: 727–746. Raven Press. New York.
23. LATHAM, A. N. 1975. Effects of in vitro change in urinary pH on the enzymatic measurement and daily variation in excretion of D-glucaric acid. J. Pharmacol. **27:** 612–615.
24. MADSEN, J. 1943. Further studies on the biochemistry of epilepsy. Acta Psychiatr. Neurol. **18:** 257–337.
25. BISGAARD, JARLOV & NORVIG BISGAARD. 1918. Cited in Ref. 24.
26. ALTENBERGER & STERN. 1928. Cited in Ref. 24.
27. MEYER, J. S. & A. G. WALTZ. 1961. Relationship of Cerebral Anoxia to Functional and Electroencephic. Abnormality. *In* Cerebral Anoxia and the Electroencephalograph. H. Gastaut & J. S. Meyer, Eds.: 307–328. Thomas. Springfield, IL.
28. DAVIS, H. & W. WALLACE. 1941. Factors affecting the electroencephalographic changes induced by hyperventilation. Am. J. Physiol. **133:** 258.
29. LUBIN, A. J. & J. C. PRICE. 1942. Effect of alkalosis and acidocis on cortical electrical activity and blood flow. J. Neurophysiol. **5:** 261–268.
30. DAVIS, H. & W. WALLACE. 1942. Factors affecting changes produced in electroencephalogram by standardized hyperventilation. Arch. Neurol. Psychiatr. **47:** 606–625.
31. SWANSON, A. G., L. S. STAVNEY & F. PLUM. 1958. Effects of pH and carbon dioxide on cerebral electrical activity. Neurology: **8:** 787–792.
32. FAURBYE, A. 1943. Blodets Reaktion ved Epilepsi. Ph.D. thesis, Cøbenhavns Universitet, Copenhagen.
33. ROSS, I. S. & L. H. LOESER. 1951. Electroencephalographic findings in essential hypoglycemia. EEG Clin. Neurophysiol. **3:** 141–148.
34. MILLICHAP, J. G. & J. A. ULRICH. 1962. Abnormal urinary excretion of amino acids in children with petit mal epilepsy: Preliminary communication. Mayo Clin. Proc. **37:** 307.
35. SIMILA, S., L. VON WENDT & S. L. LINNA. 1980. Dipropylacetate and aminoaciduria. J. Neurol. Sci. **45:** 83–86.
36. KAMIYA, J. 1969. Operant control of EEG alpha rhythm and some of its reported effects on consciousness. *In* Altered States of Consciousness. C. Tart, Ed. John Wiley. New York.
37. BROWN, B. B. 1974. New Mind, New Body. Harper & Row. New York.
38. STERMAN, M. B. & E. WYRWICKA. 1967. EEG and correlates of sleep: Evidence for separate forebrain substrates. Brain Res. **6:** 143–163.
39. WYRWICKA, W. & M. B. STERMAN. 1968. Instrumental conditioning of sensorimotor cortex EEG spindles in the waking cat. Physiol. Behav. **3:** 703–707.

40. CHASE, M. M. & R. M. HARPER. 1971. Somatomotor and visceromotor correlates of operantly conditioned 12/14 sec. sensorimotor cortical activity. EEG Clin. Neurophysiol. **31:** 85–92.
41. HARPER, R. M. & M. B. STERMAN. 1972. Subcortical unit activity during conditioned 12-14 Hz sensorimotor rhythm in cats. Physiol. Fed. Proc. **31:** 414.
42. STERMAN, M. B. & L. FRIAR. 1972. Suppression of seizures in an epileptic following sensorimotor EEG feedback training. EEG Clin. Neurophysiol. **33:** 89–95.
43. STERMAN, M. B. 1973. Neurophysiological and clinical studies of sensorimotor EEG biofeedback and training: Some effects of epilepsy. *In* Biofeedback Behavioral Medicine. L. Birk, Ed. Grune & Stratton. New York.
44. KAPLAN, B. J. 1975. Biofeedback in epileptics: Equivocal relationship of reinforced EEG frequency to seizure reduction. Epilepsia **16:** 477–485.
45. GASTAUT, H. 1975. Comments on "Biofeedback in epileptics: Equivocal relationship of reinforced EEG frequency to seizure reduction" by Bonnie Kaplan. Epilepsia **16:** 477–485.
46. UPTON, A. R. M. & D. LONGMIRE. 1975. Effects of feedback on focal epileptic discharges in man. Can. J. Neurol. Sci. **3:** 153–168.
47. LUBAR, J. F. & W. W. BAHLER. 1976. Behavioral management of epileptic seizure following EEG biofeedback training, of the sensorimotor rhythm. Biofeed. Self-Reg. **1:** 77–104.
48. FINLEY, W. W. 1976. Operant conditioning of the EEG in two patients with epilepsy: Methodologic and clinical consideration. Pavolvian J. Biol. Sci. **12:** 93–111.
49. STERMAN, M. B., L. R. MACDONALD & I. BERNSTEIN. 1977. Quantitative analysis of EEG sleep spindle activity in epileptic and nonepileptic subjects. Electroenceph. Clin. Neurophysiol. **42:** 724.
50. STERMAN, M. B. 1977. Effects of sensorimotor EEG feedback training on sleep and clinical manifestations of epilepsy. *In* Biofeedback and Behavior. J. Beatty & H. Legewie, Eds.: 167–200. Plenum Press. New York.
51. STERMAN, M. B. 1977. Clinical implications of EEG biofeedback training: A critical appraisal. *In* Biofeedback: Theory and Research. J. Beatty, Ed. Academic Press. New York.
52. KUHLMAN, W. N. & T. ALLISON. 1977. EEG feedback training in the treatment of epilepsy: Some questions and some answers. Pavlovian J. Biol. Sci. **2:** 112–122.
53. MOSTOFSKY, D. I. & B. A. BALASCHACK. 1981. Psychobiological control of seizures. Psychol. Bull. **84:** 723–750.
54. REYNOLDS, E. H. 1976. Unsatisfactory aspects of the drug treatment of epilepsy. Epilepsia **17:** 3, 13–15.
55. KUHLMAN, W. N. 1979–1980. EEG feedback training of epileptic patients: Clinical and electroencephalographic analysis. *In* Biofeedback and Behavioral Medicine.: 466–477. Aldine. New York.
56. QUY, R. J., S. J. HUTT & S. FORREST. 1979. Sensorimotor rhythm feedback training and epilepsy: Some methodological and conceptual issues. Biol. Psychol. **9:** 129–149.
57. STERMAN, M. B. & R. A. KOVALESKI. 1979. Anticonvulsant effects of restraint and pyridoxine on hydrazine seizures in the monkey. Exp. Neurol. **65:** 78–86.

58. Soulayrol, R., E. Mesdjian, H. Lob, C. A. Tassinari & J. Roger. 1965. The tryptophan loading test in epileptic children. Epilepsia **6:** 4, 310–324.
59. Holcombe, V., M. B. Sterman, S. J. Goodman & M. D. Fairchild. 1979. The immobilization response in rhesus monkey: A behavioral and electroencephalographic study. Exp. Neurol. **63:** 420–435.
60. Bowersox, S. S. & M. B. Sterman. 1981. Changes in sensorimotor sleep spindle activity and seizure susceptibility after somatosensory deafferentation. Exp. Neurol. **74:** 814–828.
61. Lubar, J. F., H. S. Shasbin, S. E. Natelson, G. S. Holder, S. F. Whitsett, W. E. Pamplin & D. I. Krulikowski. 1981. EEG operant conditioning in intractable epileptics. Arch. Neurol. **38:** 700–704.
62. Sterman, M. B. 1981. EEG Feedback: Physiological behavior modification. Neurosci. Biobehav. Rev. **5:** 405–412.
63. Clausen, O. 1951. Repiratory movements in normal, neurotic, and psychotic subjects. Acta Psychiat. Scand. Suppl. **68.**
64. Comroe, J. H., Jr. 1974. Physiology of Respiration, 2nd Edit. Yearbook Medical Publishers. Chicago.
65. Sodeman, W. A. & T. M. Sodeman. 1979. Pathologic Physiology. W. B. Saunders. Philadelphia, PA.
66. Brown, E. B. 1953. Physiological effects of hyperventilation. Physiol. Rec. **33:** 445–471.
67. Tower, D. B. 1960. Neurochemistry of Epilepsy. Chas. C. Thomas. Springfield, IL.
68. Rosett, J. 1924. The experimental production of rigidity, of abnormal involuntary movement and of abnormal states of consciousness in man. Brain **47:** 293–336.
69. Lennox, W. G., F. A. Gibbs & E. L. Gibbs. 1938. The relationship in man of cerebral activity to blood flow and blood constituents. J. Neurol. Psychiat. **1:** 221–225.
70. Tarlan, M. 1958. EEG changes in neurogenic chronic respiratory acidosis. EEG Clin. Neurophysiol. **10:** 724–729.
71. Lennox, W. G. 1928. The effect on epileptic seizures of varying the composition of respired air. J. Clin. Invest. **6:** 23.
72. Gibbs, F. A., D. Williams & E. L. Gibbs. 1949. Modification of the cortical frequency spectrum by changes in CO_2, blood sugar and O_2. J. Neurophysiol.: 49–58.
73. Holmberg, G. 1953. The electroencephalogram during hypoxia and hyperventilation. EEG Clin. Neurophysiol. **5:** 371–379.
74. Schneider, J. 1961. Urinary excretion of electrolytes in centrencephalic epileptics. Epilepsia **2:** 358–366.
75. Ikonomoff, S. I. 1970. Anticholinesterase drugs and epileptic seizures. Br. J. Psychiat. **117:** 679–680.
76. Babb, R. R. & P. B. Eckman. 1972. Abdominal epilepsy. JAMA **222:** 1, 65–66.
77. Kariga, T. 1962. Neurochemical studies of convulsion. J. Psychiat. Neurol. **64:** 707–720.
78. Mattson, R. H., G. R. Henniger, B. B. Gallagher & G. H. Glaser. 1970. Psychophysiologic precipitants of seizures in epileptics. Neurology **20:** 407.
79. Robinson, L. J. 1944. Encephalographic study during epileptic seizures related to hyperventilation. Dis. Nerv. Syst. **5:** 87–90.

80. BRODY, B. S. & J. G. DUSSER DE BARENNE. 1932. Effects of hyperventilation on the excitability of the motor cortex in cats. Arch. Neurol. Psychiat. **28:** 571.
81. WOLFF, H. G. & W. G. Lennox. 1930. Cerebral cirulation XII: Effects on pial vessels of variation in O_2 and CO_2 content of blood. Arch. Neurol. Psychiatr. **23:** 1027–1030.
82. MERRITT, H. H. 1979. A Textbook of Neurology. 6th edit. Lea and Febiger. Philadelphia, PA.
83. LIVINGSTON, S. 1956. Etiological factors in adult convulsions—An analysis of 689 patients whose attacks began after 20 years of age. N. Engl. J. Med. **256:** 1211–1216.
84. COBB, S., W. W. SARGANT & R. S. SCHWAB. 1939. Simultaneous respiratory and electroencephalographic recording in a case of petit mal. Arch. Neurol. Psychiatr. **42:** 1189–1191.
85. GIBBS, F. A., D. WILLIAMS & E. L. GIBBS. 1940. Modification of the cortical frequency spectrum by changes in CO_2, blood sugar, and O_2. J. Neurophysiol. **3:** 49–58.
86. LENNOX, W. G., F. A. GIBBS & E. L. COBB. 1938. The relationship in man of cerebral activity to blood flow and to blood constituents. A. Res. Nerv. Mental Dis. Proc. **18:** 277–297.
87. SUTHERLAND, J. M. & M. J. EADIE. 1980. The Epilepsies. Churchill Livingstone. Edinburgh.
88. RILEY, T. L. 1982. Epilepsy—or merely hyperventilation? Emerg. Med. **14:** 162–167.
89. MEDUNA, L. J. 1950. Carbon Dioxide Therapy. 6th edit. Thomas. Springfield, IL.
90. INGVAR, D. H., B. SIESJO & C. H. HERTZ. 1959. Measurement of tissue PCO_2 in the brain. Experientia **15:** 306–308.
91. BREWER, G. J. 1974. Red cell metabolism and function. *In* The Red Blood Cell. 2nd edit. Vol. **I:** 473–508. D. MacN. Surgenor, Ed. Academic Press. New York.
92. HEISTADT, D. D., M. L. MARCUS & F. M. ABBOUD. 1978. Experimental attempts to unmask the effects of neural stimuli on cerebral blood flow. *In* Cerebral Vascular Smooth Muscle and Its Control. M. J. Purves, Ed. Elsevier Medica. Amsterdam.
93. SMYTH, V. O. G. & A. L. WINTER. 1964. The EEG in migraine. EEG Clin. Neurophysiol. **16:** 194–202.
94. GOLDENSOHN, E. S. 1976. Paroxysmal and other features of the electroencephalogram in migraine. Res. Clin. Stud. Headache **4:** 118–128.
95. HOCKADAY, J. M. 1978. Late outcome of childhood onset migraine and factors affecting outcome, with particular reference to early and late EEG findings. *In* Current Concepts in Migraine Research. R. Greene, Ed.: 41–48. Raven Press. New York.
96. AMERY, W. K. 1982. Brain hypoxia: The turning point in the genesis of the migraine attack? Cephalalgia **2:** 83–109.
97. ADAMSON, W. B. & E. D. SELLERS. 1933. Observations on the incidence of the hyper-sensitive state in one hundred cases of epilepsy. J. Allergy **4:** 315–323.
98. BEAUCHEMIN, J. A. 1936. Allergic reactions in mental diseases. Am. J. Psychiatry **92:** 1191–1204.

99. Clarke, T. W. 1934, Epilepsy of allergic origin. N. Y. State J. Med. **34:** 647–651.

100. Chobot, R., H. D. Dundy & B. L. Pacella. 1950. The incidence of abnormal electroencephalographic patterns in allergic children. J. Allergy **21:** 334–338.

101. Dees, S. C. & H. Lowenbach. 1951. Allergic epilepsy. Ann. Allergy **9:** 446–458.

102. Dewar, D. C. 1941. The allergic factor in idiopathic epilepsy. J. Ment. Sci. **87:** 608–630.

103. Dewar, D. C. 1941. The allergic factor in idiopathic epilepsy. Practitioner **147:** 776–788.

104. Klein, J. 1933. Allergic epilepsy. J. Pediatrics **3:** 505–508.

105. McGee, W. A. 1949. Allergic epilepsy. N. Orleans Med. Surg. J. **101:** 601–603.

Biofeedback for Disorders of Initiating and Maintaining Sleep

ELLIS I. BAROWSKY[a]

Department of Special Education
Hunter College
City University of New York
New York, New York 10021

JOANNE MOSKOWITZ

Rockland Psychological Associates
Pomona, New York 10970

JOSEPH B. ZWEIG

Rockland Psychological Associates
Pomona, New York 10970

Disturbances of sleep in children are a primary reason for pediatric consultation. While the nature of the disturbance may vary from disorders of initiating and maintaining sleep (DIMS) to disorders of excessive sleep (DOES) or hypersomnolence to dysfunction within the sleep–wakefulness cycles (Parasomnias and Phase-lag syndrome),[1] the great majority of reports of children focus on the prevalence of insomnia. Generally, parents recognize the insomnia; the pediatric patients will rarely report the problem. It is estimated that up to 5% of the pediatric population experiences this disorder.[2]

Sleep disturbance in children can occur as a primary problem or secondary to other psychological problems, such as depression or anxiety reactions. In toddlers, up to one-third of all sleep problems are associated with other behavioral difficulties,[3] while in adolescence poor sleep has been correlated with stress and certain personality characteristics.[4] For instance, children who are diagnosed as having depression, attentional deficit disorder (ADD), and conduct disorders show a higher prevalence for sleep disorders than the general pediatric population,[5] with 13% of emotionally disturbed adolescents being referred for treatment.[6] Neurologic "soft signs" are also identified as often coincident with sleep problems, suggesting a possible underlying neurological substrate or a higher incidence among

[a] Address for correspondence: Dr. Ellis I. Barowsky, Hunter College, Department of Special Education, 695 Park Avenue, New York, NY 10021.

neurologically impaired children.[7] It should be noted, however, that transient sleep difficulties may be within the realm of normality as a reaction to environmental events that serve to arouse the child, such as anticipation of an exciting event or brief adjustment reactions to life situations. These "transient and situational" precipitants of psychophysiological arousal are generally self limiting, with the more persistent "species" requiring more treatment.

According to the Association of Sleep Disorders Centers, DIMS that are persistent result from the "mutually reinforcing factors of chronic, somatisized tension—anxiety and negative conditioning to sleep." Left untreated, the time and place designated for sleep becomes the target of anxiety, causing an arousal response within the child and perpetuating a vicious cycle of sleep inhibition—anxiety and arousal—sleep inhibition. Loss of control and feelings of helplessness develop[8] along with increased irritability, restlessness, and depression.[9]

Psychopharmacological treatment of sleep disorders secondary to depression has proven successful,[10] although less intrusive methods may be preferable for the pediatric population. Methods allowing greater control to the pediatric patient may gain greater compliance and allow the child to again feel in control, therefore less vigilant, less physiologically aroused, and the sleep situation less charged with anxiety.

Behavioral (and conditioned) concommitants of psychosomatic illness have been managed successfully using nonpharmacological techniques,[11-13] particularly with acute and chronically ill children. Some of these techniques have also been employed in reducing anxiety and inducing sleep. Guided imagery,[14] hypnotic suggestion,[15] and behavioral relaxation training[16] have all been proven effective. Children have also demonstrated the ability to master biofeedback techniques in the treatment of medical disorders where more intrusive approaches had been traditionally employed.[13]

Three case histories are presented in which the primary symptoms involved disturbed sleep patterns marked by insomnia or impaired sleep maintenance. Each patient was instructed in the use of biofeedback for monitoring body responses to their aroused state along with exercises to reduce this psychophysiological vigilance.

CASE 1

The first patient was a 17-year-old boy who had a history of adjustment difficulties in social and academic areas. He had undergone elective surgery for adenoid removal, which had impaired the quality of his speech. After surgery he developed a fear of sleep and unconsciousness associated with surgical anesthesia. When he began to enter sleep, he immediately became aroused. This series of events occurred a number of times through the night. A secondary depression developed marked by the sleep disturbance, irritability, and agitation.

CASE 2

The second patient was an 11-year-old girl who experienced sustained delays in sleep onset. Nocturnal anxieties pertaining to school achievement and anticipated school failure precipitated arousal which delayed sleep.

CASE 3

The third patient was a 9-year-old boy whose chief complaint was of delayed onset of sleep with multiple wakenings during the night. Each wakening was marked by long latencies in returning to sleep. He consequently awoke each morning, reported fatigue and headache (muscular tension in origin), and was unable to concentrate on schoolwork. His delays in entering sleep were reportedly the result of frightening imagery resulting from "scary" movies he had seen, in spite of the long periods of time between the original experience and the nightly sleep disruption.

TREATMENT

Relaxation training with concommitant biofeedback was conducted with each patient. Training involved thermal and electromyographic (EMG) feedback monitoring the changes in muscle tone and peripheral vasodilation associated with relaxation. Initial training involved frontalis EMG feedback and thermal feedback from the dominant hand during relaxation. Each child was instructed in diaphragmatic breathing and learning to discriminate between tense and relaxed muscle groups within his or her own body. Individualized visualization exercises were developed with each child's direction, incorporating experiences associated with relaxation and pleasure for the child. EMG recordings were made from the frontalis muscle[17] by means of surface electrodes interfaced with an Apple II computer by means of an Inner-Tell A 7 EMG. Peripheral temperature[18,19] was recorded by a thermistor attached to the dominant hand and interfaced to the Apple II computer by an Inner-Tell A 6 temperature trainer.

Programming of biofeedback parameters and recordings were performed by D.P. 6 Profile Systems addressing EMG and thermal parameters. Recordings were made with intercycle intervals of one minute with visual and auditory feedback presented to each child on the same schedule. The visual feedback involved the presentation of a linear array of light-emitting diodes in analogue to the increase in peripheral skin temperature. As skin temperature increased, a greater number of diodes would become illuminated. A clicking sound was provided as auditory feedback for changes in muscle tone with the click rate analagous to EMG reading and declining with reductions in tonus. Self-directed relaxation tapes for use at bedtime were provided along with instructions to carry out relaxation exercises at that time.

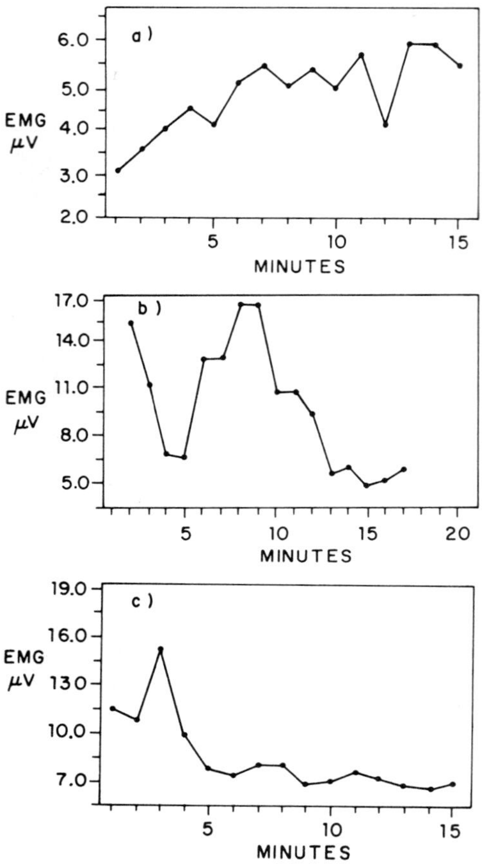

FIGURE 1. Electromyograph tracing during relaxation training. **(a)** Initial session of training for 17-year-old male patient with difficulty in maintaining sleep. Intermittent arousal with increased EMG tracing after incidents of relaxation. (*Arrow*) At this point, patient was observed to close eyes and appear to sleep. Next cycle evidenced arousal just as had been reported happened when sleep was attempted. **(b)** Third session for 11-year-old girl with difficulty initiating sleep. **(c)** Sixth session for 9-year-old boy with difficulty initiating sleep. Progressive decrease in EMG noted from initiation to termination of session.

A second phase involving weaning from therapist's presence followed, based upon the reduction in EMG and the child's self report of his readiness. During this phase additional muscle groups were used for EMG feedback (masseter and trapezius) to demonstrate generalization as well as different arousal states (eyes open and closed) as were upright and reclining postures.

RESULTS

FIGURE 1 shows computer plotting of EMG recordings during representative training sessions for each of the three children.

FIGURE 1a reveals some reduction in EMG during the first session of our third patient with attenuation becoming interrupted as he entered the initial sleep phase. EMG recordings for this patient appear to verify the self report that as he begins to fall asleep he suddenly becomes aroused, thus interrupting somnolence. This pattern is not an unusual tracing in the early phase of relaxation training. FIGURES 1b and 1c show the decremental EMG achieved within the same sessions. The initial values are shown to vary with each child and each child established his or her own baseline with reduction serving as the dependent variable. FIGURE 1b reflects reduction by the third training session for patient 2 while FIGURE 1c was recorded during the sixth session for patient 3. By session 7, the parents all reported decreased indications of child anxiety behaviors such as restlessness and avoidance of bedtime in addition to sleep occurring within 15 minutes and continuing without interruption through the night.

DISCUSSION

The rapid resumption of normative sleep patterns in children consequent to reduced psychophysiological arousal lends support to the Association for Sleep Disorders hypothesis for persistent DIMS. Attenuated muscle tonus and concommitant peripheral vasodilation are indications that the body is in a more relaxed state. While relaxation training contributes to this response, biofeedback, which according to Stroebel allows you "to listen to your body,"[20] permits the child to monitor the changes and validate his somatosensory perceptions of this state; this appears to contribute to symptom abatement. Reduced levels of arousal now under the control of the child and verified by instrumentation may reduce feelings of helplessness. Similar behavioral interruption of chronic pain helplessness cycles have been shown to facilitate coping.[13,21,22]

Further, the dependent state, which can be acquired by the pharmacotherapy patient, is also avoided, given the ability of the patient to be weaned from therapist and equipment dependency. Biofeedback has also been shown to be a method acceptable to both parent and child and is further not associated with undesireable side effects. One of the difficulties we have encountered, however, is that the relaxation often induces sleep before the "planned" end of the session. While in some respects this serves to demonstrate *in vivo* effectiveness, more reinforcement of the controlled relaxation response with the patient in an awake state is precluded. The experience of control of psychophysiological arousal is important before reentry into the milieu (sleep time and location) ultimately associated with hypervigilance. To deal with this issue, "practice" with relaxation tapes is recommended during day hours not primarily associated with entering sleep.

It should also be noted that the issues associated with persistent DIMS in our three patients represent frequent fears of children. They were neither remarkable nor atypical concerns and may well represent issues causing arousal in a number of children. The clinician should be aware of those conditions often resulting in psychophysiological arousal and stress in children and not dismiss what appear to be unremarkable life situations as benign. Further, awareness of the varied biofeedback methods in addition to firm understanding of child development should be regarded as the benchmark of the clinician, without which clinical involvement with biofeedback is inappropriate.

SUMMARY

Sleep disturbances are a frequent reason for pediatric consultation. When the disturbance persists in the form of delays in entering or maintaining sleep (DIMS), a vicious cycle develops. As part of the cycle, vigilance or arousal occurs, further inhibiting sleep occurrence. Persistent DIMS requires treatment to interrupt this self-perpetuating sequence. Interruption requires reduction in psychophysiological arousal and deconditioning of the events surrounding sleep. Electromyographic (EMG) and thermal biofeedback in conjunction with relaxation training were used with three children who maintained high levels of arousal resulting from stresses common to their developmental stages. Within seven sessions, all three patients showed attenuation of arousal and symptom abatement marked by uninterrupted sleep.

REFERENCES

1. Roffwarg, H. 1986. Diagnostic classification of sleep and arousal disorders. Sleep **2:** 1–137.
2. Bisler, E., A. Kales & C. Soldatos. 1979. Sleep disorders encountered in medical practice: A national survey of physicians. Behav. Med. **6:** 1–6.
3. Richman, N. 1981. A community survey of the characteristics of 1 to 2 year olds with sleep disorders. J. Am. Acad. Child Psychiatry **20:** 281–291.
4. Price, V., T. Coates & C. Thorsen. 1978. Prevalence and correlates of poor sleep among adolescents. Am. J. Dis. Child. **132:** 583–586.
5. Dixon, K., L. Monroe & S. Jahim. Insommiac children. Sleep **4:** 313–318.
6. Marles, P. & L. Monroe. 1976. Correlates of adolescent poor sleep. J. Abnorm. Psychol. **85:** 243–246.
7. Hauri, P. & E. Olmstead. 1980. Childhood-onset insomnia. Sleep **3:** 59–65.
8. Freedman, R. & J. D. Papsdorf. 1976. Biofeedback and progressive relaxation treatment of sleep-onset insomnia; a controlled all night investigation. Biofeedback and Self-Regulation **3:** 253–271.
9. Lamberg, L. 1984. The American Medical Association's Guide to Better Sleep. First Edit. Random House. New York.
10. Ware, J. C. 1983. Tricyclic antidepressants in the treatment of insomnia. J. Clin. Psychiatry **44:** 25–28.
11. Melamed, B. G., K. A. Matthews, D. K. Routh & B. Stabler. 1986. Introduction. Health Psychol. **5:** 181–183.
12. Fentress, D. W., J. M. Bruce, J. E. Mehegan & H. Benson. 1986. Biofeedback and relaxation-response training in the treatment of pediatric migraine. Dev. Med. Child Neurol. **28:** 139–146.
13. Barowsky, E. I., J. B. Zweig & J. Moskowitz. 1987. Thermal biofeedback in the treatment of symptoms associated with reflex sympathetic dystrophy. J. Child Neurol. **2:** 229–232.

14. PORTER, J. 1965. Guided fantasy as a treatment for childhood insomnia. Aust. N. Z. J. Psychiatry **9:** 169–172.
15. LEVINE, E. S. 1980. Indirect suggestions through personalized fairy tales for treatment of childhood insomnia. Am. J. Clin. Hypn. **23:** 57–63.
16. ANDERSON, D. R. 1979. Treatment of insomnia in a 13-year-old boy by relaxation training and reduction of parental attention. J. Behav. Ther. Exp. Psychiatry **10:** 263–265.
17. BUDZYINSKI, T. H. & J. M. STOYUA. 1969. An instrument for producing deep muscle relaxation by means of analog information feedback. J. App. Behav. Analysis **2:** 231.
18. FULLER, G. D. 1977. Biofeedback methods and procedures in clinical practice. Biofeedback Institute of San Francisco Press. San Francisco.
19. GREEN, E. E. & A. M. GREEN. 1983. General and specific applications of thermal biofeedback. *In* Biofeedback Principles and Practice. 2nd Edit. M. D. Basmajian, Ed. Williams and Wilkins. Baltimore.
20. STROEBEL, C. F. 1985. Biofeedback and behavioral medicine. *In* Comprehensive Textbook of Psychiatry. **IV:** H. I. Kaplan & B. J. Sadock, Eds.: 1467–1473. Williams and Wilkins. Baltimore.
21. HENDLER, N. 1984. Depression caused by chronic pain. J. Clin. Psychiatry **45:** 30–36.
22. BAROWSKY, E. I. 1987. Factors affecting the impact of pain and painful experiences on the exceptional child. J. Spec. Educ. **21:** 109–121.

The Concept of Mind in Comparative Psychology

KARYL B. SWARTZ

Lehman College
The City University of New York
Bronx, New York 10468

There have been many recent treatments of conscious experience in animals, including discussions of animal awareness,[1,2] animal consciousness,[3] animal representation,[4] and animal mind.[5,6] In general, this area of inquiry has suffered from a lack of consensus about what these various terms refer to (i.e., exactly how awareness, consciousness, and mind should be defined and distinguished), and doubts still exist about whether such concepts are appropriate for psychology in general, much less for animals (see Griffin[2] and Commentary, *The Behavioral and Brain Sciences,* 1978, **4:** 555–629, for discussions of definition and related issues).

One of the more well-articulated conceptualizations is Gallup's discussion of mind. Gallup[5] has argued that conscious experience is an important concept in the study of animal behavior. His theory distinguishes three overlapping yet also distinct variables: self awareness (the ability to become the object of one's own attention), consciousness (being aware of one's own existence), and mind (the ability to monitor one's own mental states). According to Gallup, self awareness is necessary for mind, and the presence of mind leads to the ability to impute such states to others.

Several points of discussion arise in attributing self awareness, consciousness, and mind to animals. They involve (1) the problem of defining precisely what is meant by the concepts, (2) the problem of operationalizing the conceptual definitions, (3) the problem of determining who (i.e., which species) possesses these attributes and under what circumstances they are demonstrated, and (4) the problem of determining the theoretical impact on comparative psychology and/or ethology of the presence of such attributes in nonhuman organisms. Each of these points will be discussed in the following sections.

THE PROBLEM OF CONCEPTUAL DEFINITION

A substantial amount of the literature has been directed toward defining awareness, consciousness, and mind. These issues have long been the domain of philosophy, having been relatively neglected by psychologists in the name of objective behaviorism. To date, psychologists interested in animal behavior have delineated different issues that must be considered when defining these constructs, and have explored the implications of pursuing different types of definitions (see Griffin[1,2] and Gallup[5]). However, the animal behavior literature still lacks clear cut and unambiguous definitions of conscious-based constructs, and the area will continue to have its critics until this state of affairs is rectified.

The fuzziness of conceptual definitions of conscious experiences in animals is actually not surprising. It has long been recognized by philosophers of science that a concept only takes on meaning in the broader context of the theoretical network in which it is embedded. Precise conceptual definitions typically emerge from preliminary working definitions that are formed during the early stages of research. As research progresses and the theoretical framework becomes more elaborated, the conceptual definitions take on clarity and meaning. The empirical study of animal conscious experience, although not new, is still relatively undeveloped, and elaborate theoretical frameworks simply do not exist. Gallup's research is an important step in this direction, since it represents a conscientious attempt to place the concepts of self awareness, consciousness, and mind into a meaningful theoretical context from which predictions of animal behavior can be derived.

The major point being made is that it may be premature to expect precise conceptual definitions for each of the labels that have arisen in this area of inquiry. Rather, it seems more productive to propose some working definitions that can guide research and then allow the conceptual definitions to emerge from the theoretical networks that result. Gallup's conceptualization of the mind represents a major stride in this direction.

THE PROBLEM OF OPERATIONAL DEFINITION

Of fundamental importance to the understanding of any psychological concept is the extent to which it can be objectively operationalized. Implicit in any operational definition are theoretical assumptions about the psychological concept being studied. In his discussion of mind in animals, Gallup has made clear what the theoretical characteristics of mind are, and the requisite characteristic for mind in his view is the capacity for self awareness. The presence of self awareness can be objectively demonstrated using his mirror recognition text.[7]

According to Gallup's theory, once an animal has self awareness, then other capabilities follow. Although the theoretical argument that Gallup proposes (i.e., that being self aware leads to attributing the same state to others) may not appear to be compelling, he provides an objective method for testing the presence of self awareness, and he makes explicit suggestions about ancillary behaviors (e.g., attribution, empathy, deception) that should be demonstrated if that theoretical link is valid. Further, Gallup is able to describe characteristics of empirical tests of the presence of mind. This ability to provide a good, operationally definable, behavioral criterion for mind is a major contribution that Gallup has made to the general area of animal conscious experience, and it takes the study of animal mind away from the realm of philosophy and brings it into the arena of objective psychological science. Further, empirical demonstrations of relationships among these behaviors should lead to clarification of some of the previously poorly defined concepts and could lead to some theoretical understanding of the distinctions among these concepts.

THE PROBLEM OF DETERMINING WHICH SPECIES HAVE MIND AND UNDER WHAT CIRCUMSTANCES THEY SHOW IT

The suggestion from Gallup's discussion is that some species have mind and others do not. That suggestion arises from the failure of animals of some species to demonstrate empirical evidence for self recognition with Gallup's mirror recognition technique. Although anecdotal evidence and laboratory training studies might suggest that self recognition is characteristic even of pigeons,[8] neither a young human infant labeling its mirror image with its own name nor a carefully trained pigeon using a mirror to peck a spot on its chest fulfill the requirements set forth by Gallup for demonstration of self awareness (see Gallup[5] for further discussion). It is clear, however, as Gallup[9] has acknowledged, that the mirror recognition procedure he developed is not the only means for demonstrating self recognition. Other measures, including one suggested by Gallup,[9] can indicate that an organism perceives itself as a distinct entity and can understand the effect of its own behavior on external objects and events. As an example, Menzel, Savage-Rumbaugh, and Lawson[10] have presented a description of chimpanzee behavior that can be interpreted to indicate the presence of self awareness. Chimps were given the task of reaching through a small window in a wall and touching a mark on the wall containing the window. The window was too small to allow the animal to see through while reaching, and the only visual information provided the animal was on a video monitor, located on the chimp's side of the wall next to the window, which displayed the scene from the other side of the wall being filmed by a closed-circuit video camera. Austin and Sherman, two language-trained chimps from the Language Research Center of Georgia State University, were able quickly to use the information from the video monitor to guide their arms to the position necessary to touch the spot, the location of which was changed on every trial. Furthermore, the chimps were able to modify their behavior appropriately when the video image was altered by a left–right reversal or an up–down reversal. The most convincing demonstration of self awareness, however, occurred when the animal was presented with two monitors, one presenting a live picture from the current trial and one presenting a videotape recording from a previous trial. The animals spontaneously developed the strategy of moving the arm back and forth at the beginning of a trial to determine which monitor was presenting live information. Such a behavior undoubtedly indicates self awareness, and tests of that sort could be modified and used with other species to provide evidence of self awareness, even in the absence of positive evidence from the Gallup mirror recognition procedure.

The importance of multiple methods of measurement has been emphasized by methodologists for some time.[11] These methodological considerations become especially important in the context of such variables as self awareness and the mind. A single method of measurement may contain sources of measurement error that are unique to that method. To the extent that a theoretical result is manifested across different sources of error (measurement methods), then our confidence in that result will increase. This argument implies that the search for multiple assessment techniques is an important direction for research in animal conscious experience.

As an example, consider research on mirror recognition in the gorilla. Several carefully conducted studies have failed to demonstrate evidence of self recognition in the mirror recognition task with gorilla subjects.[12,13] It may be the case that the gorilla does not have the capacity for self awareness, and hence, does not have mind as Gallup defines it. Based on current knowledge of gorilla behavior, including learning capacity,[14,15] in comparison to that of the other great apes, that conclusion may be premature. Although it is unclear why it might be the case, perhaps the mirror recognition procedure is inappropriate for gorilla subjects, and some other method could be used to demonstrate self awareness with that species. The same suggestion might also hold for some monkey species (see Gallup[16] and Gallup, Wallnau & Suarez[17]) and for other species (see Fox[18]). The use of multiple tests (i.e., the use of multiple methods of measurement) for self awareness should lead to a better theoretical understanding of self awareness and its relationship to other mental characteristics, within and across species.

The above point is not only related to the problem of determining what species have mind, but also the circumstances under which those species demonstrate mind. If the gorilla has mind (or evidence of mind provided by a demonstration of self awareness) but shows evidence of this capacity only under certain circumstances (i.e., under certain test conditions, with only a few selected tasks, after only a prescribed series of developmental experiences, or under some combination of selected motivational, cognitive, and experiential circumstances), the issue of mind in animals becomes more complex than just determining what species have mind and what species do not. Indeed, one of the reasons for studying mind in animals is to understand the animals, and a determination of the variables leading to the demonstration of mind in a species can provide considerable insight into the mental experience of that species.

Implicit in Gallup's discussions of mind is the suggestion that not all species have mind, and that the determination of what species have mind will provide some sort of phylogenetic discontinuity placing humans and those other species like chimpanzees who have mind on one side, and all "mindless" species on the other (note that being mindless does not preclude animal awareness, but see Gallup[5]). This perspective might also be applied to the development of mind in human infants (and other species having mind, as well). Indeed, some investigators, using a paradigm much like Gallup's mirror recognition task, have provided evidence that human infants do not recognize themselves in a mirror until around two years of age.[19,20] Thus, if self awareness is considered a prerequisite for mind, it might be said that the age of two represents an ontogenetic discontinuity for it is not until that age that the human infant demonstrates evidence of self awareness. Indeed, the age of two is generally considered to be an important transition period in development, separating infancy from childhood.[21] That age marks the end of the sensorimotor period in Piaget's theory, and such abilities as language, delayed imitation, symbolic play, and object permanence are considered behavioral indicators of substantive cognitive changes that occur during the 18-month to 24-month age period.[22] The inclusion of self awareness and mind in this set of characteristics has interesting implications for developmental theory.

THE PROBLEM OF INCORPORATING MIND INTO ETHOLOGICAL AND COMPARATIVE PSYCHOLOGICAL THEORY

Clearly, the very suggestion that animals have mind is of major importance to theories of animal behavior. Griffin[2] has quite effectively discussed many of the important theoretical implications for comparative psychology and ethology in his proposal for a "cognitive ethology" involving the acknowledgment and study of animal awareness. Psychology no longer withdraws from consideration of very complex cognitive events in humans,[23,24] including consciousness.[25] Comparative psychology has also considered complex learning processes,[26] intelligence,[27] and even complex concept acquisition[28] in animals. In light of such behaviors as mirror recognition,[7] complex natural communication,[29] and other complex cognitively based behaviors[6,30,31] demonstrated by animals such as chimpanzees, it would seem appropriate to consider conscious experience in these species. Indeed, the degree to which such capacities as consciousness, self awareness, and mind can be demonstrated in nonhuman species, the more interesting become our theories of animal behavior and comparative psychology. The utility of such concepts has not yet been fully demonstrated in theories of animal behavior, and that is the challenge for the future in this area. Gallup's work is an excellent step in that direction.

REFERENCES

1. GRIFFIN, G. R. 1976. The Question of Animal Awareness. Rockefeller University Press. New York.
2. GRIFFIN, D. R. 1978. Prospects for a cognitive ethology. Behav. Brain Sci. **4:** 527–538.

3. HUMPHREY, N. K. 1980. Nature's psychologists. *In* Consciousness and the Physical World. B. D. Josephson & V. S. Ramachandran, Eds. Pergamon Press. New York.
4. MASON, W. A. 1976. Environmental models and mental modes: Representational processes in the great apes and man. Am. Psychol. **31:** 284–294.
5. GALLUP, G. G., Jr. 1982. Self-awareness and the emergence of mind in primates. Am. J. Primatol. **2:** 237–248.
6. PREMACK, D. & G. WOODRUFF. 1978. Does the chimpanzee have a theory of mind? Behav. Brain Sci. **4:** 515–526.
7. GALLUP, G. G., Jr. 1970. Chimpanzees: Self-recognition. Science **167:** 86–87.
8. EPSTEIN, R., R. P. LANZA & B. F. SKINNER. 1981. "Self-awareness" in the pigeon. Science **212:** 695–696.
9. GALLUP, G. G., Jr. 1979. Self-recognition in chimpanzees and man: A developmental and comparative perspective. *In* The Child and Its Family. M. Lewis & L. A. Rosenblum, Eds. Plenum. New York.
10. MENZEL, E. W., JR., E. S. SAVAGE-RUMBAUGH & J. LAWSON. 1985. Chimpanzee (*Pan troglodytes*) spatial problem solving with the use of mirrors and televised equivalents of mirrors. J. Comp. Psychol. **99:** 211–217.
11. CAMPBELL, D. T. & D. W. FISKE. 1959. Convergent and discriminant validation by the multitrait-multimethod matrix. Psychol. Bull. **56:** 81–105.
12. SUAREZ, S. D. & G. G. GALLUP, Jr. 1981. Self-recognition in chimpanzees and orangutans, but not gorillas. J. Hum. Evol. **10:** 175–188.
13. LEDBETTER, D. H. & J. A. BASEN. 1982. Failure to demonstrate self-recognition in gorillas. Am. J. Primatol. **2:** 307–310.
14. RUMBAUGH, D. M. & T. V. GILL. 1973. The learning skills of great apes. J. Hum. Evol. **2:** 171–179.
15. RUMBAUGH, D. M. & C. MCCORMACK. 1967. The learning skills of primates: A comparative study of apes and monkeys. *In* Progress in Primatology. D. Stark, R. Schneider & H. J. Kuhn, Eds. Fischer. Stuttgart.
16. GALLUP, G. G., Jr. 1977. Absence of self-recognition in a monkey (*Macaca fascicularis*) following prolonged exposure to a mirror. Dev. Psychobiol. **10:** 281–284.
17. GALLUP, G. G., Jr., L. B. WALLNAU & S. D. SUAREZ. 1980. Failure to find self-recognition in mother-infant and infant-infant rhesus monkey pairs. Folia Primatol. **33:** 210–219.
18. FOX, M. W. 1982. Are most animals "mindless automatons"?: A reply to Gordon G. Gallup, Jr. Am. J. Primatol. **3:** 341–343.
19. AMSTERDAM, B. 1972. Mirror self-image reactions before age two. Dev. Psychobiol. **5:** 297–305.
20. LEWIS, M. & J. BROOKS-GUNN. 1979. Social Cognition and the Acquisition of Self. Plenum. New York.
21. VANDERZANDEN, J. W. 1981. Human Development, 2nd edit. Alfred A. Knopf. New York.
22. PIAGET, J. 1952. The Origins of Intelligence in Children. International Universities Press, Inc. New York.
23. NEISSER, U. 1967. Cognitive Psychology. Prentice Hall. Englewood Cliffs, NJ.
24. POSNER, M. 1978. Chronometric Explorations of Mind. Lawrence Erlbaum. Hillsdale, NJ.
25. RITTER, W. 1979. Cognition and the brain. *In* Evoked Brain Potentials and Behavior. H. Begleiter, Ed. Plenum. New York.

26. SCHRIER, A. M. 1984. Learning how to learn: The significance and current status of learning set formation. Primates **25:** 95–102.
27. THOMAS, R. K. 1980. Evolution of intelligence: An approach to its assessment. Brain Behav. Evol. **17:** 454–472.
28. SCHRIER, A. M., R. ANGARELLA & M. L. POVAR. 1984. Studies of concept formation by stumptailed monkeys: Concepts *human, monkeys,* and letter *A.* J. Exp. Psychol. Anim. Behav. Proc. **10:** 564–584.
29. MENZEL, E. W. 1974. A group of young chimpanzees in a one-acre field. *In* Behavior of Nonhuman Primates. Vol. 5. A. M. Schrier & F. Stollnitz, Eds. Academic Press. New York.
30. RUMBAUGH, D. 1977. Language behavior of apes. *In* Behavioral Primatology. A. M. Schrier, Ed. Lawrence Erlbaum. Hillsdale, NJ.
31. ETTLINGER, G. 1977. Interactions between sensory modalities in nonhuman primates. *In* Behavioral Primatology. A. M. Schrier, Ed. Lawrence Erlbaum. Hillsdale, NJ.

Matching to Sample by Atlantic Bottlenose Dolphins (*Tursiops truncatus*)

Chinese Characters and English Words

LEONORE LOEB ADLER[a]

Department of Psychology
Molloy College
Rockville Centre, New York 11570

HELMUT E. ADLER

Department of Psychology
Yeshiva University
New York, New York 10033

DOLPHINS AS SUBJECTS

The animals most often studied by psychologists in the past, the white rat, pigeon, dog, cat, monkey, and chimpanzee, have in recent years been joined by cetaceans, specifically the odontoceti, the order of dolphins, porpoises, and (for the most part) comparatively small whales. It has been possible to keep various species of the odontoceti, the toothed whales, in aquaria and oceanaria, although the other branch of the cetacea, the whalebone whales or mysteciti, are too large and, as food strainers of plankton, are hard to feed.

Newly captured cetaceans exhibit little fear of humans. They may have to be taught to feed on dead fish, as this is contrary to their normal feeding pattern, but they can be kept healthy and apparently at home in a large tank of salt water once they are over this hurdle. As social animals, they will interact with other members of the cetacean order, even if not their own species, including participation in social rank order establishment and sexual interaction. They will also direct social responses to familiar humans, much as a dog or a cat will do. A human trainer, in turn, can shape a cetacean's behavior, using food and praise as reinforcements.

[a] Address for correspondence: Dr. Leonore Loeb Adler, Department of Psychology, Molloy College, Rockville Centre, NY 11570 or Dr. Helmut E. Adler, Department of Psychology, Yeshiva University, 500 W. 185th Street, New York, NY 10033.

Not all cetaceans are equally adept at learning new behaviors. As in humans, there are individual differences. But once a dolphin has learned to respond to commands, it not only appears to relish performing, but if given a chance, will invent new versions of entertainment.

Dolphins exhibit a good deal of curiosity and playfulness. They appear to be eager to break the monotony of just swimming around their tank. They will, for example, frequently solicit play when a ball is available, by throwing it to a familiar person, expecting that the ball will be returned to them. They are also likely to splash an unsuspecting person standing within range, to get their attention, and in case of the belukha whale, one of the small toothed whales, to spit a mouthful of water in a playful stream at the unwary.

These behavioral traits have not only endeared dolphins to the general public, but have also formed the basis of a number of serious investigations of their cognitive functions (see Schusterman, Thomas, and Wood.)[1] The goal of these studies has been to assess the general level of abilities in cetaceans and the complexity of the tasks they can master. Ultimately, the hope is to better understand not only the behavior of cetaceans, but to assess the continuity of evolution of the higher mental processes or cognitive functioning.

Dolphin cognition, as part of a general growing interest in the field of comparative cognition, has been the subject of a number of recent studies and conferences.[1–3] Among the various behaviors that have been studied, the ability to match symbolic representations with the appropriate objects has been a focus of attention, not only in delphinids, but in primates (e.g., Savage-Rumbaugh[4,5]), pigeons (Blough[6]), and pinnipeds (Schusterman & Krieger[7]) as well.

Using computer-generated model sounds Richards and associates[8,9] found that Phoenix, a bottlenose dolphin, could learn to label objects, such as a ball, a pipe, a square loop, a Frisbee, and a person, with appropriate sounds. These whistle-like sounds represented symbolically the objects associated with them, which the dolphin had first learned to discriminate and eventually to imitate vocally.

Although it was once thought that dolphins' vision in air was poor, it is now clear that their duplex visual system functions well in air and under water.[10–12] The early work on dolphin visual information processing has been summarized by Herman.[13] Later experiments by Herman, Richards, and Wolz[14] with Akeakamai, a dolphin trained in a gesture-based sign language, showed considerable progress in complex cognitive tasks. Not only was she able to match visual signals to objects, but she was able to react to commands involving these objects. The implications of this work, particularly in comparison to other species, have been discussed by Herman.[15]

Among visual symbolic representations that have been used in studies with chimpanzees have been American sign language[16]; arbitrary systems, such as the computer-generated figures used by the Rumbaughs[4]; and the plastic nonsense symbols used by Premack and Premack.[17] Pictures of real objects (e.g., leaves, fish, Charlie Brown), as well as letters of the alphabet, have been discriminated by pigeons (summarized by Herrnstein[18]). Pigeon perception of letters of the alphabet, studied by Blough,[6] showed confusions of letters similar to that found in humans.

The study of cognitive processes in nonhuman subjects frequently has employed the conditional learning paradigm to test for concept formation, using a matching to sample task. As described by Zentall, Hogan, and Edwards[19] in the case of their work with pigeons, "In the presence of one or two (or more) stimuli, an organism is given a choice between two (or more) choice or comparison stimuli. In the presence of one sample, one of the comparison stimuli is correct (i.e., a response to it is reinforced); in the presence of the other sample, the other comparison is correct" (p. 390).

There are three components to this behavior: (1) Discrimination among the sample stimuli, (2) discrimination among the comparison stimuli, and (3) development of association behavior between the sample stimuli and the choice stimuli to which they have to be matched. In our experiment the sample stimuli were objects, the comparison stimuli were printed words or Chinese characters, and the dolphins had to associate the appropriate object with its symbolic representation.

Words are symbols, but in our style of writing the same set of letters is used in different combinations to make up the words. This fact is recognized as one of the factors that presents difficulties to the beginning reader. In the Chinese system of representation, each character stands for a word and thus differs in detail from every other character. In a study comparing the progress of second-grade inner-city schoolchildren with reading disabilities, when they were taught English material written in different Chinese characters, a clear advantage was shown for the Chinese characters over English words (Rozin, Poritsky & Sotsky[20]; see also *The Sciences*[21]).

In experiments reported in 1981 by Xing-Chu Zeng (East China Normal University, Shanghai, PRC),[22] it was found that Chinese infants, as young as six months, as well as toddlers, were able to discriminate both English words and Chinese ideographs. For example at six months, children pushed the appropriate button labeled "light" or "dark" when the corresponding stimulus word or character was presented under randomized conditions. At 18 months, children were able to discriminate or recognize more than 300 words, using such techniques as matching objects and words, pointing to an appropriate word card selected from a number of cards, matching English and Chinese words, and arranging the right letter sequence of an English word when the Chinese character was displayed.[22] Zeng reported an advantage for Chinese characters in his sample (Zeng, personal communication).

It was of interest, therefore, to study the ability of dolphins to discriminate written symbols, such as the names of objects in English block letters and Chinese characters and to associate them with the appropriate objects. Moreover, it seemed possible, in the light of the above-mentioned studies, that Chinese characters might be easier to match than English writing.

This report consists of three experiments. In Experiment I the dolphins learned to discriminate two English words in block letters and two Chinese characters. At the same time the subjects had to match the words and characters with the objects they symbolized. In Experiment II the same procedure was followed with two other objects. Experiment III demonstrated that no involuntary cues had been introduced in the previous two experiments by using a "blind" procedure in this visual discrimination task.

EXPERIMENTS I AND II

Method

Subjects

The two Atlantic bottlenose dolphins (*Tursiops truncatus*) that served as subjects for this experiment were long-time residents at the Mystic Marinelife Aquarium, Mystic, Connecticut. Kimo, a 175-kg male, and Sassy, a 150-kg female, were born in the wild and caught in the Florida Keys. Their ages at the beginning of the study were estimated at eleven years for Kimo and ten-and-a-half years for Sassy. As is customary in work with rare species, the same animals were used for a number of experiments. These animals become "test wise" and are more quickly able to learn the nature of the task than naive animals. Some negative transfer may occur in the initial shaping program, but this soon extinguishes. The dolphins had previously participated in studies of observational learning,[23] concept shift,[24] reversal and nonreversal shift,[25] and oddity problems.[26] As part of their daily routine, they were trained to give public demonstrations at the aquarium (from 10 A.M. to 4 P.M. every hour), which they carried out after they had taken part in the experiments earlier in the morning. The routine changed, however, for each public demonstration as different animals participated in exhibiting their skills and their accomplishments.

Apparatus

Testing was done at the edge of either the kidney-shaped main pool, 21.3 m (70 ft) in length, 12.2 m (40 ft) in width, and 6.1 m (20 ft) in depth, or in one of two circular holding pools, 9.1 m (30 ft) in diameter and 2.7 m (9 ft) deep. The dolphins were tested individually. Two belukha whales were present at times during some of the tests, but as far as could be determined, their presence did not affect the results.

The test stimuli were mounted on panels of brown fiberboard, 30½ cm × 122 cm (11⅞″ × 48″) in dimension. These targets were suspended by ropes from sawhorses positioned in such a way that they hung above the waterline at the edge of the pools.

Two sets of targets were used in each of the two experiments. Training targets carried a stimulus word or a Chinese character on one side, right or left, and a blank white square on the other side. Test targets had two stimulus items, one on each side, right and left. The letters or ideographs were cut from black plastic tape and mounted on white plastic squares of the same size 21.6 cm × 21.6 cm (8½ × 8½). The letters of characters were made up of strokes 1 cm (⅜″) wide and were centered in the white squares.

The stimulus items for Experiment I, a ball and a fish, were familiar stimuli for the subjects. For Experiment II the equally familiar stimulus objects were a pole and a ring. The English words were block printed:

BALL – FISH POLE – RING

The Chinese equivalents were[b]:

魚	波	桿	圈
yü(fish)	*ch'iu*(ball)	*kan*(pole)	*ch'ün*(ring)

Each stimulus appeared equally often on the right or left side, English paired with English and Chinese paired with Chinese in the test sessions.

Procedure

The dolphins were familiar with the targets and the routine of the experiments. Their behavior had originally been shaped to approach the targets and to indicate their choice by touching with their rostrum or beak the stimulus item they had selected. Correct choices were reinforced by the blowing of a whistle, followed by a small piece or raw fish (usually herring, capelin, or mackerel). A correction procedure was used in Experiments I and II, but not during the testing session of Experiment III. In the correction procedure, the dolphins were permitted to correct their choices until they indicated the correct stimulus item and received their reinforcement. Immediately after the correct choice had been made and reinforced, the next target was presented until the series, in a predetermined random order, was completed. The dolphin, which had either been waiting in front of the testing station or had swum away to another part of the pool, usually returned as soon as the next target was presented to make the next choice.

[b] Due to an inadvertent lexicographic mix-up, the character for "wave" was used instead of the idiograph for "ball." It is, of course, self-evident that this substitution could not affect the dolphins' performance. We thank Yin Mei Lin for pointing out this discrepancy, and also the Far East Department of the Library of St. John's University in Jamaica, New York for the help extended to us in identifying the correct characters (reference: *Mathews' Chinese-English Dictionary*. 1963. Harvard University Press. Cambridge, MA).

The *training sessions* were divided into two phases. During the first phase of Experiment I the appropriate object, either the ball, 12.7 cm (5″) in diameter, or the fish, usually a large mackerel, 25.4 cm–38.1 cm (10″–15″) long, were held over the word or the ideograph. However, in order to test informally for generalization, Sassy was shown a capelin, 10.2–12.7 cm (4″–5″) long. She touched the appropriate stimulus (either English or Chinese) correctly regardless of the size of the object she saw. The same was true with the stimulus object ball, which was sometimes substituted with a larger ball in random order.

A block of 24 trials was given for ten days. The second phase consisted of training with the object held in the center of the targets between the word or character and the blank square. For ten days blocks of the 24 trials were given. Words and ideographs were presented in random order for an equal number of times.

The *testing sessions* followed immediately after the last training session. In Experiment I the first test session had 16 trials. This was followed by three more blocks of tests of 20 trials each. Either fish or ball were held over the center of the target. The stimulus items, both fish and ball, were presented together on the fiberboard target, though the sides were changed frequently, in order to avoid a position habit. According to a predetermined random order, the fish or ball were shown, which was the cue to choose the appropriate stimulus and to make the correct response. Every day the same procedure was followed.

In Experiment II the training sessions were shortened to five blocks of 24 trials, with the objects being either a small, thin wooden pole, 66 cm × 2.5 cm (22″ × 1″) long and wide, or a plastic ring, 30.5 cm (12″) in diameter. Both objects were wrapped in white and green strips of plastic tape to give a candy-striped appearance that differentiated them from the other aquarium equipment. The stimulus objects were held up first over the item, and then in the center between the word or ideograph and the blank square, as in Experiment I.

The testing sessions followed immediately after the last training session and consisted of two daily blocks of 20 trials and one of 16 trials.

Immediately following the last testing sessions of Experiment II, the dolphins were retested on the ball and fish for 12 trials each. After a lapse of four months and 20 days, they were given a delayed retest of eight trials on ball and fish, followed by eight trials on pole and ring (see TABLE 1).

Results

In the first block of the test trials, both Kimo and Sassy indicated the correct choice in the first 16 consecutive test trials. In a total of 60 trials subsequently, spread over three days, Kimo made two incorrect choices while Sassy made only one error. The combined percentage of correct responses was 98.7% for Sassy and 97.4% for Kimo (see TABLE 2).

TABLE 1. Summary of Procedure

Experiment I: Ball & Fish
- 10 blocks of training with object over symbol
- 10 blocks of training with object in center
- 4 blocks of test sessions

Experiment II: Pole & Ring
- 5 blocks of training with object over symbol
- 5 blocks of training with object in center
- 3 blocks of test sessions

Retest: Ball & Fish
- 1 block of testing

Delayed Retest: Four months and 20 days later
- 1 block of testing on Ball & Fish
- 1 block of testing on Pole & Ring

Sassy was 100% correct on the English word for ball and the Chinese characters for ball and for fish. Kimo scored 100% correct for the English words ball and fish. The differences in correct responses were so small that no significant differences could be detected between the different stimulus objects. It was also apparent that the dolphins discriminated English words and Chinese characters equally well.

In Experiment II Kimo made 19 correct responses in the first 20 trials. Sassy had a perfect score, 20 correct out of 20 trials of the first session. In 36 subsequent trials Sassy had three incorrect choices, while Kimo made one wrong response. The overall percentage of correct responses was 94.6% for Sassy and 96.4% for Kimo.

Both Sassy and Kimo were 100% correct when the ring was shown, whether the stimulus was the English word or the Chinese character. Again, no significant differences could be found between stimulus objects. English and Chinese presentations were equally well discriminated (see TABLE 2).

The retest on ball and fish, following the conclusion of Experiment II, showed perfect retention. Both dolphins performed without error.

On the delayed retest, a four-month and 20-day interval after the conclusion of Experiment II and retest, the dolphins were first given a short refresher of eight trials with the stimulus object over the item, using the training targets. This was followed by eight trials with the stimulus object in the center. The test trials, following immediately after the retraining trials, resulted in seven correct responses out of eight presentations of the ball and fish in English and Chinese. In tests of the ring and pole, Sassy made no incorrect choices, while Kimo made one error.

TABLE 2. Discrimination of Words or Characters[a]

Words/Characters	Sassy	Kimo
Experiment I		
BALL	100	100
波 (Ball)	100	95
FISH	95	100
魚 (Fish)	100	95
Combined	98.7	97.4
Experiment II		
POLE	93	93
桿 (Pole)	86	93
RING	100	100
圈 (Ring)	100	100
Combined	94.6	96.4
Retest		
Ball and Fish	100	100
Delayed Retest		
Ball and Fish	87.5	87.5
Ring and Pole	100	87.5

[a] Expressed as percent correct choices.

Discussion

The near-perfect performance on the test trials by both dolphins provides evidence that the discrimination of the representation of two items, either as English words or Chinese characters, did not present an exceptionally difficult problem. The number of training trials was reduced in Experiment II, since it was felt that half the number of sessions would be sufficient, especially since it could be assumed that a learning set[27] would facilitate the acquisition of the second discrimination.

Rozin *et al.*[20] attributed the superiority of Chinese characters to the fact that the relationship between character and word was easier to grasp than that between symbol and sound. Because sound production was never an aspect in our experiments, any superiority of Chinese characters over English letters would have to depend on visual characteristics.

No differences were discernable between the English words and the Chinese characters in our results. Zeng (personal communication) had found that the Chinese infants learned to recognize Chinese characters faster than English words. He attributed this difference to the fact that each Chinese character differed from every other one, while English words were made up of the same letter units with the sequence of their occurrence determining the meaning of a word. In the present experiment all English words were four letters long. They shared some common features, such as the I's and L's. The Chinese characters all appeared to be distinctly different.

The question may be posed whether the dolphins were able to form categories or whether they merely associated specific objects with their respective English or Chinese symbols. We can only point to some informal observations, for instance, in the cases with the "fish" and the "ball" stimuli. Each day a different fish was held up. Some were large and some were small; some were mackerels and some were capelins. The dolphins seemed to understand the concept "fish," or some other common concept such as "food," which they showed by their responses—even by trying to snatch, at times, the fish stimulus object from the experimenter's hand. In this way they succeeded on occasion to receive an unscheduled reinforcer. The "ball" also was switched randomly at times, from the small-sized stimulus object to a large-sized ball.

The delayed tests, especially the four-month, 20-day interval, can be interpreted as evidence for the dolphins' excellent visual memory.

The "Clever Hans" Phenomenon (an Experimenter Expectation)

In Berlin, Germany, Herr Wilhelm von Osten had created a sensation in 1904 with the activities of his horse Hans, dubbed the "kluge" Hans, or Clever Hans, as he has gone down in history.[28] Hans communicated by tapping with his right hoof, as well as by head movements. His mathematical ability was astounding; for example, he would correctly answer questions such as How much is $\frac{2}{5} + \frac{1}{2}$? In addition, he read German, but only the small letters, not the capitals; he also could spell—when shown a picture of a horse, he would promptly spell *p-f-e-r-d.*

Carl Stumpf, Professor of Psychology at the University of Berlin, assigned one of his students, Oskar Pfungst, to undertake an experimental study of the horse's reputed abilities. Pfungst came up with the answers, based on good experimental technique and clever experimentation. He first established that Hans did very poorly when asked to answer questions in which the examiner did not know the answer. Pfungst then concluded that the horse was responding to involuntary movements of the questioners.

Clever Hans has become synonymous with unconscious cuing; but as Sue Savage-Rumbaugh points out,[4] alleging a Clever Hans effect does not prove its presence. Potential inadvertent cues may be present, but may not necessarily be used by the subject or even make it easier to solve a problem. The fact that Hans picked up subtle cues is just as remarkable as it would have been for him to perform all the feats as claimed.

EXPERIMENT III

Since the time that the previous research was conducted, Kimo had died from an infection. While there were other dolphins who could work in experiments, Experiment III concentrated on work with Sassy to check on the possibility of unwitting cues or, in other words, a "Clever Hans" effect.

Subject and Experimenters

The follow-up study was carried out three years later. In the absence of Kimo, therefore, Sassy served as the subject in this phase, as she had done in the original research. However, this time the experimenters worked with a female volunteer-assistant, a high school graduate in her late teens, who was entering college the next fall.

Procedure

While the setting was unchanged and the same targets were used, the procedure was changed radically. This time one experimenter, standing behind the sawhorse at the edge of the pool, turned the target-boards with the stimulus items. For each trial a different pair of stimulus items was presented, similar to the original research. The stimuli were either two English words in block letters or two different Chinese characters. No training procedure or "refresher course" was given. All eight items were presented in random order in a series of "practice runs," (contrary to the previous procedure of Experiments I and II, when only four items were used, i.e., two words/characters, in English and Chinese). The appropriate or identifying stimulus object for each trial was held up by the volunteer-assistant. As had been suggested, she wore sunglasses at all times to avoid any possible eye contact.[14] She stood about three to four feet behind the first experimenter. Close to the volunteer-assistant stood the second experimenter. Neither the volunteer-assistant nor the second experimenter could see the responding dolphin from where they stood. Of course, the first experimenter could see neither of the other two. The second experimenter, who knew the random order of the stimulus objects, showed the pad with the next stimulus to the volunteer-assistant, in order not to give any audible cues. After being informed about the next stimulus, she held up the

FIGURE 1. Spatial arrangements for the "blind" procedure during the follow-up study with Sassy. (See text for a complete description of the procedure.)

appropriate object. The dolphin, out in the pool, could observe easily which item was held up. The subject then swam to the target in order to point with her rostrum to either of the stimulus items. At this point neither the volunteer-assistant nor the second experimenter could see the dolphins, nor could Sassy see them. Since the first experimenter did not know which of the two stimulus items was the designated stimulus, she could not readily reinforce the dolphin's correct responses. Therefore, she called out to identify the stimulus Sassy pointed to. In return the volunteer then replied to the dolphin's response with either "correct" or "wrong." (No correction was allowed for "wrong" responses. In Experiments I and II the first experimenter blew the whistle and threw a small piece of fish as reinforcer to the dolphin before turning the target-boards for the next trial.) This procedure assured a completely blind procedure for all four participants, including the dolphin (see FIG. 1).

Anybody who has worked with animals generally, and dolphins specifically, knows that the personality and behavior of a trainer or an experimenter can influence the behavior of the animal. In order to give Sassy a chance to get used to the new procedure and to the volunteer-assistant, she was

TABLE 3. Follow-up with "Blind" Procedure with the Dolphin Sassy as a Subject[a]

Correct Responses for First Six Trails	Percent	Correct Responses for 12 Trials	Percent
6	100.00	11	91.66

[a] Figures are for the last day of testing, which was videotaped.

given several trials for four days, followed by the testing/taping session on the fifth day. (A videotape was used in order to have a permanent record.)

Results

The results with the new volunteer-assistant showed that the subject Sassy was aware of the changes. Her initial responses (for six trials) each day were better than her later ones (for 12 trials). She increased in overall accuracy during the five days of this follow-up study. On the last day (testing/taping) Sassy gave 100% correct responses for the first six trials.

However, she made one wrong response during the next six trials, for a total of 92% (rounded) accuracy during these twelve trials (TABLE 3).

DISCUSSION

Several interesting results emerged. It did not take long for the dolphin to get used to the new routine, though she seemed aware of the presence of the third person. Sassy made no errors in the initial six test-trials, while she made one wrong choice in the subsequent six test-trials. To comment on this effect can only be speculative at this point. However, the results of this follow-up study with a completely blind procedure proved beyond any doubt that the dolphin could discriminate among four English words and among four Chinese characters by using visual channels for her differential and accurate responding. It also implied that the results of Experiment I and II were beyond reproach, though the experimenters concede that there could have been opportunity to give unconscious cues by the experimenters. The results of the present study, Experiment III, with a completely blind procedure should lay to rest any suggestions of a "Clever Hans" effect.

SUMMARY

Two bottlenose dolphins (*Tursiops truncatus*) learned to match to sample by associating English words in block letters and Chinese characters with corresponding objects. In Experiment I a fish and a ball served as stimulus objects. After a training procedure that paired objects and symbols, the dolphins had to choose the appropriate word or character to match the respective object. In Experiment II a pole and a ring were used as additional stimulus objects, with a shortened training session. Both experiments resulted in almost perfect matchings. Chinese characters showed no advantage over English words; both were mastered equally well. A delayed retest almost five months later showed excellent visual memory. After a time interval of three years, Experiment III was conducted. Only one dolphin was available. All four previous stimulus objects were used. However, this time a "blind" procedure was employed to rule out involuntary cues. The results clearly showed that there had never been any "Clever Hans" effect.

ACKNOWLEDGMENTS

The authors wish to thank the volunteer, Ms. Trista Giovanniello, for her assistance with Experiment III. Special thanks are extended to the staff of the Mystic Marinelife Aquarium for their help and cooperation during all phases of this research. Finally we would like to acknowledge our deep gratitude to our collaborator "Sassy" who died February 17, 1987 in childbirth.

REFERENCES

1. SCHUSTERMAN, R. J., J. A. THOMAS & F. G. WOOD, Eds. 1986. Dolphin Cognition and Behavior: A Comparative Approach. Erlbaum. Hillsdale, NJ.
2. ROITBLAT, H. L. 1985. Introduction to Comparative Cognition. Freeman. New York.
3. ROITBLAT, H. L., T. G. BEVER & H. S. TERRACE, Eds. 1984. Animal Cognition. Erlbaum. Hillsdale, N.J.
4. SAVAGE-RUMBAUGH, E. S. 1981. Can apes use symbols to represent their world? *In* The Clever Hans Phenomenon: Communication with Horses, Whales, Apes, and People. T. A. Sebeok & R. Rosenthal, Eds. Ann. N.Y. Acad. Sci. **364:** 35–39.
5. SAVAGE-RUMBAUGH, E. S. 1984. Acquisition of functional symbol usage in apes and children. *In* Animal Cognition. H. L. Roitblat, T. G. Bever & H. S. Terrace, Eds.: 291–310. Erlbaum. Hillsdale, NJ.
6. BLOUGH, D. S. 1983. Pigeon perception of letters of the alphabet. Science **218:** 397–398.
7. SCHUSTERMAN, R. J. & K. KRIEGER. 1984. California sea lions are capable of semantic comprehension. Psychol. Rec. **34;** 3–23.
8. RICHARDS, D. G. 1986. Dolphin vocal mimicry and vocal object labeling. *In* Dolphin Cognition and Behavior: A Comparative Approach. R. J. Schusterman, J. A. Thomas & F. C. Wood, Eds.: 273–277. Erlbaum. Hillsdale, NJ.
9. RICHARDS, D. G., J. P. WOLZ & L. M. HERMAN. 1984. Vocal mimicry of computer-generated sounds and vocal labeling of objects by a bottlenosed dolphin, *Tursiops truncatus.* J. Comp. Psychol. **98:** 10–28.

10. Herman, L. H., H. F. Peacock, M. P. Yunker & C. J. Madson. 1975. Bottlenosed dolphin: Double-slit pupil yields equivalent aerial and underwater diurnal acuity. Science **189:** 650–652.
11. Dral, A. D. G. 1975. Vision in Cetacea. J. Zoo Anim. Med. **6:** 17–21.
12. Rivamonte, L. A. 1976. Eye model to account for comparable aerial and underwater acuities of the bottlenose dolphin. Netherlands J. Sea Res. **10:** 491–498.
13. Herman, L. M. 1980. Cognitive characteristics of dolphins. *In* Cetacean Behavior: Mechanisms and Functions. L. M. Herman, Ed.: 363–429. Wiley. New York.
14. Herman, L. M., D. G. Richards & J. P. Wolz. 1984. Comprehension of sentences in bottlenose dolphins. Cognition **16:** 1–90.
15. Herman, L. M. 1986. Cognitive and language competencies in bottlenose dolphins. *In* Dolphin Cognition and Behavior: A Comparative Approach. R. J. Schusterman, J. A. Thomas & F. G. Wood, Eds.: 221-252. Erlbaum. Hillsdale, NJ.
16. Gardner, R. A. & B. T. Gardner. 1969. Teaching sign language to a chimpanzee. Science **165:** 664–672.
17. Premack, D. & A. J. Premack. 1983. The Mind of an Ape. Norton. New York.
18. Herrnstein, R. J. 1984. Objects, categories and discriminative stimuli. *In* Animal Cognition. H. L. Roitblat, T. G. Bever & H. S. Terrace, Eds.: 233-261. Erlbaum. Hillsdale, NJ.
19. Zentall, T. R., D. E. Hogan & C. A. Edwards. 1984. Cognitive factors in conditional learning by pigeons. *In* Animal Cognition. H. L. Roitblat, T. G. Bever & H. S. Terrace, Eds.: 389–405. Erlbaum. Hillsdale, NJ.
20. Rozin, P., S. Poritsky & R. Sotsky. 1971. American children with reading problems can easily learn to read English represented by Chinese characters. Science **171:** 1264–1267.
21. Anonymous. 1971. The Sciences **11:** 20–21.
22. Zeng, X. C. 1981. Some studies on early learning and development. Unpublished manuscript.
23. Adler, H. E. & L. L. Adler. 1978. What can dolphins (*Tursiops truncatus*) learn by observation? Cetology **30:** 1–10.
24. Adler, L. L. & H. E. Adler. 1981. Concept shift in Atlantic bottlenose dolphins (*Tursiops truncatus*) (Abstract). Poster presented at the 89th Annual Meeting of the American Psychological Association, Los Angeles, CA.
25. Adler, L. L. & H. E. Adler. 1982. Cognitive functioning in bottlenose dolphins (*Tursiops truncatus*) *In* Evolution and Determination of Animal and Human Behavior. H. D. Schmidt & G. Tembrock, Eds.: VEB Deutscher Verlag der Wissenschaften. Berlin. (Simultaneously published by Elsevier, Amsterdam.)
26. Adler, H. E. & L. L. Adler. 1989. Responding to oddity problems in dolphins (*Tursiops truncatus*). Submitted for publication.
27. Herman, L. M., F. A. Beach III, R. L. Pepper & R. B. Stalling. 1969. Learning—set formation in the bottlenose dolphin. Psychonom. Sci. **14:** 98–99.
28. Pfungst, O. 1965. Clever Hans: The Horse of Mr. von Osten. R. Rosenthal, Ed. (C. L. Rahn, Trans.) Holt, Rinehart & Winston. New York. (First published 1911.)

Nutritional Requirements for Normative Development of the Brain and Behavior

BRIAN L. G. MORGAN[a]

Institute of Human Nutrition
Columbia University
College of Physicians & Surgeons
New York, New York 10032

Brain growth is time dependent. Different developmental processes occur at specific chronological ages, and once the time for a phase of growth has passed, it cannot be restarted. The period of brain growth in children is from 12 weeks of pregnancy until three years of age. Hence, if a child is undernourished throughout this period, brain growth will be impaired. Furthermore, attempts at nutritional rehabilitation after this time will not have any beneficial effects on brain growth. Behavioral development is similarly time dependent with certain types of behavior appearing at specific times, although the timing of behavioral development is much more variable than it is for brain growth. It cannot be overemphasized that good nutrition during pregnancy and infancy is critical to normal brain development. Although some gross malnutrition does exist in the United States, marginal undernutrition is more common and can lead to small but significant decreases in brain development, which in turn lead to impaired behavioral development. Unfortunately such marginal retardation is difficult to pick up until after two or three years of age with the clinical tests currently available. By this time brain development is nearly complete. Hence, developing a test to pick up impaired brain growth due to malnutrition earlier in life when nutritional rehabilitation can have beneficial effects is a necessity.

Most of the information that has been collected over the last few years concerning the effects of nutrition on brain development arose from an interesting theory put forward by Winick and Noble.[1] They suggested that growth in any tissue, including the brain, could be divided into different phases. In the first phase, hyperplasia alone occurred at the time of cellular proliferation. Then each tissue went through a phase in which hyperplasia was accompanied by an increase in cell size or hypertrophy. This was followed by a phase of hypertrophy alone after which the tissue was said to

[a] Current affiliation: University of Miami Medical School, Miami, FL 33139.

have achieved its maximum or mature size. This was found to apply to all tissues although each had its own characteristic timetable of development.

The theory applies to brain growth, but here it is further complicated by the existence of two different populations of cells, namely neurons and glia. The neurons divide from weeks 12 to 26 of gestation and the glial cells from about 26 weeks of gestation to five months of life.[2] As the forebrain grows, the initial period of cellular division is of neurons and the latter is mainly of glial cells. Different areas of the brain have their own individual growth curves. They grow at different times and at different rates. Hence, the brain is more complicated than other tissues in this respect.

Malnutrition during the period of cellular development leads to decreased cell numbers. Initially the reduced cell numbers were believed to be the underlying reason why undernourished children sometimes show behavioral defects, but later data brought this under question. For instance, the human male brain weights 1400 g, and a woman's brain is about 150 g smaller, but obviously women are no less intelligent than men. Even when calculations are made for brain to body ratios, women still have relatively smaller brains. Anatole France, well known to have been a genius, is reputed to have had a brain weighing less than 1000 g. Clearly, brain function does not correlate with brain size.

The protein content of the brain and the protein-to-DNA ratio, which is a good estimate of cell size, are decreased in malnourished children.[3] Malnourished children also have reduced brain cholesterol content, which indicates decreased myelination.[4] In addition, they have lower RNA content.[3] Observations of the ratio of head circumference to brain growth revealed that the two measurements were well correlated,[3] and this method has been used routinely as a measure of brain growth in children.

According to Winick's theory, it follows that if a child is malnourished during the whole period of his brain growth (for the first three years) and rehabilitated after this time, catch-up growth will not be achieved and the brain will not grow to its usual size. As a result intellectual achievement will not reach normal levels. This was tested by Winick[5,6] in a group of Korean orphans that had been taken into the Holt Adoption Agency in Korea after being malnourished for various periods of time. There were essentially two populations. One population was a group of children that had been taken to the Holt Agency during the first one to two years of their lives. These children were rehabilitated in Korea and adopted into American families before the age of three. These children were divided into the following categories: severely undernourished, moderately undernourished, and well-nourished. Severely malnourished children were characterized as having heights and weights below the third percentile, moderately undernourished were children from the fourth percentile to the twenty-fourth percentile, and well-nourished children were those from the twenty-fifth percentile and above. All of these children spent about eight years in American schools and then were assessed for IQ and growth.

All children surpassed height and weight values compared to the values for well-nourished children living in Korea. Furthermore even the malnourished children scored above the IQ scores for normal American children. Of course, these children were adopted into middle-class homes in the United States, which is considered an "optimal environment" for brain and behavioral development. All of the children in the study did very well, but the children who were well nourished did statistically better than those who were severely malnourished.

The second population of children had been brought to the Holt Agency after the third year of life when brain growth had ceased. These children were classified into the same three groups as the other population, were rehabilitated, brought to the United States, and adopted into middle-class homes. After eight years in U.S. school systems, their heights and weights again were found to have surpassed that of the Korean norm. However, these children did not do quite as well in terms of IQ scores as did the children that had been adopted earlier. In this case the severely malnourished children did not reach the American norm, although the other two groups did fairly well. Once again, all groups surpassed the scores for well-fed Korean children.

It is difficult to determine whether the improvement in IQ was due to environmental stimulation or nutritional rehabilitation. Both groups did better than their Korean counterparts. However children that were nutritionally rehabilitated when their brains were still growing definitely did better than those that were rehabilitated after this time. Hence, it looks like both environmental stimulation and nutrition have an effect on behavioral development. The study also provided circumstantial evidence to support the notion of time dependency of growth.

Winick, Jaroslow, and Winer[7] did a further study to demonstrate the importance of nutrition and environmental stimulation. This involved studying children that had been fostered either into multiple foster homes or single foster homes. When IQ is plotted against percentile height rank for these children, those children fostered into a very unstable environment (multiple foster homes) showed a fairly good correlation between IQ scores and percentile height rank. This may also be interpreted as demonstrating that IQ improves with nutritional status. Children brought up in single foster homes, a very stable environment, showed absolutely no correlation between IQ and percentile height rank. This data, therefore, tends to confirm that environmental stimulation can overcome some of the effects of malnutrition.

Some time ago I hypothesized that the development of neuronal processes and the resulting synaptic interconnections between them was more critical to brain function and behavior than cell numbers per se. One way to measure the degree of synaptogenesis is to look at brain ganglioside content, specifically G_{D1a} gangliosides.[8] Several different kinds of gangliosides are present in the brain. Basically gangliosides are lipid-type moieties incorporating an oligosaccharide chain and one, two, three, or four moieties of *N*-acetylneuraminic acid denoted as NeuNAC (monosialo, disialo, and trisialo gangliosides, respectively). Our initial studies[9] were an attempt to increase the amount of gangliosides present in the brains of undernourished rat pups by injecting NeuNAC at the time of rapid brain growth.

Rat dams were undernourished throughout pregnancy and lactation. Their offspring were divided into two groups. Half received a daily intraperitoneal injection of NeuNAC from days 7–21 postnatally, and the other half were given a placebo injection of saline, which was used as the solvent for the NeuNAC. Litters of control animals that had been well fed during pregnancy and lactation were similarly treated. Open-field activity measurements indicated that the effect of injecting control rats with NeuNAC was to produce rat pups that behaved "super-normally." Undernourished animals similarly treated with NeuNAC displayed the same activity as the well-fed control animals. The mean duration of time spent with a novel object was also enhanced by the administration of NeuNAC. Neurochemical analyses of the brains of these animals revealed that the only variables affected by the NeuNAC injection were the levels of ganglioside and glycoprotein NeuNAC. Improvement in behavior was associated with an increase in each of these variables. No changes occurred in brain DNA, RNA, or protein.

This effect of NeuNAC could have been a temporary pharmacological effect or a permanent effect owing to incorporation into the developing neural membranes. To differentiate between these two possibilities, groups of animals similarly treated as explained above were placed in individual cages at 21 days of age and fed stock diet until six months of age. At this point they were tested in a Y maze. The rats given NeuNAC during days 7–21 of their lives learned a maze more quickly than controls given placebo injections of saline. These changes in behavior were once again associated with an increase in brain ganglioside and glycoprotein NeuNAC levels. Hence, early administration of NeuNAC had a permanent effect on brain composition and behavior. If the NeuNAC was injected after 30 days of age, by which time the rat brain has completed its growth, neither behavior nor brain biochemistry was affected. Hence the effect was time dependent.

Because environmental stimulation seems to improve behavior, we examined the effects of environmental stimulation on brain NeuNAC.[10] In order to provide relatively stress-free forms of environmental stimulation, we used the technique of providing rat pups with two "mothers" during the lactation period, as described by Plaut.[11] This involves training virgin rat dams to be nonlactating aunts. In this way litters of rat pups were accompanied by two "mothers" in their cages. The effect of putting two female rats in with a litter of pups is to increase the attention received by each pup, which is equivalent to environmental stimulation.

In this experiment we had basically the same groups as in the previous experiment: two undernourished groups and two well-fed groups. At two days after birth one undernourished and one well-fed group were given an aunt, which stayed in the cage with the mother and litter until weaning at 21 days postnatally. There was the same degree of change in behavior in the environmentally stimulated pups at 21 days of age as was seen in the pups given injections of NeuNAC. Environmental stimulation improved behavior in an open field both in terms of activity as well as mean duration of time spent with a novel object. Brain biochemistry also revealed the same pattern. When a change in behavior occurred, there was a corresponding increase in ganglioside NeuNAC and glycoprotein NeuNAC. Once again no other changes in neurochemistry arose from environmental stimulation.

When pups subjected to environmental stimulation in early life were weaned at 21 days and grew to six months of age in individual cages on a regular chow diet, the same patterns of behavior and neurochemistry were found as in the NeuNAC administration experiments. When there was an improvement in the ability to learn a Y maze, the levels of ganglioside NeuNAC and glycoprotein NeuNAC increased. Increases in brain NeuNAC and improvement in behavior seemed to be correlated in this study in the same way as in the previous NeuNAC administration experiments.

Radioactive tracer studies were carried out to ascertain the location of incorporation of NeuNAC injected during the brain growth period.[12] It was found that over 80% became incorporated into the synaptosomes. Measurement of total brain NeuNAC content also showed that most of it was in the synaptosomes. Similar results were obtained for both undernourished and control rat pups. Clearly NeuNAC exerts its effects on behavior via the synaptosomes.

Other studies were designed to examine the effects of undernutrition on the rate-limiting enzymes of ganglioside metabolism.[13] Undernutrition delayed the development of these enzyme systems and reduced their peak activity. This delay in enzyme development is an exception to the generalized phenomenon of time dependency of brain growth processes.

NeuNAC is very acidic, and although a rat seems to tolerate it well, much further study needs to be undertaken before human trials may be considered. However, one immediate application would be to use NeuNAC as a measure of the functional development of the brain. Head circumference measurements give us no indication of brain composition, but if brain NeuNAC could be correlated with serum NeuNAC this would provide a sensitive measure of synaptogenesis. Measurements on rats has revealed that such correlations do exist.[14] There are straight line correlations between serum NeuNAC and brain wet weight, ganglioside NeuNAC, and glycoprotein NeuNAC. This test awaits human trials. If cord blood NeuNAC content could be shown to correlate with fetal synaptogenesis, this would provide pediatricians with a precise method of measuring fetal brain growth at a time when growth is in its most rapid phase and growth retardation arising from undernutrition could be alleviated by nutritional supplementation.

REFERENCES

1. WINICK, M. & A. NOBLE. 1965. Quantitative changes in DNA, RNA, and protein during prenatal and postnatal growth. Dev. Biol. **12:** 451–466.
2. DOBBING, J. & J. SANDS. 1973. The quantitative growth and development of the human brain. Arch. Dis. Child. **48:** 757–767.

3. WINICK, M. 1976. Nutrition and cellular growth of the brain. *In* Malnutrition and Brain Development: 63–97. Oxford University Press. New York.
4. DICKERSON, J. W. T., A. MERAT & H. K. M. YUSUF. 1982. Effects of malnutrition on brain growth and development. *In* Brain and Behavioral Development. J. W. T. Dickerson & H. McGurk, Eds.: 73–108. Surrey University Press. London.
5. WINICK, M., K. K. MEYER & R. C. HARRIS. 1975. Malnutrition and environmental enrichment by early adoption. Science **190:** 1173–1175.
6. LIEN, N. M., K. K. MEYER & M. WINICK. 1977. Early malnutrition and late adoption. A study of their effects on the development of Korean orphans adopted into American families. Am. J. Clin. Nutr. **30:** 1734–1739.
7. WINICK, M., A. JAROSLOW & E. WINER. 1978. Foster placement, malnutrition, and environment. Growth **42:** 391–397.
8. MORGAN, B. L. G. & J. W. T. DICKERSON. 1982. Comparative aspects of brain growth and development. *In* Brain and Behavioral Development. J. W. T. Dickerson & H. McGurk, Eds.: 48–72. Surrey University Press. London.
9. MORGAN, B. L. G. & M. WINICK. 1980. Effects of administration of *N*-acetylneuraminic acid (NANA) on brain NANA content and behavior. J. Nutr. **110:** 416–424.
10. MORGAN, B. L. G. & M. WINICK. 1980. Effects of environmental stimulation on brain *N*-acetylneuraminic acid content and behavior. J. Nutr. **110:** 425–432.
11. PLAUT, S. M., D. W. GRAHAM & K. Y. LEINER. 1972. Effects of prenatal maternal handling and rearing with aunts on behavior, brain weight and whole brain serotonin levels. Dev. Psychobiol. **5:** 215–221.
12. MORGAN, B. L. G. & M. WINICK. 1981. The subcellular localization of administered *N*-acetylneuraminic acid in the brains of well-fed and protein restricted rats. Br. J. Nutr. **46:** 231–238.
13. MORGAN, B. L. G. & D. J. NAISMITH. 1982. The effect of early postnatal undernutrition on the growth and development of the rat brain. Br. J. Nutr. **48:** 15–23.
14. MORGAN, B. L. G., G. L. BORIS & M. WINICK. 1982. A useful correlation between blood and brain *N*-acetylneuraminic acid contents. Biol. Neonate **42:** 299–303.

Attributions and Information Processing as a Function of Observers' Involvement Level

A Re-examination of Actor–Observer Attribution Differences

HONG-JEN CHEN

Market Research Department
Rorer Pharmaceuticals
Fort Washington, Pennsylvania 19034

BRIAN T. YATES

Department of Psychology
The American University
Washington, D.C.

INTRODUCTION

In social psychology, Heider's[1] *The Psychology of Interpersonal Relations* generated significant interest in research on lay epistemology—how "people in the street" determine causal explanations for observed events. Briefly, attribution theory attempts to formalize the rules that the average person uses to infer the cause or causes of observed behaviors or events. Attribution theories view human perceivers as intuitive psychologists who explain behavior and draw inferences about themselves, others, and their social environments.

The attribution theories formulated by past researchers[1-6] deal primarily with the "objective" ways in which the human observers make attributions. These theories are often termed "normative" because they describe the appropriate procedures in which information is processed. For over three decades, researchers have been guided by Kelley's[3] normative causal analysis model. Kelley argued that this causal analytic process involves three types of behavioral information: consensus, distinctiveness, and consistency. Consensus refers to the responses of other persons to the same stimulus event; that is, to what extent are other people's reactions the same as the target person in the same situation? Distinctiveness refers to whether a behavior is a response to a particular stimulus. Consistency refers to whether a behavioral occurrence (in response to the same stimulus) has been repeated over time and across different situations. This attribution model depicts the process of how people use the three types of behavioral information to infer causality (e.g., Kelley,[3,4] Ferguson & Wells,[7] McArthur,[8] and Pruitt & Insko[9]).

According to Kelley's model, the three kinds of information may take on one of two values: high or low consensus, high or low distinctiveness, and high or low consistency. Eight information configurations can be generated from the model. These different combinations of the three types of information should lead to different attributions.

To test this hypothesis, earlier studies generally provided subjects with situational scenarios and combinations of consensus, distinctiveness, and consistency information and asked the subjects to make attributions for the events.[7–9] For example, McArthur[8] asked subjects to make attributions for events qualified by high or low levels of consensus, distinctiveness, and consistency information. The results supported the predictions of Kelley's model. The information patterns of high consensus, high distinctiveness, and high consistency (HHH) produce greater external attribution than other information combinations. This pattern indicates that the actor's response is common among the responses of other persons, consistent with, and distinct from his or her responses to other stimuli. The low consensus, low distinctiveness, and high consistency (LLH) pattern indicates that few others consistently did what that person does. This pattern was attributed to ability or effort, internal characteristics of the person.

It should be noted that most studies demonstrating normatively justified causal inferences presented the subjects with well-organized stimulus materials.[10,11] By doing so, the experimenter manipulates consensus, distinctiveness, and consistency information apparent to the observer subjects. The subjects usually did not have to decide the relevance of the available information and did not have to collect, store, and retrieve information. Furthermore, the subjects did not observe, estimate, or summarize data for the observed events. This strategy is reasonable for an investigator to determine a subject's ability to make causal analyses uncontaminated by motivations. However, such a strategy seems certain to present an inflated view of the capacity of persons for everyday causal analysis. In their daily lives, people must use information that is often "insufficient" and/or irrelevant to the inferential task.

Zuckerman and Mann[12] argued that although many investigators showed that providing subjects with information will lead to a specific attribution pattern, no studies have examined the effect of attributions on information processing. They employed an ingenious experimental procedure, which was a reversal of past research procedures. Instead of providing subjects with consensus, distinctiveness, and consistency information, they examined how people use attributed causality to infer the three types of behavioral information. These inferences were concerned with whether an actor's behavior toward a given stimulus in a given set of situations can be generalized to people other than the actor, to other stimuli, and to other circumstances. In their study, subjects were required to read descriptions of several stimulus events (i.e., "Nancy enjoys the jazz concert"). Along with the description of each event, an explanation regarding the cause of the event was provided (i.e., "something about Nancy causes her to enjoy the jazz concert"). Subjects were then asked to rate three nine-point scales of consensus, distinctiveness, and consistency.

With some exceptions, the findings suggested that attributions affect estimates of behavioral information. For example, the actors tended to infer high consensus information; that is, they felt that the majority of people share their behavior. Although the results are consistent with Kelley's model, numerous attribution studies have revealed that the human observers do not always follow the same procedures outlined by Kelley and others. In fact, the attribution process is frequently marked by persistent errors and biases. Some of these errors and biases derive from limitations on perceptual and cognitive processes, others stem from individual motivations, and a few may come from both motivational and cognitive factors. Research has suggested attribution errors or biases are most pronounced when they involve people's attribution for their own and others' behaviors. The attributional difference between self and others is termed the "actor–observer" effect.

The actor–observer effect shows that a person's attributions for others' behavior are caused by relatively enduring dispositional factors and attributions for one's own behavior are more situational. Research has found that the divergent perceptions of actors and observers are both due to perceptual differences (e.g., Storms[13] and Wyer, Henninger & Hinkle[14]) and to informational differences (e.g., Eisen[15]). Storms[13] used a videotaping procedure that enabled both actors and observers to view their own behaviors later. The technique successfully reversed the actors' and the observers' visual fields and thus reversed their attributions.

Sherrod and Farber[16] have found that observers made less dispositional attributions to an actor's failure when they later became actors. Similarly, actor-subjects reinterpreted the same behavior as caused by external reasons. Sherrod and Farber explained their results in terms of information differences between the actors and the observers. They suggested that the shift from observer role to actor provided former observers access to additional information about the actor and the environment. This newly discovered information about the setting and the actor thus altered former observers' attributions.

Instead of using perceptual and information models, many researchers have argued for a self-serving or ego-defensive bias model.[17–19] In 1958, Heider wrote that causal attributions are often influenced by subjective needs and wishes as well as by objective elements. The literature on actor's attributions of success and failure (e.g., Bradley[20] and Snyder, Stephan & Rosenfield[21]) labeled the effects of a person's needs and wishes on attribution as defensive, egocentric, egotistic, or self-serving—terms often used interchangeably. Specifically, this research suggests that actors enhance or protect their self-esteem by taking credit for successes while denying responsibility for failures.

A person's success boosts his self-esteem when he is causally responsible for it. Therefore, the motivation to enhance self-esteem should result in a person's attribution of success to his own actions. Likewise, failure affects self-esteem negatively unless the person avoids responsibility for it. Such attributions are viewed as self-protecting or self-serving.[22] The notion that an actor's internal attribution of success and external attribution of failure are self-serving is supported by McFarland and Ross,[23] Nicholls,[24] and Riemer.[25] They showed that such attributions relate to a more positive affective state of an actor. In a review, Zuckerman[26] also argued that the need to maintain self-esteem directly affects the attribution of task outcomes.

Furthermore, actor/observer divergent attributions owing to perceptual differences can be minimized when the "involvement" factor is introduced. Observer effects can also be weakened or reversed. Active (involved) observers make different attributions than passive (uninvolved) observers. Many researchers have argued that it is critical to identify two types of observers, active and passive. This is because the active observers are more likely to be affected by their personal interest in the actor's responses.[2,27–30]

Carver, DeGregorio, and Gillis[31] argued for a need to identify two types of observers, head coach and assistant coaches. The head coach's job is to select able players and decide on team strategies. The assistants' tasks, on the other hand, are to train the individual players and improve on their skills. Carver *et al.*[31] found that these two kinds of observers showed diverse attribution patterns. The results were interpreted in terms of the self-serving model. To avoid responsibility, the assistant coaches attributed the players' poor performance to lack of ability. The head coach, however, attributed the players' failure to lack of effort but not to their inability. This attribution tendency is self-serving in nature.[31]

The self-serving explanation is not without problems, however. Since the head coach and the assistant coaches have different behavioral requirements in the team, information they have concerning the players' effort and ability is different. The assistant coaches work with the players more closely so that they may know much about the players' ability and effort. The head coach, on the other hand, may have a broad picture of the team rather than individual players' past winning and/or failing records. It is possible that such differential information availability contributed to the Carver *et al.* research findings. Carver *et al.* did not offer clear evidence to rule out this possibility.[31]

Research has supported the notion that a person's interests and subjective needs affect the attribution process in many ways. These interests determine when a person is motivated to make attributions. Additionally, they determine whether a motivated person seeks open-ended causal understanding, or whether he is predisposed to particular attributions.

In addition, past research has usually assumed that persons confronted with attributional questions will engage in spontaneous information searches. Wong and Weiner's[32] five experiments suggested that individuals would actually do so. However, no study provides substantial evidence of persons actively performing spontaneous information searches nor demonstrates what information has been sought.

Research has been hindered by the lack of a common method to investigate mediation[33] or to measure when, rather than whether, people engage in a process. Questioning people about inferences may show that they are able to make the inference, but does not show whether they do. Empirical estimates of the processing time people need to make causal judgments after an event would be helpful to answer such questions. Such parameter estimates could provide important evidence about the attributional processes.

Moscovitch[34,35] and Silberman *et al.*[36] suggested that reaction time to the stimulus is a good indicator of whether the information it provides is processed. Therefore, it would be an important contribution to attribution theory to measure time (latency or reaction time) taken to attribute cause or causes of an event observed under various circumstances and to determine the information processed to arrive at such causal attributions. Therefore, the present study measured the time people spent searching for information and generating causal attributions in two motivational states—high versus low personal involvement.

To control for the differences in information availability, we exposed involved and uninvolved observer subjects to same information concerning the actor. This was done by having observers view a videotape of an actor's success or failure performance. To directly investigate effects of motivation on observer's attributions and information processing, Experiment 1 manipulated two independent variables, involvement level of observers and an actor's test outcome, and measured four dependent variables—attribution time, attribution-scale response, the information inferences after attributions, and inference time. The two involvement conditions were involved observer and uninvolved observer. The test outcome was divided into two dimensions, positive and negative. The attribution time included attribution question-reading/comprehension time (Time 1) and attribution scale response time (Time 2). All subjects were asked to estimate Kelley's three information dimensions presumably used to reach a particular attribution. The time needed to read/comprehend and respond to the information question were also recorded. To further examine the effect of motivation, all observers were asked to take the test and serve as actors in Experiment 2.

It was hypothesized that the involved and the uninvolved observers in the Experiment 1 would have dissimilar attribution. That is, the involved observers tended to attribute an actor's poor test score to bad luck and a good test score to ability. In other words, success was attributed internally and failure externally. The uninvolved observers, however, attributed the actor's failure to his lack of ability and success to good luck or easiness of the test.

Subjects' information-processing patterns and time spent in each condition corresponded to the attributions made by the subjects. The most plausible attribution took subjects less attribution and information search time (time to read/comprehend and to respond on the rating scales) because it required less reasoning. The most plausible attribution was defined as the attribution that the subjects believed most strongly to be the cause of a given test result. For example, the involved observers were inclined to attribute an actor's positive test outcome more to ability and effort than to easiness of the test and luck. They would thus take less time to reach the ability and high effort attributions than the time needed to attribute such outcome to the easiness of test and luck. However, both involved and uninvolved observers would have similar attribution patterns and information searching times when they later served as actors in Experiment 2.

EXPERIMENT 1

Design

Experiment 1 involved the manipulation of two independent variables: observer involvement level and actor's test outcome. The observers' attributions, the types of information used to make a particular attribution, and the time spent in processing information were measured. A 2 (involved observer versus uninvolved observer) $\times$ 2 (positive versus negative test outcome) factorial design was employed. In Experiment 2, all observers were required to serve in the actor role after completing Experiment 1. This procedure was to reveal change in observers' attributions when they became actors.

Subjects

The subjects were 50 undergraduate students recruited from introductory psychology classes. Subjects participated in the study individually under the supervision of a research assistant. Three assistants were trained to conduct all phases of the experiment including how to operate the experimental apparatus smoothly without error. The experimental data collection procedures were automated to prevent errors. In addition, a double-blind procedure was employed in which the research assistants were given false hypotheses concerning the purpose of the study. The experiment was described as a study to measure the ability of the subjects to identify another person's anxiety level during the test. All subjects were thoroughly debriefed upon the completion of the study.

Experimental Procedure

The subjects were randomly assigned to each of four experimental conditions—involved observer with positive test outcome, involved observer with negative test outcome, uninvolved observer with positive test outcome, and uninvolved observer with negative test outcome.

Subjects assigned to the "involved observer" condition were required to take the Social Intelligence Test (SIT). However, before taking it, they were asked to view and evaluate a brief segment of a videotaped session (3 min) of another student's performance. They were informed in advance that the SIT is a valid measurement of a person's social intelligence and is used to predict social skills.

After the viewing session, they were shown the person's test outcome, either positive or negative. Those designated to observe a positive test outcome were shown a test score and told that the person did very well, better than 90% of all those tested in the past four years. Subjects designated to observe a negative test outcome were shown a low test score and told that the person did very poorly on the test, near the lowest tenth percentile of the curve. A professionally printed chart of past collective test results was shown to all the subjects to help support the validity of the test outcome.

After this false test outcome manipulation, the observer was asked to answer some attributional questions projected on a screen. An electronic apparatus measured the time (in hundredths of a second) for the information search, the actual interval (latency) subjects needed to read/comprehend an attribution question (Time 1). The apparatus also recorded the attribution scale response and the response time (Time 2).

The detailed procedure each subject followed to answer the slide-projected attributional questions is as follows: First, the subjects were given a set of practice questions to familiarize them with the experimental procedure. Each subject was seated in front of a control panel and pushed a switch to advance the slide for a question (i.e., How difficult do you find the test?). With the activation of the switch, the first digital timer started measuring reading and comprehension time (Time 1). After reading the question, the subject pressed a switch to advance the projector. A nine-point scale for answering the attributional questions was projected on the screen, and a second timer started running (Time 2) until the subject pressed one of the nine switches that represented his response to the question. This response stopped the second timer, which recorded latency of the attribution response (Time 2). The question comprehension time and the scale response time was assumed to represent information searching time (in hundredths of a second). Scale responses to the questions and the two response times constitute the main dependent measures in the study.

Uninvolved observers were instructed that their task was to evaluate a brief videotaped session of a student's performance and that they would not take the test themselves. After the viewing session, they were shown the person's test score, either positive or negative. They then answered the attribution questions as did the subjects in the other conditions.

Results

Attribution Responses

A 2 (role: involved observer and uninvolved observer) × 2 (feedback: positive and negative) MANOVA was performed on the four attribution

TABLE 1. Mean Responses on the Ability, Effort, Test Difficulty, and Luck Attribution Scales by Feedback and Involvement Level in Experiment 1

	Ability		Effort		Difficulty		Luck	
Involvement Feedback	+	−	+	−	+	−	+	−
Involved observer	6.23	2.92	6.23	3.23	1.77	3.92	2.54	4.00
Uninvolved observer	3.08	6.80	2.75	5.60	4.83	2.10	5.33	2.60

NOTE: Entries are mean attribution responses on a nine-point scale ranging from one to nine in each condition. Higher scores indicate stronger agreement on the scales.

items: ability, effort, test difficulty, and luck. With the use of Wilks' criterion, it was found that the role factor did not have an effect on the combined dependent variables (ability, effort, test difficulty, and luck attributions). The results, however, indicated that these four dependent factors were significantly affected by the feedback factor ($F(4, 41) = 3.93$, $p < 0.05$) and by the role and feedback interaction ($F(4, 41) = 23.84$, $p < 0.001$).

Univariate analysis showed that the feedback factor significantly affected the effort, ability, and luck attributions ($F(1, 44) = 7.84$, $p < 0.01$; $F(1, 44) = 4.92$, $p < 0.05$; $F(1, 44) = 5.95$, $p < 0.05$), but not the test difficulty attribution. Additionally, role-by-feedback interaction effects on the four attribution items were at the 0.01 level (Fs $(1, 44) = 25.77$, 63.28, 15.54, and 32.49).

Subjects' ability, effort, luck, and test difficulty attributions under different role and feedback conditions are presented in TABLE 1. Involved observers tended to perceive ability and high effort (working hard) as factors that contributed to an actor's good test scores and were less willing to believe that inability and not working hard caused the actor's poor scores. In addition, they were less inclined to view the actor's high test score as a result of good luck and more willing to attribute poor test scores to bad luck. They were also less inclined to attribute good test scores to the easiness of the test and more inclined to attribute poor test scores to test difficulty. Results of post hoc multiple comparisons[37] indicated that these differences all reached the 0.01 level.

The uninvolved observers, however, reacted differently. They attributed an actor's poor test score to his or her lack of ability and viewed a positive test score as the result of good luck. They perceived the actor's poor performance to be a result of not trying hard (low effort) and attributed an actor's positive test score to the simplicity of the test. They also tended to attribute the actor's success to good luck, which was significantly different from the luck attribution the involved observers attributed to the actor.

TABLE 2. Mean Question Reading/Comprehension Times (Time 1s) on the Four Attribution Questions by Feedback and Involvement Level in Experiment 1

	Ability		Effort		Difficulty		Luck	
Involvement Feedback	+	−	+	−	+	−	+	−
Involved observer	964.46	1181.23	987.15	1351.77	470.85	784.85	956.08	829.38
Uninvolved observer	1297.69	837.55	1489.69	1201.27	551.15	871.73	669.92	841.18

NOTE: Entries are mean question reading/comprehension times (time 1s) in hundredths of a second. Higher values indicate longer reading time.

Multiple *t*-tests indicated that the differences reached the 0.01 level. However, as shown in TABLE 1, test difficulty attributions by the uninvolved observers for an actor's good and poor test results did not differ significantly.

Attribution Question Comprehension Time

Analyses of the scale response latencies (time 2s) on all dependent measures did not reveal any significant differences between involved and uninvolved observers.

A summary table of "the reading/comprehension" times (time 1s) for the four attribution items is presented in TABLE 2. These times were measured in hundredths of a second so that, for example, the value 1210 means 12.1 seconds. MANOVA was performed on the time 1s for the four attribution items showed a feedback main effect and a role-by-feedback interaction effect, Wilks' Lambdas $F(4,43) = 3.13$, $p < 0.05$ and $F = (4,43) = 5.30$, $p < 0.01$.

Univariate analysis of variance showed time 1s on the "ability" and the "effort" attribution items showed significant two-way interaction effects, $Fs(1,46) = 6.64$ and 6.24, $ps < 0.05$. Analysis of reading/comprehension time (time 1) of the "test difficulty" question showed a feedback main effect, $F(1,46) = 7.36$, $p < 0.001$. Both the involved and the uninvolved observers who witnessed an actor receiving a negative test outcome took longer to read the question than did those who observed a positive test result. Analysis of reading time (time 1s) on the "luck" attribution question did not reveal any significant differences between the two observer conditions.

The involved observers needed slightly more time to read/comprehend (finish reading) the "ability" attribution question when observing an actor's negative test score than when viewing a positive test score, $p < 0.05$. Analysis of the question comprehension times (time 1s) for the attribution of effort indicated a two-way interaction effect, $F(1,46) = 4.98$, $p < 0.01$. The involved observers took more time to read the question concerning "effort" attribution when the actor's test score was poor than when the score was positive. The involved observers generally took less time to comprehend the "effort" attribution question when they observed a high test score than when they observed a low test score. Post hoc comparison revealed a significant difference between positive and negative test outcome conditions at the 0.05 level.

Contrarily, post hoc comparisons indicated that the uninvolved observers took more time to read the attribution questions after viewing an actor's good performance than after viewing a poor performance, $p < 0.05$. The uninvolved observers took a longer time to read an "effort" attribution question after observing a positive performance than after observing a negative one.

Information Estimates

A 2 (role: involved observer versus uninvolved observer) + 2 (feedback: positive versus negative test outcome) MANOVA was performed on the three information estimates: consensus, distinctiveness, and consistency. The Wilks' criterion showed that the combined dependent variables were not affected by the role factor, but by the feedback ($F(3,44) = 4.05$, $p < 0.05$) and the role by feedback interaction ($F(3,44) = 17.19$, $p < 0.001$).

To investigate the effects of each main effect and interaction on the individual dependent variables, univariate analysis of variance was performed. Main effects on the feedback variable were found on the distinctiveness, the consistency, and the consensus information at the 0.05, 0.01, and 0.05 levels ($Fs(1,46) = 5.09$, 21.74, and 17.46, respectively). Two significant interaction effects at the 0.01 level were obtained for the consensus and the distinctiveness information ($Fs(1,46) = 7.93$ and 34.58).

To contrast our results with Kelley's[3,5] model, means of individual information dimensions were used as cut-off points to divide the values in TABLE 3B into two levels: high versus low. The means for the consensus, the distinctiveness, and the consistency information were 4.31, 3.88, and 4.91. Values above and below the means were viewed as high and low on the scale, respectively.

TABLE 3A presents the information combinations as predicted by Kelley's model. TABLE 3B indicates that the involved observers who viewed an actor's positive test scores estimated low consensus and low distinctiveness information; that is, they thought that few people obtained the same good score as the actor did, and that the actor generally did well on other tests ($p < 0.05$). On the other hand, the information combination estimated for the negative test scores was high consensus and high distinctiveness information. In other words, they tended to believe that many others had also done as poorly as the actor did. They also claimed that the actor's poor test performance was a rare incident ($p < 0.05$).

TABLE 3. Predicted and Obtained Estimates of the Kelley's Information Dimensions by Feedback and Involvement Level in Experiment 1

		Information Estimates					
		A. Predicted Estimates			B. Obtained Estimates		
Involvement	Feedback	Consensus	Distinctiveness	Consistency	Consensus	Distinctiveness	Consistency
Involved observer	+	Low	Low	High	4.46 High	1.85 Low	5.69 High
	–	High	High	High	4.46 High	5.31 High	3.77 Low
Uninvolved observer	+	High	High	High	5.38 High	5.38 High	5.85 High
	–	Low	Low	High	2.91 Low	1.91 Low	5.18 High

NOTE: Entries are mean scale responses on a nine-point scale ranging from one to nine in each condition. Higher scores indicate higher estimates. For convenience, information estimates in TABLE 2B are classified into high and low dimensions using individual means of the three information dimensions (consensus, distinctiveness, and consistency) as cut-off points (4.31, 3.88, and 4.91, respectively).

Consistent with the Kelley's model, the uninvolved observers' information inferences were high consensus and high distinctiveness when they observed an actor's positive test performance; that is, they believed that many others had also done as well on the test as the actor did and that the actor did not always perform well on other tests. When the actor scored low on the test, the uninvolved subjects thought that he or she was one of the few people who had done poorly and that the actor always did poorly on other tests. In other words, a poor performance led to an inference of low consensus and low distinctiveness.

The analyses of the times needed to respond to the questions concerning the use of Kelley's three kinds of information were not statistically significant on consensus and consistency information. Distinctiveness information, however, yielded a main effect on the involvement variable, $F(1,46) = 8.065$, $p < 0.001$.

EXPERIMENT 2

To further examine the effect of motivation, all observers were asked to take the test and serve as actors in Experiment 2.

After completing the evaluation session, the involved observers took the test and became actors in Experiment 2. The uninvolved observers were told that a student scheduled to be the next subject could not come and were asked to help the experimenter by also taking the SIT test. The SIT consists of three sections of questions on personal beliefs and value judgments. Since the correct answers were unknown to the subjects, the experimenter could manipulate the subjects' test scores.

All subjects had approximately 30 minutes to complete the test. After taking the test, the subject waited alone for 10 minutes awaiting a computer analysis of his test to be completed in another room. The subject was then given a false test outcome, either positive or negative. Those designated to receive a positive test outcome were shown a test score and told that they did very well, better than 90% of all those tested in the past four years. Subjects designated to receive a negative test outcome were shown a low test score and told that they did very poorly on the test, near the lowest tenth percentile of the curve. A professionally printed chart of past collective test results was shown to all the subjects to help support the validity of the test outcome.

After this false test outcome manipulation, the subjects were asked to answer some attributional questions projected on a screen. The procedure subjects in Experiment 2 followed was the same as that of Experiment 1.

Results

A 2 (involved versus uninvolved observer) × 2 (positive versus negative test outcome experienced) MANOVA was conducted. In addition, a series of 2 (involved versus uninvolved observer) × 2 (positive versus negative test

TABLE 4. Mean Responses on the Ability, Effort, Test Difficulty, and Luck Attribution Scales by Feedback and Involvement Level in the Experiment 2

	Ability		Effort		Difficulty		Luck	
Involvement Feedback	+	−	+	−	+	−	+	−
Involved observer	5.43	2.75	5.57	2.67	1.07	1.17	1.57	4.17
Uninvolved observer	5.21	3.33	6.14	3.00	2.36	3.00	1.85	4.40

NOTE: Entries are mean attribution responses on a nine-point scale ranging from one to nine in each condition. Higher scores indicate stronger agreement on the scales.

outcome experienced) ANOVAs were performed on all of the attributional questions as well as the kind of information used.

Attribution Scale Response

The test outcome factor manifested a significant main effect on "ability" attribution, $F(1,44) = 13.23$, $p < 0.001$. Ability was considered a more important causal factor for the subjects' own positive test scores than for their negative test scores.

Post hoc multiple t test revealed that ability was considered a causal factor by the subjects given good test scores in Experiment 2. As TABLE 4 indicates, the subjects were more likely to deny that lack of ability caused their poor test performance, $p < 0.05$.

They also felt that effort was a more important causal factor when they did very well on the test than when did poorly, $F(1,44) = 27.78$, $p < 0.001$. They perceived that effort (trying hard) was a causal factor for their positive test scores, whereas it was not viewed as a causal factor for their negative test scores, $p < 0.01$. Additionally, the analyses indicated that all the subjects (former observers) had similar involved patterns and reacted similarly to those of the involved observers in Experiment 1. The subjects felt more strongly that "bad" luck was more a causal factor in their failure than was "good" luck in their success, $F(1,44) = 32.88$, $p < 0.001$. They did not, however, differ significantly on the test difficulty attribution scale.

Attribution Question Comprehension Time

The analyses of the response times in making attributional ratings (time 2s) did not reveal any statistically significant results between groups. According to TABLE 5, however, the subjects took longer (time 1) to read and comprehend the attribution question concerning their own ability when

TABLE 5. Mean Question Reading/Comprehension Times (Time 1s) on the Four Attribution Questions by Feedback and Involvement Level in Experiment 2

	Ability		Effort		Difficulty		Luck	
Involvement Feedback	+	−	+	−	+	−	+	−
Involved observer	756.64	925.25	846.79	1096.17	403.29	798.67	849.71	635.83
Uninvolved observer	772.14	901.90	902.79	1154.50	443.85	705.20	580.64	733.40

NOTE: Entries are mean question reading/comprehension times (time 1s) in hundredths of a second. Higher values indicate longer reading time.

they did poorly on the test than when they did well, $F(1,44) = 7.42$, $p < 0.01$.

Reading/comprehension time for the test difficulty item was significantly longer when the subjects received negative test scores than when they received positive test scores, $F(1,44) = 47.90$, $p < 0.001$. The corresponding measure for the attribution of effort, however, did not reach statistical significance.

An interaction was found on reading/comprehension (time 1) for the luck attribution, $F(1,44) = 4.47$, $p < 0.04$. The involved subjects took less time to consider the question concerning an attribution to luck for poor test scores than for good test scores. Similarly, the uninvolved observers spent less time considering the same question when they did poorly on the test than when they did well.

Estimates of Kelley's Informational Dimensions

When receiving positive test scores, the former involved subjects' estimate of information usages were low consensus, low distinctiveness, and high consistency. The subjects felt that their positive test results were more consistent with their past test performances than were their poor test results, $F(1,44) = 43.401$, $p < 0.001$. Post hoc comparisons confirm such differences in the information usage for making attributions ($p < 0.01$).

As TABLE 6 suggests, the involved observers perceived their negative test results as more distinctive than did the uninvolved observers who received positive test scores, $p < 0.05$.

The formerly uninvolved observers reacted similarly to the positive and negative test outcome. Multiple t comparisons confirm such differences in the information usage for making attributions ($p < 0.01$).

The time 1 measures on the estimates of the information were also analyzed. TABLE 7 suggests that the subjects (former involved and uninvolved observers) spent more time trying to estimate the distinctiveness

TABLE 6. Predicted and Obtained Estimates of the Kelley's Information Dimensions by Feedback and Involvement Level in Experiment 2

		Information Estimates		
Involvement	Feedback	Consensus	Distinctiveness	Consistency
Involved observer	+	3.93 Low	3.93 Low	5.79 High
	−	4.50 High	5.00 High	2.58 Low
Uninvolved observer	+	3.79 Low	2.50 Low	6.64 High
	−	3.89 Low	3.20 Low	2.50 Low

NOTE: Entries are mean scale responses on a nine-point scale ranging from one to nine in each condition. Higher scores indicate higher estimates. For convenience, information estimates are classified into high and low dimensions using individual means of the three information dimensions (consensus, distinctiveness, and consistency) as cut-off points (4.03, 4.17, and 4.57, respectively).

TABLE 7. Mean Information Processing Times on the Kelley's Information Dimensions by Feedback and Involvement Level in Experiment 2

		Information Estimates		
Involvement	Feedback	Consensus	Distinctiveness	Consistency
Involved observer	+	901.43	977.43	898.86
	−	1075.00	1211.17	1137.25
Uninvolved observer	+	900.14	716.71	927.57
	−	1003.30	1196.60	1198.80

NOTE: Entries are mean question reading/comprehension times on the Kelley's information dimensions in hundredths of a second.

information $F(1,44) = 37.439$, $p < .001$ and the consistency information, $F(1,44) = 6.185$, $p < 0.05$, after receiving a low test score than after receiving a high test score. Measures of reading time (time 1) for the consensus item did not differ significantly between groups.

GENERAL DISCUSSION

Attribution Responses

Weiner[6] argued that causal factors could be classified in four categories: ability, effort, luck, and test difficulty. Although these four causal categories have been widely accepted by past researchers, it is important to note that this list of perceived causes is not exhaustive. A person may often assign causality to sources not readily classifiable within these four categories. For example, failures or negative results might be attributed to fatigue (which is distinguished from effort expenditure), bias (which is distinguished from test difficulty), misread instructions (which is distinguished from bad luck), and so forth. However, Weiner and his associates[6,38] contended that the four causal elements account for the major sources of variance in attributing cause or causes of success and failure.

Using similar measures, the present results generally support past research findings. The subjects evaluated ability, effort, luck, and test difficulty after either taking a test (Experiment 2) or observing another person's performance (Experiment 1). The results suggest that attributions vary with the performance outcomes.

In Experiment 1, the involved observers' attributions of an actor's test score followed the attribution and information-processing pattern of the actors in the Experiment 2. The uninvolved observers, however, attributed the actor's failure to lack of ability and success to good luck or easiness of the test. When serving as actors in Experiment 2 and when both the involved and the uninvolved observers received low test scores, they generally perceived the test as more difficult than when they received high test scores. They were likely to attribute a poor test score to bad luck and a good test score to ability. In other words, success was attributed internally and failure externally. The results confirm the investigator's hypothesis that involvement has an important effect on attributional processes.

Attribution theorists assume that persons are motivated to seek meaning for both their own behavior and that of other persons. Thus, attributional processes are important to the individual's understanding and interpreting the possible cause or causes for his own actions, feelings, and attitudes.

As Heider[1] stated in his "naive psychologist" model, attributions of causality are influenced by subjective needs as well as by objective evidence. The literature on attribution of success and failure (e.g., Bradley[20] and Hastorf, Schneider & Polefka[39] and Snyder, Stephan & Rosenfield[21]) has labeled the effects of subjective needs on attribution as defensive, egotistic, or self-serving. Specifically, these researchers suggested that people try to enhance or protect their self-esteem by taking credit for success and denying responsibility for failure. Thus, the actors (former observers) in Experiment 2 attributed success more to their own ability than to luck, because this attribution enhanced their self-esteem. Conversely, they avoided embarrassment and loss of self-esteem by attributing failure to bad luck and/or test difficulty.

An attribution made by a person with a personal stake in a situation, either present or future, will be different than that of an uninvolved person. This notion was supported by the first experiment's finding that the involved observers tended to deny an actor's personal responsibility for his failure by perceiving the test as unreliable. Observers also gave an actor more personal credit when he did well on a test and accorded him less blame when he did poorly.

In short, this study sought to show how personal involvement directly influences the attribution of test results. It suggests that the magnitude of this effect depends on the extent to which involvement is aroused and thus influences attributional decisions. Specifically, when such a motivational state is not aroused, the uninvolved subjects are less concerned whether their attributions would affect the actor's self-esteem. The study has shown that uninvolved observers attributed an actor's high test score to good luck or easiness of the test and a poor test score to lack of ability. Such differential attributions following one's own or another's success or failure is a clear indication of motivational bias. This study supports the notion that attributional differences between actors and observers are, in part, the result of motivational (differential involvement) differences. The results further confirm past findings that actor–observer attributional differences are affected by differences in their involvement states.

Perhaps the involved observers are reluctant to attribute failure to an actor's lack of ability because they identify with him. Involved observers facing a difficult test may be reluctant to blame an actor for failing the same test, since they may shortly be subject to a similar appraisal.

On the other hand, the attributions of uninvolved observers, who did not anticipate taking the test, were unaffected by such motivational considerations. They were less generous to the actor and attributed the actor's positive test score to good luck and/or test simplicities (external attributions) and a poor test score to "not trying hard" and/or "lack of ability" (internal attributions).

The importance of motivation in the attributional process can also be substantiated indirectly by many previous studies. For example, Gould and Sigall[40] tested such motivational factors by instructing observers to empathize or not empathize with a target man who either succeeded or failed to make a good impression on a woman. Empathic observers attributed the target man's success to internal factors and his failure to external factors, while nonempathic observers made internal attributions for both success and failure. As Gould and Sigall suggested, the empathy may have made the subjects share an emotional experience which leads to the sharing of a self-enhancing outcome. Arkin, Gabrenya, and McGarvey[41] have also shown that observers who share social perspective with an actor made more flattering attributions about the actor's performance than observers whose role and social perspective were more distinctive from those of the actor. Of course, to the extent that the observer's generosity matches the actor's self-serving bias, no actor–observer differences would be evident. Again, this notion is confirmed by our study.

The importance of the involvement (motivational) factor can further be demonstrated by comparing the uninvolved observers' responses between Experiment 1 and Experiment 2. Both involved and uninvolved observers were asked to take the SIT test and were given false test results, either positive or negative. The actors (former involved and uninvolved subjects) in Experiment 2 reacted similarly to the involved observers in Experiment 1. Again the results of the second experiment confirm our hypothesis that involvement mediates attribution and information processes.

There is another explanation for the finding that the actors in the second experiment and involved observers of the first experiment show similar attribution patterns, while uninvolved observers reacted differently. In their review, Miller and Ross[18] questioned whether there are nonmotivational interpretations of self-serving attribution. They postulated three informational (nonmotivational) processes to account for the association between success and internal attribution: (a) people expect success more often than failure (Parducci[42]), and they tend to take responsibility for results they expect (Feather[43]), (b) people are more likely to perceive covariations (Kelley[4]) between their behavior and increasing success than between their behavior and constant failure, and (c) erroneous conceptions of contingency lead people to infer personal responsibility from the co-occurrences of their responses and desired outcomes (i.e. success), whereas the co-occurrences of responses and negative outcomes (i.e. failure) are ignored.[44,45]

Because the involved observers were instructed to focus on the actor's behavior, in accordance with Miller and Ross's "erroneous conception of contingency," involved observers may become more aware of the covariation between the actor's behavior and his success than the covariation between the actor's behavior and his failure. Consequently, they may give the actor more credit for success than for failure. Although the uninvolved observers received instructions the same as those of the involved observers, their reactions were quite different. The interpretation of Miller and Ross[18] fails to explain the findings that the uninvolved observers in Experiment 1 attributed the actor's success to external factors (test simplicity and/or good luck) and attributed his failure to internal factors (lack of ability and/or effort).

Attribution Question Reading/Comprehension Time

The present study suggests that attributional response measures used in past research can be substantiated with another type of measure—attribution response time. The important methodological advantage of the reaction time paradigm is that effects of motivation (involvement) on information processing and attribution processes can be tapped by such measurement.

For example, it was found that the actors and the involved observers generally took less time to consider attributional questions when the test results were positive than when they were negative. However, the uninvolved observers took longer to read/comprehend the attributional questions when an actor's test score was positive than when it was negative. The findings suggest that the motivational state of involvement can be tapped by response latency measures as well as rating scales.

The study suggests, therefore, that an attribution is more readily made when it does not appear to have a negative effect on the attributor and will not require much time to consider. However, an attribution that has a possible negative personal implication may be more carefully considered before it is made, and the response time will be longer.

The results suggest that attributions are generally made during the reading/comprehension of attributional questions. This was evidenced by the fact that response latencies on the rating scales (time 2), as distinct from reading/comprehension times, did not differ significantly between experimental groups. Reading/comprehension times (time 1s), however, were different under different experimental conditions. Attributions made during reading/comprehension may have different temporal characteristics, depending on the motivational state of observers, and that these temporal differences can be detected by straightforward latency measures.

The suggestion that this type of information processing is part of the normal question comprehension process cannot rest exclusively on the findings; however, it is supported by relevant theory. The cognitive literature on comprehension (e.g. Kintsch[46]) emphasizes the role of inferences in comprehension. The potential importance of linkages between such theory and the social psychological literature on attribution has perhaps not yet been widely recognized. The results presented here confirm the plausibility of that body of cognitive theory as it applies to specific types of attributional responses that have been studied by social psychologists.

Kelley's Normative Information Model

This study did not find strong support for Kelley's normative model. The results suggest that the data supplied by Kelley[3] and others (i.e. McArthur[8]) may have been contaminated by experimental artifacts.

Many researchers have expressed a passing interest in the theories of naive epistemology. Attribution theorists such as Heider,[1] Jones and Davis,[2] Jones *et al.*,[47] and Kelley[3,5] have pursued this topic most vigorously and systematically. Since Kelley's work in 1967 and 1973, the primary focus of attribution research has been the logical rules or "schemas" that a layman employs to make causal inferences and social interpretation from particular data configurations.

Much of social psychologists' current interest in the intuitive scientists' activities, have been guided by a normative model of causal analysis. The central organizing device of this model is Kelley's[3] normative model. The three dimensions of Kelley's model are (a) "distinctiveness," the degree to which an effect occurs in the presence of one particular causal factor and not in the presence of others; (b) "consistency," the degree to which an effect is observed reliably when a particular causal factor is present; and (c) "consensus," the degree to which people other than the target actor show the effect. The normative model requires that people use each component of the model to determine cause or causes.

The normative approach guided most early attribution work and yielded a somewhat flattering portrait of the lay person's capacity to use normative causal inferential principles. Because it has been often reviewed, it is not necessary to relate earlier attribution research in any detail. Suffice it to say, however, that Kelley's initial papers[3–5] supported by other major studies (i.e., McArthur,[8] Orvis, Cunningham & Kelley[11] and Weiner *et al.*[38]) provide ample evidence that subjects' causal inferences are often directionally responsive to the three informational dimensions that normatively "ought" to influence them—distinctiveness, consistency, and consensus. For example, a subject is told that "John is enthralled by a particular painting, that he is enthralled by few other paintings, that he always has been enthralled in the past by this particular painting, and that almost all other people are enthralled by the painting." The subject would attribute John's positive response more to the painting rather than to John's predisposition to be enthralled by paintings.[8] Similarly, if a subject is told that Jane succeeded at a test that most people fail and that she did not have to try hard to succeed, the subject is more likely to attribute her success to ability rather than luck, effort, or an easy test.[38]

Most studies demonstrating normatively justified causal inferences presented the subjects with streamlined, well-organized stimulus materials. The subject usually did not have to decide the relevance of the available information and was spared the tasks of information collection, storage, and retrieval. Most importantly, the subject did not observe, estimate, or summarize data for the observed events. This strategy is reasonable for an investigator who wishes to determine a subject's ability to make causal analyses, uncontaminated by motivations. However, such a strategy seems certain to inflate the estimated capacity of persons for everyday causal analysis. In their daily lives, people must use information that is biased, insufficient, or of questionable relevance to the inferential task.

In the typical attribution study, the experimenter supplies the relevant data and, by doing so, manipulates response consistency, distinctiveness, and consensus apparent to the social observer. This strategy (e.g. McArthur[8]) has obvious and undeniable advantages if the experimenter's primary interest is the subject's data analysis and interpretation. The strategy also has serious costs, because it demands that one overlook certain potentially crucial phases of attribution that precede data analysis—collecting, coding, and retrieving information from memory.

A reasonable assumption is that the same behavior is not repeated in the exact same fashion. For example, no one takes the same statistics course more than twice. Thus, if a person fails a statistics test, it is unlikely that the person can follow Kelley's normative rules to relate the event to the same past events. It is possible to speculate that when an event occurs a person may associate the event with similar events in the past. This thus leads to distorted attributions. In other words, subjects may imagine a behavioral history for themselves or others in order to derive an attribution for an observed event. This phenomenon explains why this study did not yield strong support for Kelley's model. Since the present study did not provide subjects with systematic information as McArthur[8] did, subjects may have constructed the information combinations needed to generate the attributions requested in the experiment. This study thus suggests that the data supplied by Kelley[3] and others (i.e. McArthur[8]) may have been the result of ignoring the importance of motivational factors in a situation where consensus, consistency, and distinctiveness are ambiguous.

The importance of this study is very clear in that it directly examines the effect of involvement on the observers. The results suggest that a person processes information differently when attributions bear personal relevance.

SUMMARY

Attribution theories postulate that human actors and observers process information differently and make different causal judgments about observed behaviors and events. However, past research has failed to address whether an important factor—motivation—affects such information processing, and thus make the actor and observers different in their attributions. Does the motivational factor make people more willing to process information? Two experiments were designed to show how a motivational factor, personal involvement, directly influences a person's information processing of attributions for an actor's performance. To measure when actor and observers process information to arrive at a specific attribution, a reaction time paradigm was adopted. It was hypothesized that the time needed to arrive at a specific attribution would depend on the extent of the subject's involvement in the task attempted by the actor. The implications of the results in explaining actors' and observers' attributional differences are discussed.

REFERENCES

1. Heider, F. 1958. The psychology of interpersonal relations. Wiley. New York.
2. Jones, E. E. & K. E. Davis. 1965. From acts to dispositions. *In* Advances in Experimental Social Psychology. L. Berkowitz, Ed. Vol. 2: 219–266. Academic Press. New York.
3. Kelley, H. H. 1967. Attribution theory in social psychology. *In* Nebraska Symposium on Motivation, Vol. 15. D. Levine, Ed. University of Nebraska Press. Lincoln, NB.
4. Kelley, H. H. 1971. Attribution in Social Interaction. General Learning Press. Morristown, NJ.
5. Kelley, H. H. 1973. The processes of causal attribution. Am. Psychol. **28:** 107–128.
6. Weiner, B. 1972. Theories of Motivation: From Mechanism to Cognition. Markham. Chicago.
7. Ferguson, T. J. & G. L. Wells. 1980. Priming of mediators in causal attribution. J. Pers. Soc. Psychol. **39:** 461–470.
8. McArthur, L. Z. 1972. The how and what of why: Some determinants and consequences of causal attribution. J. Pers. Soc. Psychol. **22:** 171–193.

9. PRUITT, D. J. & C. A. INSKO. 1980. Extension of the Kelley attribution model: The role of comparison-object consensus, target-object consensus, distinctiveness, and consistency. J. Pers. Soc. Psychol. **39:** 39–58.
10. HANSEN, R. D. & J. M. DONOGHUE. 1977. The power of consensus: Information derived from one's own and others' behavior. J. Pers. Soc. Psychol. **35:** 294–303.
11. ORVIS, B. R., J. D. CUNNINGHAM & H. H. KELLEY. 1975. A close examination of causal inference: The roles of consensus, distinctiveness, and consistency information. J. Pers. Soc. Psychol. **32:** 605–616.
12. ZUCKERMAN, M. & R. W. MANN. 1979. The other way around: Effects of causal attributions on estimates of consensus, distinctiveness, and consistency. J. Exp. Soc. Psychol. **15** 582–597.
13. STORMS, M. D. 1973. Videotape and the attribution process: Reversing actors' and observers' point of view. J. Pers. Soc. Psychol. **27:** 165–175.
14. WYER, R. S., JR., M. HENNINGER & R. HINKLE. 1977. An information analysis of actors' and observers' belief attributions in a role-playing situation. J. Exp. Soc. Psychol. **13:** 199–217.
15. EISEN, S. V. 1979. Actor–observer differences in information inference and causal attribution. J. Pers. Soc. Psychol. **37(2):** 261–272.
16. SHERROD, D. R. & J. FARBER. 1975. The effect of previous actor/observer role experience on attribution of responsibility for failure. J. Pers. **43(2):** 231–247.
17. AJZEN, I. & M. A. FISHBEIN. 1975. A Bayesian analysis of attribution processes. Psychol. Bull. **82:** 261–277.
18. MILLER, D. T. & M. ROSS. 1975. Self-serving biases in the attribution of causality: Fact or fiction? Psychol. Bull. **82:** 213–225.
19. TILLMAN, W. S. & C. S. CARVER. 1980. Actors' and observers' attributions for success and failure: A comparative test of predictions from Kelley's cube, self-serving biases, and positivity bias formulations. J. Exp. Soc. Psychol. **16:** 18–32.
20. BRADLEY, G. W. 1978. Self-serving biases in the attribution process: A re-examination of the fact or fiction question. J. Pers. Soc. Psychol. **36:** 56–71.
21. SNYDER, L., W. G. STEPHAN & D. ROSENFIELD. Egotism and attribution. J. Pers. Soc. Psychol. **33:** 435–441.
22. WEARY, G. 1980. Examination of affect and egotism as mediators of bias in causal attributions. J. Pers. Soc. Psychol. **38:** 348–357.
23. MCFARLAND, C. & M. ROSS. 1982. Impact of causal attributions on affective reactions to success and failure. J. Pers. Soc. Psychol. **43:** 937–946.
24. NICHOLLS, J. G. 1975. Causal attributions and other achievement related cognitions: Effects of test outcome, attainment value, and sex. J. Pers. Soc. Psychol. **31:** 379–389.
25. RIEMER, B. S. 1975. Influence of causal beliefs on affect and expectancy. J. Pers. Soc. Psychol. **31:** 1163–1167.
26. ZUCKERMAN, M. 1979. Attribution of success and failure revisited, or: The motivational bias is alive and well in attribution theory. J. Pers. **47:** 245–287.
27. CHAIKIN, A. L. & J. COOPER. 1973. Evaluation as a function of correspondence and hedonic relevance. J. Exp. Soc. Psychol. **9:** 257–264.
28. CUNNINGHAM, J. D., P. A. STARR & D. E. KANOUSE. 1979. Self as actor, active observer, and passive observer: Implications for causal attributions. J. Pers. Soc. Psychol. **37(7):** 1146–1152.
29. HILL, C. T. & J. M. JONES. 1973. Effects of prejudice and perspective on attribution of intentionality. Proc. 81st Annu. Convention Am. Psychol. Assoc. **8:** 347–348.

30. MILLER, D. T. & S. A. NORMAN. 1975. Actor–observer differences in perceptions of effective control. J. Pers. Soc. Psychol. **31:** 503–515.
31. CARVER, C. S., E. DEGREGORIO & R. GILLIS. Field-study of evidence of an ego-defensive bias in attribution among two categories of observers. Pers. Soc. Psychol. Bull. **6(1):** 44–50.
32. WONG, P. T. P. & B. WEINER. 1981. When people ask "why" questions, and the heuristics of attributional search: Mediators of bias in causal attributions. J. Pers. Soc. Psychol. **40:** 650–663.
33. TAYLOR, S. E. & S. T. FISKE. 1975. Point of view and perception of causality. J. Pers. Soc. Psychol. **32:** 439–445.
34. MOSCOVITCH, M. 1972. Choice reaction time study assessing the verbal behavior of the minor hemisphere in normal adult humans. J. Comp. Physiol. Psychol. **80:** 66–74.
35. MOSCOVITCH, M. 1973. Language and the cerebral hemisphere: Reaction time studies and their implications for models of cerebral dominance. *In* Communication and Affect: Language and Thought. P. Pliner, L. Krames & T. Alloway, Eds.: 97-125. Academic Press. New York.
36. SILBERMAN, E. K., H. WEINGARTNER, R. STILLMAN, H. CHEN & R. M. POST. 1983. Altered lateralization of cognitive processes in female depressed patients. Am. Psychiatr. J. **140(10):** 1340–1344.
37. GLASS, G. V. & K. D. HOPKINS. 1984. Stat. Methods Educ. Psychol. Prentice-Hall. Englewood Cliffs, NJ.
38. WEINER, B., I. FRIEZE, A. KUKLA, L. REED, S. REST & R. M. ROSENBAUM. 1971. Perceiving the Causes of Success and Failure. General Learning Press. New York.
39. HASTORF, A. H., D. J. SCHNIDER & J. POLEFKA. 1970. Person Perception. Addison-Wesley. Cambridge, MA.
40. GOULD, R. & H. SIGALL. 1977. The effects of empathy and outcome on attribution: An examination of the divergent-perspectives hypothesis. J. Exp. Soc. Psychol. **13:** 480–491.
41. ARKIN, R. M., W. K. GABRENYA, JR. & B. MCGARVEY. 1978. The role of social perspective in perceiving the causes of success and failure. J. Pers. **46:** 762–777.
42. PARDUCCI, A. The relativism of absolute judgments. Sci. Am. **219:** 84–90.
43. FEATHER, N. T. 1969. Attitude and selective recall. J. Pers. Soc. Psychol. **12:** 310–319.
44. JENKINS, H. M. & W. C. WARD. 1965. Judgment of contingency between responses and outcomes. Psychol. Monogr. **79** (1, Whole No. 594).
45. SMEDSLUND, J. 1963. The concept of correlation in adults. Scand. J. Psychol. **4:** 165–173.
46. KINTSCH, W. 1974. The Representation of Meaning in Memory. Erlbaum. Hillsdale, NJ.
47. JONES, E. E., D. E. KANOUSE, H. H. KELLEY, R. E. NISBETT, S. VALINS & B. WEINER, Eds. 1972. Attribution: Perceiving the Causes of Behavior. General Learning Press. Morristown, NJ.

Sociopsychological and Structural Factors Related to Women's Vocational Development

MICHELE A. PALUDI

Department of Psychology
Hunter College
City University of New York
New York, New York 10021

INTRODUCTION

The study of women's career development is of very recent origin, despite the fact that the field of vocational psychology itself is over 70 years old.[1] This relative neglect of the career psychology of women is a result of two widely accepted assumptions: (a) The primary career roles of women centered around domestic and childcare responsibilities; and (b) the theories developed to describe young men's career development would automatically generalize to the description of women's career development.[2,3]

Personal and public attitudes toward women's career psychology began to change in the late 1960s and early 1970s, signaled and stimulated by the reemergence of the women's movement.[4] These attitudinal changes are mirrored in the proportion of women, including women with preschool children, engaged in paid employment outside the home. Since 1970, for example, approximately four million women have joined the workforce.[5] In addition, women outnumbered men in all age groups among adult learners, constituting 57% of the total.

Therefore, regarding the first assumption, "women's place" has been extended outside the home to college, graduate school, and the workforce. As for the second assumption, this "male as normative" view has actually characterized much of psychology as a discipline.[6-8] Gender differences observed in career psychology include the following:[1] (a) a relatively restricted range of career alternatives pursued by women in comparison to a much larger range pursued by men; (b) women continue to be concentrated in female-populated fields whose status and market value is low; (c) women are less well represented at each higher degree level; (d) women are more likely than men to be enrolled in public institutions and to attend college on a part-time basis; (e) female-populated professions offer limited career mobility; and (f) women's intellectual capacities are not reflected in their educational and occupational successes; their aspirations are relatively lower than men's of comparable ability.

These gender differences have been interpreted as supporting the "homogenization of American women."[9] That is, women are typically socialized by family, peers, and teachers to pursue the same role regardless of their individual capabilities. According to this and other research, women's career psychology is predictable, not on their characteristics as individuals, but on the basis of their sex. Also, women's career development has involved one additional step than that of men's[10] and is the product of two sequential decisions: (a) deciding whether or not they want a career and (b) deciding what occupation or career to pursue. Men, in contrast, begin instead with decisions about what career they would like to pursue.

Thus, vocational psychologists have recognized the need for theory and research focused specifically on women's career development. Among the many topics related to this inquiry are women's aspirations,[11] motivation,[12] and attributions[13] as well as barriers to women's success.[14,15] What follows is an overview of research on women's career development my colleagues and I have conducted. The focus of this research is mainly concerned with sociopsychological and structural factors that differentially affect women's achievement and the career pathways they follow. Sociopsychological or person-centered issues we have studied include fear of success and failure, achievement orientation, causal attributions of success and failure, and employed mothers' role strain and job satisfaction. Structural or institution-centered explanations we have investigated include evaluations of women's achievement, discrimination in the workplace, the availability of role models and mentors in academia, and gender and sexual harassment in academia.

I will summarize these areas by addressing the results of some of our recent research on women's career development. The implications of this research will also be discussed. Finally, I will offer several recommendations concerning further directions for theory and research in the area of women's career development.

OVERVIEW OF RESEARCH ON WOMEN'S CAREER DEVELOPMENT

Achievement Striving

In 1986 Jean Fankell-Hauser and I conducted an in-depth interview study on women's achievement orientation that served as one of the initial studies in our program of research on women's career development.[16] We recognized that individuals differ in the strength of their striving for achievement. In addition, people differ in the roles that elicit their striving. Therefore, we believed that women's achievement striving could best be predicted from information about these women's own specific interests, activities, and aspirations. The main purpose of our research was to develop an idiographic approach to the measurement of women's success striving. We accomplished this by using biographical interviewing.[17] This enabled us to identify personal, parental, and peer influences on women's success striving.

We interviewed 80 women, 10 each from the following age groups: late teens, 20s, 30s, 40s, 50s, 60s, 70s, and 80s. The mean age was 46.8 years. This sample included women who were beginning their careers, who were in the middle of their achievement paths, and who had been retired. Also included in this sample were women who were or had not been employed outside the home. We used the following standardized interview items with each woman:

- What, specifically, do you want to accomplish in the next few years?
- What specific steps do you plan to take to achieve these goals?
- What blocks in yourself will you have to overcome to achieve these goals?
- What blocks in the world will you have to overcome to achieve these goals?
- How do you feel about the possibility of achieving these goals? Of failing to achieve them?
- How do your parent(s) feel about the possibility of your achieving these goals? Of failing to achieve them?
- How does your mate feel about your achieving these goals?
- How do your children feel about you achieving these goals?
- How do your women acquaintances feel about you achieving these goals?
- How do your men acquaintances feel about you achieving these goals?
- Who, if anyone, are the people (or person) you would like to be like? That is, who are the people you try to model yourself after? Describe the different role models you've had over the course of your life.
- Have you ever been in a situation where you were about to succeed at something and wondered if it was worth it or got afraid of the success or something it might produce?

Women's responses to the interview items were content-analyzed for the types of achievement goals described, blocks preventing them from attaining their goals, support and encouragement, and the positive reactions to achievement striving they received. One theme that emerged from the interview items concerned developmental discontinuities in women's achievement striving. Compared to older women, younger women were more concerned with competitive achievement. Older women (in the 50-to-80 age groups) reported that their achievement striving increased when they were in the "child launching" phase of their relationships. They reported feeling accepted at that stage by both male and female peers and relatives. This finding supports the hypothesis that older women become role innovators or pioneers.[18]

Achievement striving was also likely to be characteristic of women whose parents reinforced and encouraged achievement efforts and who were reared in dual-earner families. These women viewed their relationship with their parent(s) as warmer, closer, more sharing, and more supportive than did other women. Similar findings were reported by Hennig and Jardim[19] in their study of successful older business women and their fathers.

Women voiced their realization that masculine achievement-striving behavior is limited. The biographical interviewing technique did not emphasize the dichotomous acceptance or rejection of success and fear of success. In addition, the technique does not obscure the importance of investigating different types of achievement. Instead, the interviewing approach helps to explore the personality characteristics that predispose women of several cohorts toward achievement-striving behavior, taking into account the effects of family, friends, and role models.

Furthermore, the biographical interviewing method suggested that the fear of success component of women's achievement motivation should be abandoned. In 1968 Matina Horner proposed that women are more likely than men to be afraid of success—that success will lead to unpleasant consequences, including unpopularity and a loss of femininity.[20] However, Diane Hruska, Brooke Guda, Laura Bowman, and I recently completed an updated review of the literature on fear of success that supported the findings from the interview study.[21] On the basis of a review of studies, we drew the following conclusions:

- inconsistent data exists to support the hypothesis that fear of success is less likely among black women and more likely among white women.
- fear of success has shown no consistent relationship to ability—IQ, career goals—in women,
- inconsistent data exists to support a relationship between fear of success and gender role identity;
- no reliable age or gender differences in fear of success have been observed; and
- whether fear of success taps a motive or cultural stereotype is not clear.

We found more support, both from the literature review and interview study for Jean Lipman-Blumen's theory concerning direct and relational achieving styles.[22] Direct achieving styles are used by people who confront achievement tasks very directly; a direct achiever may enjoy winning over competitors or may simply enjoy the thrill of accomplishment. Relational achieving styles are used by people who seek success through their relationships with others, for example, working in collaboration with other people. Women seem to show wide variability in the kind of achieving style they prefer.

Role Conflict in Employed Women

We believed that the politically motivated response to research on fear of success masked a more general phenomenon implicit in it: role conflict.

The conflict surrounding achievement strivings arise from attempts to implement values, goals, and aspirations that appear to be mutually exclusive or at least in conflict with one another. Fear of success may be thought of as a conscious solution to a realistic role conflict; of women's reluctance to violate important social norms where these violations would be costly. Men may be more conforming to the stereotypic core elements of the male role in society which mandates that they appear self-confident, worry-free, and fearless in achievement situations.

Therefore, we believed we should investigate such role conflict and decided to ask employed mothers to address the interrelationships among their work and family roles. Ruth Anderson-Kulman and I published the results from this line of research in 1986.[4] We assessed how factors associated with the mother's employment (e.g., part or full time), job satisfaction, and commitment to work influenced the family in terms of its cohesiveness and degree of conflict. We also included single mothers as a target group and assessed the similarities and differences between single and married, employed mothers.

Few differences were found between single versus married women, or those who worked part time or full time. The women worked predominantly in white-collar occupations and ranged in age from 20 to 42 years (mean age: 30 years). Job satisfaction among employed mothers was found to be predictive of family cohesion, such that greater maternal job satisfaction was associated with greater cohesiveness among their families. Maternal role strain was also found to be associated with familial conflict as less role strain among employed mothers was predictive of lower levels of family conflict.

The areas of conflict endorsed by the mothers indicated that managing the household and home cleaning were major sources of stress among the sample as a whole. In addition, a majority of women reported experiencing conflict about care of sick children. The most commonly reported problems among the mothers were child related. Other problems included issues with time management, stress, and fatigue. The lack of time appears to be most accentuated in areas that are self-related—community activities, reading, hobbies, and physical fitness.

The finding that greater job satisfaction was associated with lower levels of role strain among employed mothers leads one to seek ways to enhance the level of satisfaction with one's work because this may be expected to promote positive coping among employed mothers and their families. Personal belief systems about women's role as mothers also have a profound effect on women's achievement. In dual-working families the woman continues to assume most of the home and parental role responsibilities. Even in marriages among the more educated and liberal professionals, egalitarian role relations in the workplace and the home are uncommon. Thus, the demands of parenting continue to have a far greater impact on the achievements and career paths of women than of men. Men assume they will combine a career and family without undue difficulty; women assume that combining a career and a family is nearly impossible and a feat only to be achieved by "superwomen." A not so surprising result of these strongly held assumptions is the lower marriage rate among professional women in comparison to their male peers; a secondary result is the increasing prevalence of childlessness among professional couples.[1]

Role Models and Mentors

How persons think about their circumstances and act upon them is influenced by social ideology, social norms, and social organization. It is well documented that gender role socialization influences the personality development of women and men, as well as the observed gender-role-related differences in various achievement areas.[23] Carol Gilligan[24] also describes how childhood social contexts can account for the development of many psychological gender differences, particularly those reflecting the greater imbeddedness of women in social contexts in contrast to the more individualistic, mastery-directed activities of men. These early influences form an important background against which to consider the personality variables often investigated in relationship to women's achievement and professional development.

One example of this influence is the availability of role models or mentors on women's vocational development.[25-27] Recently, Marilyn Haring-Hidore and I[28] reported that women are looking for models who combine professional and personal roles and who are likely to affirm them as professionals and encourage and support their professional goals. Women have reported to us that such affirmation is more likely to come from women than from men. Moreover, women role models, so selected, would be more able than others in the work or educational environment to show sensitivity to women's concerns such as discriminatory practices against women.

The difficulties women have in locating and establishing relationships with role models are compounded when it comes to mentors.[29] Indeed, the mentor process is largely unavailable to women. Mentors are seen as essential because they generate power. A structural barrier related to mentoring in its dynamics and effects is the social organization of collegial ties. With whom do men and women interact in their work environment? And, how open is the male buddy system to women peers? Women are often isolated from informal collegial contacts. Consequently, women may receive less encouragement for their achievements and/or be avoided by their male colleagues. Men may also be ambivalent about interacting with women since they may believe it threatens the role expectations of male dominance.[28,30]

Furthermore, when women are present in particular positions, they become tokens and, as such, may be evaluated more critically and experience greater pressure to conform to gender-role stereotypes. And, because the career span (and lifespan) transitional phases are different for women, women tend to have additional and/or different needs from a mentoring relationship. For example, Erkut and Mokros[31] and Paludi, Meyers, Speicher, and Kindermann[32] reported that reentry women seek a mentor who will assist them in planning their futures so that they will be successful. Networking among professional women is gaining in popularity, with a number of organizations being formed expressly for this purpose.[33] Findings from recent research in our collective by Joni Kindermann and me[34] underscore the importance of the sex of the role model and mentor for the career advancement of women as well as to women's self-assessment of competency, aspirations, and self-worth.

Attitudes and Attributions About Women's Achievement

Research by Cindy Clow and me[30] suggests that male faculty are less likely to hold liberal views than female faculty about women's roles and degree of career commitment. Women students may receive less professional support from male than from female faculty. Indifference in academic settings may undermine women's commitment to their professional careers and contribute to self-fulfilling prophecies about not being competent enough to succeed in male-populated careers.

We have found that one of the greatest structural barriers to women's achievement involves attitudes about women's abilities and women's roles. Related to these attitudes is the differential evaluation of individuals on the basis of sex. Lisa Strayer and I[15] have found that men are rated higher than equivalent women in performing certain tasks and job qualifications. Similarly, women receive lower recognition and economic rewards for their work than men, and lower prestige, knowledge, and expertise are attributed to them as well. Widely accepted stereotypes depict men, but not women, as having the requisite skills and characteristics for managerial and leadership positions.[35] These stereotypes persist even though gender differences are *not* found in leadership ability or job performance!

One implication of these studies and others by Kay Deaux and her colleagues (e.g., Deaux & Emswiller[13]) is that when women's accomplishments are legitimized through awards or high status, prejudice against women is somewhat minimized. Although prejudice in evaluations may be minimized for successful individuals, differential sexist attributions regarding the reasons for success may remain. Given the current social climate where overt prejudice no longer is socially acceptable, prejudice is more likely to be seen indirectly in terms of attributions made rather than directly in terms of differential evaluations.

In sum, because women are expected to conform to the gender role stereotypes, when they don't, they may be negatively evaluated. And, more to the point, most women—or men—are not award winners. Sexist prejudice against these women is still prevalent. Ann McNeer, Ingeborg Hrabowy, Valerie Johnson, and I[36] have found this attributional prejudice against women's performance in children as young as eight years old. Girls' and women's success are attributed to luck rather than skill. As a result of male teachers and employers attributing women's successes to luck rather than skill, women's level of aspiration remains low. Therefore, many women never establish any occupational life plan or prepare themselves for a career. Another consequence of attribution patterns concerns employment. Virginia O'Leary[37] reported that people were more likely to give promotions to employees whose success had been attributed to ability. If men are more likely than women to have their success explained in terms of ability, than they are more likely than women to receive promotions.

The differential evaluation of women and men not only influences decisions about ability and achievement but also tends to devalue female-related activities and topics. Research we have conducted on mentoring, for example, suggests that attributions made by male mentors for female protégées are different from attributions they make for their male protégés.[30] Male mentors indicated they perceive a woman apprenticing herself to them as requiring help, remedial assistance. Male protégés, however, are perceived by male mentors as persons whose career requires development. Women may thus be seen as needing the mentoring they get. This raises a serious paradox, as Marianne LaFrance[38] has recently commented: As women continue to get the mentoring they need, they will be seen as needing the mentoring they get.

Similar concerns were recently raised by Phyllis Bronstein and her colleagues.[39] Male mentors, in their letters of recommendation of female protégées for faculty positions, described the woman's family responsibilities as a burden. For men, a family life was presented as an asset. One needs to wonder at the reactions of persons reading these descriptions, persons who will consider which applicant would be more willing to relocate and who would make the most promising and productive colleague. What is also interesting is that none of the female applicants mentioned lifestyle or family status in their vita or cover letters; male mentors, however, mentioned it. These mentors may have been unaware of the unintended effects these statements would have.

SOME CONCLUDING REMARKS AND RECOMMENDATIONS FOR FUTURE RESEARCH

Now that I have summarized some of the results from our program of research, I would like to make some suggestions for future work for our research team and for the field of women's career development as well.

First, in the next phase of research on women's careers, we don't need another correlational study between one construct, for example, fear of success and a personality variable. Such research does not help clarify achievement and career-related concepts and theories. What is needed is more research relating the various scales to behavior. Careful consideration should be given to the reason for the selection of behaviors to be sampled in such research. Achievement and career constructs do not correlate with everything.[40]

Second, we should question the appropriateness of control groups used. The samples of women and men or women and women who are compared on some career-related measure should be evaluated carefully. Researchers may be creating the differences in these areas of research on women's career development. This especially applies to research done with college students enrolled in introductory psychology classes. Men may be represented in a wider range of natural and physical sciences while women may be concentrated in the social and behavioral sciences. Thus, one part of the distribution in interests, abilities, and traits may be sampled for men, another women.

Third, the person-centered (or sociopsychological) explanations and the situation-centered (or institutional) explanations for women's career development suggest different strategies for improving women's employment conditions. The person-centered explanations propose that women can advance by taking courses to make them more assertive or more skilled in conducting meetings or seeking a mentor. However, women who "improve" themselves still face hostility on the job. Person-centered approaches stress that women should adopt a traditionally male approach to problems.

The situation-centered explanations propose different strategies. These strategies include training managers to use objective rating scales, presenting affirmative action policies appropriately, and eliminating women's token status. These suggestions sound excellent, but they are unlikely to occur spontaneously. Feminist objectives will not be achieved without structural changes in the economy and society. Of the barriers, the external ones are most important and most serious, yet people often deliberately ignore them to "blame the victim" than to institute social change.

Fourth, research needs to be conducted on women of color and their career development. Women of color are not the unified group they are portrayed as being. Each of the racial and ethnic groups represents a different pattern of involvement with education and the labor force.

Fifth, we should abandon the intent of making women in the workforce and in education high in both feminine and masculine personality characteristics—independence and dependence, assertive and passive, depending on the situation. Androgyny is not the ideal human situation we thought it seemed to be; it does not lead to degenderizing behavior.[41] We should be able to figure out what behavior at the workplace or classroom is ideal for adults, without having to rely on terms such as femininity and masculinity.

Equally disastrous is that the concept of androgyny provides a double prescription for behavior. It's no longer sufficient for women to be feminine because androgyny demands that all adults have to meet both standards. Women can now be judged incompetent for two reasons, not just one.[42]

Androgyny also tempts us to believe that the solution to sex bias lies in changing the person. Androgyny is not a solution to our present social problems in the area of women's career development. This argument is consistent with the one I made earlier concerning the reality that situation-centered explanations for the treatment of women in the workplace may be more valuable than person-centered explanations.

Sixth, we need to assist institutions in understanding women's unique career patterns. Institutions do not take into account that most women have children and grandchildren for whom they are primarily responsible and thus women may need to or want to take some time out from full-time careers for child rearing to go to work or school part time. By having only one career pattern in mind—characterized by full time, uninterrupted work—institutions may shut women out of many careers.[43]

Finally, the areas that are considered successful usually have a masculine bias. Success may be represented by achievement at a prestigious occupation, academic excellence, and other accomplishments that are associated with masculine values. Consequently, accomplishments that are associated with traditionally feminine values receive little or no attention. Women may manage a household and children, and yet this kind of accomplishment is not studied in the topic of achievement motivation and work.[1] We need to redefine achievement and achievement-related issues in a way that does not keep women's lives and realities invisible. Traditional educational and occupational policies reflect the separation of work and family life and the societal expectation that mothers remain at home to care for their children. Thus, a general incompatibility exists between the school or workplace and family demands which is exacerbated by the relative lack of provisions to ease women's integration of these roles. These conditions may be expected to produce greater potential stress and conflict among student and working mothers, who hold the primary responsibility for child rearing and child care. Many universities and businesses have adopted family-oriented policies such as job sharing, flexible work hours, or employer-sponsored day care as an employee benefit. These organizations have found positive ramifications for the schools and businesses as well as for parents, including lower absenteeism, higher morale, positive publicity, lower rate of turnover, child care hours that conform to work hours, and access to quality infant and child care.[4]

Our analyses have alerted us to thinking about behaviors that reflect achievement orientations over and above educational and occupational performance. We hope that these insights will help promote new kinds of research on women, work, and careers.

REFERENCES

1. BETZ, N. & L. FITZGERALD. 1987. The Career Psychology of Women. Academic Press. New York.
2. HOLLAND, J. L. 1973. Making Vocational Choices: A Theory of Careers. Prentice Hall. New York.
3. SUPER, D. E. 1957. The Psychology of Careers. Harper. New York.
4. ANDERSON-KULMAN, R. E. & M. A. PALUDI. 1986. Working mothers and the family context: Predicting positive coping. J. Vocat. Behav. **28:** 241–253.
5. HACKER, A. 1986. Women at Work. N. Y. Rev. Books. August: 26–32.

6. Makosky, V. & M. A. Paludi. 1990. Feminism and women's studies in the academy. *In* Foundations for a Feminist Restructuring of the Academic Disciplines. M. A. Paludi & G. A. Steuernagel, Eds.: 1–37. Haworth Press. New York.
7. Matlin, M. 1987. The Psychology of Women. Holt, Rinehart & Winston. New York.
8. Wallston, B. S. & K. Grady. 1985. Integrating the feminist critique and the crisis in social psychology: Another look at research methods. *In* Women, Gender, and Social Psychology. V. E. O'Leary, R. K. Unger & B. S. Wallston, Eds.: 7–33. Erlbaum. Hillsdale, NJ.
9. Bem, S. L. & D. Bem. 1970. Case study of a nonconscious ideology: Training the woman to know her place. *In* Roles Women Play: Readings toward Women's Liberation. M. H. Garskof, Ed.: 84–96. Brooks/Cole. Belmont, CA.
10. Kriger, S. F. 1972. Achievement and perceived parental childrearing attitudes of career women and homemakers. J. Vocat. Behav. **2:** 419–432.
11. Gottfredson, L. S. 1981. Circumscription and compromise: A developmental theory of occupational aspiration. J. Counseling Psychol. **28:** 545–579.
12. Books, L. 1988. Encouraging women's motivation toward nontraditional careers: A model for assessment and intervention. J. Career Dev. **14:** 223–241.
13. Deaux, K. & T. Emswiller. 1974. Explanations of successful performance on sex-linked tasks: What is skill for the male is luck for the female. J. Personality Soc. Psychol. **29:** 80–85.
14. Fitzgerald, L. F., S. Shullman, N. Bailey, M. Richards, J. Swecker, Y. Gold, M. Ormerod & L. Weitzman. 1988. The incidence and dimensions of sexual harassment in academia and the workplace. J. Vocat. Behav. **32:** 152–175.
15. Paludi, M. A. & L. A. Strayer. 1985. What's in an author's name? Differential evaluations of performance as a function of author's name. Sex Roles **12:** 353–361.
16. Paludi, M. A. & J. Fankell-Hauser. 1986. An idiographic approach to the study of women's achievement striving. Psychol. Women Q. **10:** 89–100.
17. Levinson, D., C. Darrow, E. Klein, M. Levinson & B. McKee. 1978. The Seasons of a Man's Life. Knopf. New York.
18. Kaufman, D. & B. Richardson. 1982. Achievement and Women: Challenging the Assumptions. Free Press. New York.
19. Hennig, M. & A. Jardim. 1977. The Managerial Woman. Anchor/Doubleday. New York.
20. Horner, M. S. 1968. Sex differences in achievement motivation and performance in competitive and noncompetitive situations. Unpublished doctoral dissertation. University of Michigan. Ann Arbor, MI.
21. Paludi, M. A., D. Hruska, B. Guda & L. Bowman. 1986. Fear of success: An updated review. Paper presented at the annual meeting of the Eastern Psychological Association. April. New York.
22. Lipman-Blumen, J., A. Handley-Isaksen & H. J. Leavitt. 1983. Achieving styles in men and women: A model, an instrument, and some findings. *In* Achievement and Achievement Motives. J. T. Spence, Ed.: 147–204. Freeman. San Francisco.
23. Betz, N. Women and career development. *In* Handbook on the Psychology of Women. F. L. Denmark & M. A. Paludi, Eds. Greenwood Press. Westport, CT. In press.

24. GILLIGAN, C. 1982. In a Different Voice. Harvard University Press. Cambridge, MA.
25. BROOKS, L. & M. HARING-HIDORE. 1987. Mentoring in academe: A comparison of mentors' and protégés' perceived problems. Int. J. Mentoring **1:** 3–9.
26. COLLINS, E. G. & P. SCOTT. 1978. Everyone who makes it has a mentor. Harv. Business Rev. **54:** 89–101.
27. GILBERT, L., J. M. GALLESSICH, & S. EVANS. 1983. Sex of faculty role model and students' self-perceptions of competency. Six Roles **9:** 597–607.
28. HARING-HIDORE, M. & M. A. PALUDI. 1989. Sex and sexuality in mentoring and tutoring: Implications for opportunities and achievement. Peabody J. Educ. **64:** 164–172.
29. PALUDI, M. A., B. WAITE, R. HOEWING-ROBERSON & L. JONES. 1988. Mentors vs. role models: A clarification of terms. Int. J. Mentoring **2:** 20–25.
30. CLOW, C. & M. A. PALUDI. 1986. Mentoring: An intergenerational perspective. Unpublished data. Kent State University. Kent, OH.
31. ERKUT, S. & J. R. MOKROS. 1981. Professors as models and mentors for college students. Working Paper No. 65. Wellesley College Center for Research on Women. Wellesley, MA.
32. PALUDI, M. A., D. MEYERS, H. SPEICHER & J. KINDERMANN. 1990. Mentoring and being mentored: Issues of sex, power, and politics for older women. Women and Aging: In press.
33. DEFOUR, D. C., M. A. PALUDI, M. HARING-HILDORE, B. SHOLLEY & B. FLOYD. 1989. Feminist mentoring: Toward an ethic of care. Symposium presented at the Annual Meeting of the Southeastern Psychological Association. April. Washington, DC.
34. KINDERMANN, J. & M. A. PALUDI. 1989. Same-sex and cross-sex mentor–protégé relationships: Implications for causal attributions for success. Unpublished manuscript. Hunter College. New York.
35. O'LEARY, V. E. 1988. Women and work. *In* Handbook on the Psychology of Women. F. L. Denmark & M. A. Paludi, Eds. Greenwood. Westport, CT.
36. PALUDI, M. A., A. MCNEER, V. JOHNSON & I. HRABOWY. 1984. Children's causal attributions of successful performance: Replication and refinement. Paper presented at the annual meeting of the Southwestern Society for Research in Human Development. March. Denver, CO.
37. O'LEARY, V. E. 1987. Personal communication.
38. LAFRANCE, M. 1987. The paradox of mentoring. Paper presented at the Interdisciplinary Congress on Women. July. Dublin, Ireland.
39. BRONSTEIN, P., L. BLACK, J. PFENNIG & A. WHITE. 1986. Getting academic jobs: Are women equally qualified and equally successful? Am. Psychol. **41:** 318–322.
40. PALUDI, M. A. 1984. Psychometric properties and underlying assumptions of four objective measures of fear of success. Sex Roles **10:** 765–781.
41. LOTT, B. 1987. Women's Lives: Traditions and Alternatives. Brooks/Cole. Monterey, CA.
42. SEDNEY, M. A. 1989. Conceptual and methodological sources of controversies about androgyny. *In* Representations: Social Constructions of Gender. R. K. Unger, Ed.: 126–144. Baywood. Amityville, NY.
43. PALUDI, M. A. 1987. Women and the mentor-protégé relationship. Paper presented at the Interdisciplinary Congress on Women. July. Dublin, Ireland.

PART III. APPLIED AND CLINICAL PSYCHOLOGY

Introduction

Social and Biological Trends in Applied and Clinical Psychology

JEFFERSON M. FISH

Department of Psychology
St. John's University
Jamaica, New York 11432

Traditionally, clinical and applied psychologists have used personality concepts in an attempt to explain and change the behavior of individuals. While such endeavors have continued, many psychologists have regarded these concepts as vaguely defined, difficult to measure, and culture-bound. In response, two differing trends have become apparent in the field, both of which are represented in the papers in this section.

The first trend is an outwardly or socially oriented one, of looking at the behavior in question from the perspective of the social context of which it is a part. The insights of social psychology, sociology, anthropology, and even economics and history become relevant once one views the individual as part of a larger social field. From this perspective, the individual's behavior constitutes part of interactive sequences involving others, which jointly weave a social fabric. Interactive concepts, such as those from systems theory, become useful in understanding pieces of this fabric, and then explain the individual's behavior along with that of relevant others.

The second trend is an inwardly or biologically oriented one, of looking at the behavior in question from the perspective of the biological processes underlying it. The insights of physiological psychology and the biomedical sciences become relevant once one views individual behavior from a biological perspective.

Interestingly, while these two trends are moving in independent—some would say opposite—directions, both have the virtue of emphasizing directly observable phenomena. Social interactions and biological processes are observable in ways that personality is not.

Considering the papers in this section in terms of these two trends, one can see that those by Peele and Salzinger are representative of the social trend, and those by Barowsky and by Katahn and McMinn are representative of the biological trend.

Stanton Peele's discussion of the concept of addiction, which combines a review of data from a variety of sources, along with a fascinating historical and cross-cultural look at the concept, challenges currently widespread views. Given the public policy debate concerning addiction,[1] his paper is a useful contribution to the political process as well as to scientific understanding.

Suzanne Salzinger's review of social networks and their implications for child rearing and child behavior illustrates well the impact of systems theory and ecological thinking on applied child psychology. Once one views the child and parents as parts of larger social networks, it becomes possible to understand new aspects of the development of children's normal and abnormal behavior. A mother's child-rearing practices, for example, can be looked at, not as an expression of her personality, but as behavior subject to feedback from a variety of others (including her child) with whom she regularly interacts.

In contrast to these papers, those by Ellis Barowsky and by Katahn and McMinn illustrate the biological trend in clinical psychology. Barowsky's paper explores the extension of biofeedback training, which—for whatever reasons—has been used mainly with adults, to a variety of childhood problems. Katahn and McMinn look at biological factors in obesity and reconsider the problem of maintaining weight loss from this perspective.

In sum, the papers in this section not only provide an overview of their various subject matters, but also illustrate the ways in which problems in applied and clinical psychology are currently being investigated and conceptualized.

REFERENCE

1. Nadelmann, E. A. 1989. Drug prohibition in the United States: Costs, consequences, and alternatives. Science **245:** 939–947.

Social Networks in Child Rearing and Child Development

SUZANNE SALZINGER

New York State Psychiatric Institute
New York, New York 10032
and
Department of Psychiatry
Columbia University
New York, New York 10032

Studying social networks as they relate to child rearing and child development focuses our attention on a set of variables that have been much neglected in the developmental literature. It is not that no one has examined any of the social contextual variables that influence the child's development, but the selection of those variables has been so strongly dictated by the popular epigenetic developmental theories of the last 50 years that many aspects of the child's social context have been left largely unexplored. The purpose of this paper is to point out the advantages of a systematic network approach by illustrating its utility across a wide range of child rearing and child developmental issues.

Although the definition of personal social network has varied somewhat from investigator to investigator, there is general agreement on some basic characteristics. In its most widely accepted form, it can be considered to be the "set of connections among persons who are defined relative to an initial person, and who are connected either directly or indirectly to that individual."[1] The network forms around the shared activities[2] and foci[3] that link members together, resulting in empirically derived clusters of persons, which provide the individual with varying degrees of social access[4] to network members and thereby to the functions they represent. The characteristics of a given network, it should be noted, are not determined only by the characteristics of the individual members of the network, but by the characteristics of the connections between members of the network as well.

NETWORK STRUCTURE

A consideration of the types of connections that can occur among network members gives some idea of how they determine the character of networks and the influence and impact the networks thereby exert on individuals. A connection, for instance, can be unidirectional, such as that between the traditional school teacher and pupil, where the influence on the pupil is considerably greater than the influence on the teacher; or a connection can be reciprocal, as intimate connections are; or connections can be joint, or shared, as when an individual converses with two members of the network simultaneously. This latter type of connection, it should be noted, affords an individual more information than if the contacts are separate, by virtue of the fact that the individual becomes privy to the additional connection, or link, between the other two network members. And finally, connections can be indirect. That is, an individual may have no direct exposure to the connection between a network member and another person, but at the same time have access to that connection through direct contact with one of the network members.

Networks generally consist of all the above types of connections combined in various proportions, and, as a result, they assume certain characteristics as a whole which can be used to describe or measure them. These are the network's structural characteristics. They consist of such parameters as size, strength of contact (e.g., frequency and duration of contacts), density, cluster structure, and connectedness between clusters (i.e., boundary density).

As with types of individual connections, it is fairly obvious that differences in these parameters produce very different networks. In fact, a pronounced predominance of any one parameter could provide an individual with an extremely deviant network. As early as 1970, Cassel had already suggested that distorted networks might well account for an individual's susceptibility to illness.[5,6] Since then, there have been many studies that have explored this issue. For example, it has been shown, not surprisingly, that small size and infrequent contact with network members are the primary indications of social isolation and are typical of networks of the aged[7] and of schizophrenics.[8] Other results have been less expected. Contrary to popular belief, large networks, usually associated with support, need not always be advantageous; whether they are or not depends upon how well they meet the needs of a given person at a particular stage of life or in a particular social situation. Take, as an example, Weinraub and Wolfe's study of single parents which found that, for such women, having many social contacts was associated with low maternal nurturance.[9] Extremely dense networks, where members are all closely interconnected, tend to be very stable and may well provide their members with strong emotional support in the ordinary course of events. However, due to their limited capacity for taking in new members, they may be unable to change in response to new circumstances when it becomes necessary to do so.[10] As an illustration, Wilcox found that women's adjustment to divorce was better if their post-divorce networks were actually less, rather than more dense.[11] A pronounced lack of connectedness across the clusters in a network may insulate an individual's connections with one portion of the network (e.g. family) from his or her connections with other parts of the network (e.g. friends) such that what occurs in one part of the network is relatively unaffected by what happens in other parts.[12] Such deficiencies in boundary density have been found to be associated with aberrant parenting. Other examples can be found in the discontinuity between home and workplace that often exists for fathers, and between most therapeutic settings and the home for patients in psychotherapy. Although the ties linking clusters in the network to each other are fewer in number and usually weaker in strength than connections within clusters, they have been shown to play an important and necessary role in the development and maintenance of networks[13] and consequently in the ability of the networks to provide social and instrumental support and corrective feedback for maladaptive behavior.

NETWORK FUNCTIONS

Networks serve different functions for the individual. One of their most general functions is to provide *social access*[4] to parts of the network and the social context beyond. In the latter case they mediate between the individual and social institutions and formal social groups or organizations. It is not uncommon to find studies that assess the relationship between institutions and individuals as if it were a direct relationship. In fact it is not, and the independent measurement of social networks as an intervening variable affords us a powerful tool for understanding these correlations. An example of such work is provided by Garbarino,[14] who found that one of the major factors differentiating two economically comparable neighborhoods that differed in the risk for child abuse was the characteristics of the social networks of residents. In the low-risk neighborhood, but not the high-risk neighborhood, active involvement with network members presumably provided increased access to social support in the form of informal social contact as well as social services, thereby better protecting families from some of the more stressful aspects of childrearing in working-class families.

Not only do networks provide direct access to support, but the current literature clearly shows that the social support provided by social networks plays an indirect *buffering* role, as well, in the overall maintenance of health, by protecting the individual against the effects of stress.[15,16]

Personal networks also function to *transmit information, values, and cultural norms* among members. This occurs directly through communication with networks members and by modeling, a mode of transmission that depends upon the observation of the behavior of valued individuals. The observational learning paradigm,[17] which underlies modeling, has been widely applied and reported in studies of the modification of children's behavior, although it accounts for changes in the behavior of adults as well.

Another basic and extremely important function is that networks provide *feedback for behavior*. Feedback from different parts of the network tends to reinforce different aspects of behavior. Feedback from intimates and family tends to maintain the status quo; feedback from the more extended network of acquaintances tends to facilitate behavioral change. The implications of this contrast have been nicely illustrated by Wahler and his colleagues in studies of the generalization of therapeutically achieved modification of poor parenting practices. They found, at followup, that generalization from the therapeutic situation to the home was most likely to occur for noninsular mothers, who presumably received more support for their changed parenting behavior from their more extended network, than for insular mothers, for whom feedback (often negative) was provided mainly by close relatives.[18] Personal networks are the most *immediate source of all social reinforcement,* and, as such, in a very fundamental sense, they help to define the person for him/herself. On the basis of a recent comprehensive review of the literature concerned with the association between health and social support, Cohen and Wills[15] concluded that the degree of social integration, in and of itself, in a large social network is positively related to an individual's general feelings of stability and well-being, and thereby directly related to health. The most dramatic example of this comes from the now classic large epidemiological study of Alameda County residents in California[19] and the subsequent replication of the work in Tecumseh County, Michigan,[20] which showed that, after controlling for possible confounding risk factors for morbidity, restricted networks were associated with a significant lowering of mortality age. House,[21] in a fairly recent and thoughtful discussion of the entire issue of the relationship between health and social relationships, summarizes the evidence for their direct positive association and asks that research be pointed toward a more precise understanding of what the fundamental underlying mechanisms might be.

THE CASE FOR THE INCLUSION OF NETWORK MODELS IN CURRENT THEORIES OF DEVELOPMENT

Despite the fact that there is accumulating evidence of the importance of the entire social network for the growth of children, the dominant model of child development in this country during the first half of the century has been a linear epigenetic one, in which very early mother–child interaction is considered to have the most significant and lasting effects on the child's later behavior and development.[22–24] That is to say, the child's initial relationship with the mother, or with the earliest attachment figures, with respect to bonding and attachment, largely determines the way in which the child will respond to other aspects of the social and physical environment, thus having broad effects on the development of social and cognitive skills.[25–27]

The epigenetic, or attachment model, has generated a wealth of experimental and observational research on the interaction between mothers and children and its significance for the learning of new behavior.[28] Certainly it has been important, and it has taken us quite far, particularly with respect to understanding the early development of children's independent exploration of the world.[29,30] There are two problems with it. The predictability of the later characteristics of offspring based exclusively upon early mother– or parent–child relationships has been disappointing.[31] But perhaps an even more serious problem with the model is that it supports a concept of development that is unable to account for all the apparent discontinuities in behavior that are characteristic of development, not only within a single generation but between generations as well.[32]

As investigators began to examine early mother–child interaction in more detail, it became apparent that at least two factors besides the mother's behavior had to be considered if one were to understand developmental changes in the child's behavior. First, it became clear that the influence of the infant's behavior on that of the caretaker was just as important as that of the caretaker on the infant, thus leading to continuous dynamically produced changes in the social context surrounding the child. This understanding of the process of development was first clearly spelled out by Bell[33] and has become widely known as the transactional model. And second, the mother's social context, aside from that provided by the child, was found to affect the interaction between her and her child. This was demonstrated, for example, in Crockenberg's study[34] showing that the adequacy of maternal social support was strongly related to the security of mother–infant attachment. Not only has it been found that maternal social support affects mother–child attachment, but other characteristics of the networks of both parents have been found to have even wider effects on children's outcome, being significantly associated with children's happiness, negative emotions, school adjustment, networks, and social skills.[35] In view of these observations, it became clear that the field needed a different theoretical base. It was not entirely the case that the epigenetic, or attachment, model needed to be replaced, but rather that it needed to be incorporated into a broader model, one which considers the impact of multiple variables at whatever time each becomes appropriate during development. An ecological model was needed—one which describes, in addition to organismic factors, the child's position, or place, with respect to variables generated within ever widening environmental contexts. Bronfenbrenner's seminal work provided such a model.[36] The applicability of such an expanded model by Belsky[37] to at least one serious child-rearing issue, namely child maltreatment, has proved very heuristic in generating research leading to a greater understanding of the maltreatment process.[38]

STUDIES BASED ON A NETWORK MODEL

Studies of personal social networks imply an acceptance of an ecological model for the understanding of human development. They are based on an attempt to systematically quantify the entire social context of the developing individual in terms of its structure and function at particular points in time and to measure its impact on development by relating it to the acquisition of new behavior and subsequent changes in the behavior of the individual. Studies of social networks have thereby served to focus our attention on domains that have been largely unexplored.

Lewis and his colleagues,[39,40] among the earliest investigators in the area, adopted a network model for a series of studies in child development in which they attempted to map the various functions that different network members serve for the growing child. That matrix will, no doubt, be completed by the work of many other investigators. Although we already have a substantial amount of information on the role that mothers play in the development of the child, for instance, we still lack comparably rich data on other members of the child's network. Happily, that situation is changing as other investigators have begun to provide us with data on the functions of other people in the infant's and child's life. We now know, for instance, with respect to early development, from the work of Lamb[41] and Lewis[42] among others, that whereas mothers function more in a caretaking role, fathers function more to facilitate play for their infants, a function which, in turn, can be seen as enhancing cognitive development. In addition to parental influences, many investigators have now turned their attention to peer influences in childhood, as well.[43-46] The description of network function becomes still more complex as we begin to consider recent cohort effects as mothers enter the workforce and fathers and extrafamilial adults begin to take over more of the caretaking role for infants and young children. As with all ecological variables, networks are not static, but change in response to the general demands of the social, economic, and personal situations in which families find themselves.

An illustrative example of the relative suitability of a social network and an epigenetic model is to be found in some research that was carried out by Lewis and Shaeffer on the effect of early mother–child relationships on the social behavior of children.[47] The study was designed to test the epigenetic hypothesis that abusive interactions between mothers and their young children would have a negative effect on the children's general social behavior, not only with their mothers, but with other children as well. Comparisons were made of the behavior of abused and neglected children and nonmaltreated children aged 8 to 32 months, in a day care center that both groups attended. Observations were made daily during maternal departure, separation, maternal reunion, and free play. The mean number of 10-second periods of occurrence of selected maternal behaviors directed toward their children and the children's behavior directed toward each other were compared over a period of 12 days of five-minute observations for each child. As expected, abusing mothers showed more negative behavior and less positive behavior toward their children during both departure and reunion, and their children showed fewer attachment behaviors toward their mothers. On the other hand, somewhat unexpectedly, no significant differences were found between the maltreated and nonmaltreated children's behavior with peers during free play. These data demonstrate that maternal abuse need not result in poor interpersonal relationships overall, as predicted by the epigenetic model. Instead, in this case, a consideration of the results in terms of a social network model suggests that the concommitant interaction with nonabused peers, occurring on a regular basis in the day care setting, contributed independently toward the normal development of that particular class of social behavior in these children. Other evidence that experience with peers can compensate for poorly developed social skills can be found in Furman's work with socially withdrawn preschool children. Two groups of such children were given peer therapy consisting of social play experiences with younger children or children of the same age and compared to a similar group of children who were not treated. The peer therapy for both groups was found to substantially improve the children's social skills, particularly for the group whose therapeutic playmates were younger than they.[48] Still other examples of the mediating role that significant network members play in overcoming the deleterious effects of early stressful relationships with parent figures were shown by Tizard and Hodges in their study of adopted institutionalized children[49] and in Rutter's work on orphaned girls in which their own later parenting behavior was found to be positively affected by the choice of stable partners.[32]

Some fascinating early experimental work on nonhuman primates has also shown that both maternal and peer contact contribute separately to the development of social skills, that peer contact can protect against depression brought about by separation from mothers, and that contact with normal socially skilled peers can reverse the effects of early isolation.[50]

What these studies indicate is that the social network is specialized with respect to function, that different portions of it may well serve to facilitate the independent development of different behavioral repertoires for the individual during both the initial acquisition of behavior and the later modification of that behavior; and, furthermore, that portions of the network may take over functions for each other if, in the course of development, the network is deficient or becomes distorted.

Still another study of networks demonstrates their usefulness in understanding the development of a specific aspect of behavior—in this case language—in children between the ages of 20 and 24 months who are just learning to speak.[51] The study was designed as a two-stage study, an ecological study in Bronfenbrenner's sense of the term.[36] The first stage was concerned with the extent to which the mother's social network determines the child's social network, and the second stage was an examination of the association between the child's social network and early language function. Parenthetically, it should be noted that in order for different portions of an infant's network to exert a specialized influence on very early behavioral development, the network ought to show some diversity of its own very soon after the baby's birth. Evidence that this happens at a very young age was found in some data collected by Gutwirth and Hammer[52] from a mother's log of both her own and her baby's daily contacts shortly after the baby was born. Tabulations of the number of people seen by this baby and her mother during the time the baby was between the ages of three and seven months showed that, although it is certainly true that the baby's and the mother's networks were both quite restricted and practically identical at first and continued to be highly correlated throughout this early period, the rate at which they accumulated new contacts began to accelerate after four months. By the end of seven months, the baby's network was already comprised of about a hundred people. This is well below the age of the children in the study we intend to describe.

For that study, 10 middle-class children, 20 months of age, and their mothers were studied. The networks of the mothers and children were measured separately and related to samples of the children's speech which were obtained in a standard setting. Audio recordings were made in each child's home during two one-hour sessions, separated by a four-month interval, with the child's mother present and another mother and baby invited by the mother.

The mother's networks were elicited by a standard structured interview that required the mother to list all the people with whom she had maintained regular contact during the past year, to designate those among them with whom she had frequent contact (at least once a week), and to indicate those who were seen frequently with her child.

Reports of the child's contacts with people were elicited by telephone from the mother for the preceding day for each of the seven different days of the week and were highly correlated with reports of the size of her child's network given in her interview. Most, but not all, of the children had more contact with adults than with children, as might be expected for children under two years of age. Still, the networks were diverse enough to examine the differential effect of their different parts on language function.

Correlations between the mothers' and children's' networks showed that the size of the mother's total network did not significantly predict either the total size of the children's networks (r = 0.07) or the child's total contacts with people over a seven-day period (r = 0.43). However, considering the child's contacts with children and adults separately, it was found that the child's contact with adults did indeed seem to depend upon the size of the mother's frequently seen active network (r = 0.82, $p < 0.01$). On the other hand, the child's contact with children was already found to be independent of the mother's network by the age of 20–24 months. One other observation is of interest, although the individual correlations upon which it is based are not statistically significant, and that is that there is a difference in the direction of the association between maternal contact with close and distal parts of her network and children's contact with peers. The number of close adults seen weekly by the mother is inversely related to both the number of children in the child's network (r = −0.30) and the proportion of children in the network (−0.44), whereas the number of more distant adults in the mother's network is positively correlated with children's contact with children (r = 0.39). These data are consistent with other findings in the literature that suggest that it is the mothers' more extended network, rather than her more intimate one, that is responsible for providing opportunities for children to socialize with other children.

Two basic dimensions of the children's speech were examined in the study: (1) the extent to which speech was used to communicate and (2) its adequacy and comprehensibility. In order to measure these dimensions, the speech was divided into utterances defined by a change in speaker, by

TABLE 1. Correlations between the Child's Network and the Child's Speech at 20 and 24 Months

	# Diff Adults		# Diff Children		# Adult Contacts		# Child Contacts		Prop. Child Contacts	
Utterances	20	24	20	24	20	24	20	24	20	24
# Inadequate	−0.09	−0.80[a]	−0.35	−0.55[b]	−0.35	−0.78[a]	−0.48	−0.28	−0.45	0.08
Prop. adeq.	0.37	0.58[b]	0.22	0.24	0.69[c]	0.63[b]	0.47	0.00	0.19	−0.35
# Personal	−0.22	−0.37	−0.26	−0.73[c]	−0.26	−0.11	−0.03	−0.54	−0.04	−0.65[c]
Prop. social	0.46	0.36	0.25	0.75[c]	0.44	0.09	−0.02	0.56[b]	−0.26	0.67[c]

[a] $p < 0.01$.
[b] $0.05 < p < 0.10$.
[c] $p < 0.05$.

extended pauses, or by a change in topic. The utterances were then classified as social if they were addressed to another person and as adequate or comprehensible if they could be understood by the person they were addressed to, the coder, or the child's mother.

Correlations between the child's network and the child's speech are shown in TABLE 1. By two years of age it was found that the number of different adults in the child's network and the number of contacts the child had with them was positively associated with the proportion of the child's speech that is adequate and comprehensible and negatively related to the number of inadequate and incomprehensible utterances the child uses. On the other hand, the number of different children in the child's network, the number of contacts they have with them, and the proportion of the child's contacts with other children were all found to be positively associated with the proportion of speech that is social by 24 months, even though at that time the child's social speech is still being addressed primarily to adults rather than to other children. Contact with children was also found to be negatively associated with the absolute number of personal utterances the child uses. For the earlier period, at 20 months, these relationships were found to be much less clear.

The use of the network model for this study enables one to see that the types of social contact that children have at this early age with different parts of their network selectively affect the development of an important behavior, and that these effects become progressively stronger with age. The results suggest that social contact with adults serves a teaching function, providing both a model of the language and the feedback required to shape children's language to conform to the adult standard for communicative competence, whereas contact with children serves quite another function, that of increasing children's motivation to communicate by providing them with the social discriminative stimuli necessary for communication to occur. The study also highlights the important fact that even by 20 months, the child's network has become somewhat independent of the mother's in at least one critical respect—namely, that the contact children have with their peers need no longer depend only on the people the mother sees.

Nevertheless, given the fact that mother's networks do have some influence on their children's networks, and that the children's networks, in turn, selectively and differentially reinforce the development of behavior, it becomes important to know something about the characteristics of mothers' networks in general. Some relevant descriptive data were collected by Hammer[53] on the networks of a small number of women with coresident children, aged 14 and under, and women without children. Although the two sets of networks do not appear to differ in size, the distribution of contacts is different for mothers and non-mothers, a shift occurring from the less intimate contacts characteristic of work to the more intimate contacts of kin and friends for women who are mothers. These data were corroborated by other small samples of networks also studied by Hammer and a larger community sample studied by Fischer in northern California.[53] In addition, other work from an international survey carried out by Szalai[54] in 44 different cities on the time spent with adults, showed that, whereas working men and women spent as many as seven to eight hours a day with other adults, housewives spent only three. In summary then, it would appear that mothers seem to have the same size networks as non-mothers, although they differ with respect to both the composition of their networks and the time they actually spend with other adults.

Keeping in mind that the networks of normal housewives may thereby be somewhat limited to begin with, I would like to consider some research from our own laboratory on the social networks of mothers in families with maltreated children.[12] Although many network studies describe the impact of various portions of children's networks (e.g., fathers, mother, peers) on the development of special functions, such as language, play, cognition, and social skills, few focus primarily on the effects of the structural parameters of networks themselves. Instead, they concentrate on the particular characteristics of selected types of network members. Our own study, which deals with parental social isolation and insularity,[18] so frequently reported to be characteristic of maltreating parents,[14] is concerned with the structural parameters of parental networks. It is based on a behavioral model that hypothesizes that deficient social connections distort parental networks in such a way that they fail to provide parents with appropriate feedback for their interactive behavior with their children or with models for alternative competent parenting behavior. Nor do their networks provide parents with the positive reinforcement necessary for changing their behavior or for maintaining changes in their behavior once they have occurred.[18] In keeping with this model, we have operationally defined isolation in terms of the structural network parameters of size and frequency of contact and insularity in terms of boundary density. Isolation was characterized as small network size and infrequent contact with network members, and insularity was characterized as a deficiency in the interconnectedness between parts of the network, particularly between the immediate family and the rest of the network.

It was expected that the extended network would be likely to provide more diverse input than the immediate network because the latter is comprised of persons holding many of the same values and sharing the long-term constraints of the same social context. The persistence of severe maltreatment, which is socially unsanctioned by the extended network, would suggest that sufficient positive immediate feedback for the parents' antisocial behavior is being derived from the close network, and that it is relatively stronger than any negative feedback that might be forthcoming from the more extended network.

Therefore, one would expect the social networks of the mothers in households where severe maltreatment is occurring to show the following characteristics: First, the networks should be relatively small and the frequency of contact with network members will be limited. Second, the networks should be comprised predominantly of family members, or conversely, of fewer peers. Third, one would expect relatively less interconnectedness among various portions of the network (the subnetworks). And finally, the interconnections between the more extended parts of the network, that is, those not necessarily representing shared values, and the more immediate familial network should be sparse.

The social networks of a lower middle-class suburban group of 32 mothers in a hosptial-based outpatient family crisis clinic, whose children had recently suffered maltreatment, were elicited by structured interview and compared, with respect to the hypotheses set forth above, to the social networks of 24 demographically similar mothers in families where there was no known current maltreatment occurring.

Four network parameters were measured: size, cumulated days of contact with network members during the past year, connectedness across subnetworks (defined as the average number out of a total of 10 subnetworks that a member of any subnetwork is connected to), and joint connection to the home subnetwork (defined as the number of network members who are regularly seen by the mother with members of the home subnetwork).

As hypothesized, it was found that the clinic mothers were much more isolated than the control mothers. They have, on the average, far fewer people in their networks (M = 21.4 and M = 37.0, $p < 0.005$), and their overall days of contact with members of their network is less (M = 2,997 and M = 4,540, $p < 0.005$).

The differences between the two groups with respect to isolation appear to be more pronounced for the peer portion of the network than the family portion. Bi-serial correlations between each of the isolation measures and the occurrence of maltreatment were carried out separately for the family and peer portions of the network. In the case of size, even though there is a significant association with maltreatment for both portions of the network, the proportion of the variance accounted for by the peer portion is 38%, compared to only 15% for the family. In the case of total amount of contact,

TABLE 2. Size of the Subnetworks for Clinic and Control Mothers

	Clinic Mothers		Control Mothers		
Subnetworks	*n*	Mean	*n*	Mean	*t*
Home	32	3.7	24	3.5	−0.775
Close family	32	3.4	24	4.3	1.730
Distant family	32	4.7	24	8.0	4.984[a]
Close friends	32	2.6	24	3.4	1.746
Work	32	0.3	24	3.2	5.330[a]
School	32	0.1	24	1.2	3.047[b]
Neighbors	32	1.6	24	1.8	0.483
Organizations	32	0.7	24	3.3	2.804[b]
Other acquaintances	32	2.2	24	7.5	5.632[a]
Professionals	32	2.0	24	0.9	−3.819[a]

[a] $p < 0.001$.
[b] $p < 0.01$.

there is an even greater difference in the strength of the association with maltreatment. Essentially none of the variance is attributable to the amount of contact with family members and as much as 28% of the variance is attributable to the lack of contact with peers.

A more detailed comparison of network size by individual subnetworks is revealing. The apparent pronounced deficiency in the peer network is seen to pertain especially to the more distal parts of the network. There were, in fact, no significant differences found for the size of the close family, close friends, or neighbors (see TABLE 2).

Again, as hypothesized, the comparison between the insularity of the clinic mothers and the control mothers showed that the clinic mothers were much more insulated than the control mothers. Their subnetworks were less well connected to each other than those of the control mothers (M = 2.6 and M = 3.1, $p < 0.005$), thereby insulating the mother's relationship with members of any one subnetwork from the impact or influence of members of the other subnetworks. Also, the number of members of other subnetworks who were actually seen along with the home subnetwork were far fewer for the clinic than the control mothers (M = 7.9 and M = 21.3, $p < 0.0005$).

In order to assess the relative strength of the association between insularity and maltreatment for the family and peer portions of the network,

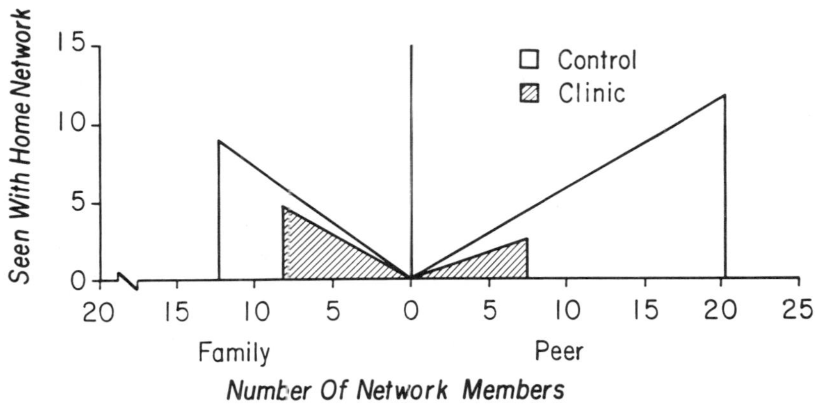

FIGURE 1. Number of family and peer network members who are seen with home network.

biserial correlations between each of the insularity measures and the occurrence of maltreatment were computed separately for the family and peer portions of the network. It appears that it is the insularity of the family from the rest of the mother's network that accounts for the greater part of the variance associated with maltreatment. The lack of interconnectedness between the family and the other subnetworks accounts for 25% of the variance (27% for the home family) as opposed to only 10% of the variance attributable to a lack of peer connectedness. Furthermore, although the amounts of contact with the home subnetwork were found to be significantly associated with maltreatment, the lack of connection with peers accounts for a good deal more of the variance, 32%, than the lack of connection with the extended family, 19%.

A summary of the joint impact of isolation and insularity for the two groups of mothers is shown in FIGURE 1. The abscissa represents isolation, as indicated by the average size of the peer and family networks (excluding members of the home subnetwork), and the ordinate represents insularity, as indicated by the number of network members seen with the home network. Although the networks of the clinic mothers can be seen to be more limited on each dimension than those of the control mothers, a consideration of the joint contribution of both dimensions reveals the striking fact that overall, it is the impact of the peer network that is most lacking for the clinic mothers.

In keeping with a network model, these findings suggest the following implications for both parenting behavior and child development in families where child maltreatment has occurred. The mothers in families where this type of nonsanctioned social behavior occurs are likely to have less actual contact with normal models of child rearing than mothers in other families because the limited social contact they have is confined primarily to their closest connections, most of whom are familial and probably share many of the same values. Because their insularity functions to separate their social behavior at home from other contacts, the feedback and reinforcement that is afforded mothers for their normal parenting behavior is probably deficient for these mothers. Their behavior is likely to be controlled almost exclusively by the aversive reinforcement contingencies in effect within the context of their immediate family.[55] Furthermore, their current coercive cycles of behavior[56] will, in all likelihood, be resistant to change, lacking the more varied discrepant input afforded by the more distal parts of their peer and family network. The attempt to modify such seriously deviant childrearing practices through professional input, even though intensive, is probably not sufficient to both change the behavior and maintain that change in the absence of enrichment of the natural extended support systems of these mothers.

CONCLUSIONS

First, a disclaimer—this paper was not intended to be an exhaustive review of network effects in child rearing, nor was it to be a test of the relative efficacy of various models of child development. Rather, it is an attempt to show that the addition of a social network model to the traditional theories of child development expands the ability of such theories to account for both normal and abnormal child-rearing patterns and their effects upon children. It brings our theoretical base more in line with newer ecological system models of development by providing a means to independently quantify the social contexts of children (and parents) and to test their effect on child outcome.

In keeping with an ecological approach, I have considered studies that have examined both child and maternal network variables. Child network variables have, for the most part, been shown to have *direct* effects on child behavior. Various portions of the network have facilitated different areas of function, illustrated most clearly in the work on language development of normal children and the social behavior of abused children. Parent network variables, on the other hand, have been shown to have primarily *indirect* effects on child behavior. Parent networks provide the child with opportunities to socialize with adults, thereby facilitating the acquisition of competent behavior; impoverished extended parental networks fail to provide corrective feedback for poor parenting, raising the risk for child abuse, among other things, and subsequent poor child outcome; and lack of maternal support networks affects maternal nurturance.

It is hoped that the empirical examples cited here have demonstrated the efficacy of the consideration of network variables across a wide spectrum of development and child rearing issues. They have been helpful in gaining an understanding of the persistence of some of the most deviant of parenting practices as well as for elucidating factors contributing to the development of some normal behaviors during childhood. In conclusion, the empirical data that have been generated so far within the framework of a social network model suggest that such a model has heuristic value for further understanding of a wide range of problems concerned with both child rearing and child development.

ACKNOWLEDGMENTS

The author is grateful to Sandra J. Kaplan, M.D., Director of the North Shore University Hospital Family Crisis Program and to the entire staff and the students in the program, especially to Connie Artemyeff, Deborah Wexler, and Terrel Kaplan for their work on the social networks of maltreating parents. I am also indebted to Muriel Hammer, Ph.D., for many years of collaborative thought devoted to the measurement of social networks and their implications for mental health.

REFERENCES

1. Kapferer, B. 1973. Social network and conjugal role in urban Zambia: Towards a reformulation of the Bott hypothesis. *In* Network Analysis: Studies in Human Interaction. J. Boissevain & J. C. Mitchell, Eds.: 83–110. Mouton. The Hague.
2. Fischer, C. S. 1977. Networks and Places: Social Relations in the Urban Setting. The Free Press. New York.
3. Feld, S. L. 1981. The focussed organization of social ties. Am. J. Sociol. **86:** 1015–1035.
4. Hammer, M. 1980. Social access and the clustering of personal connections. Soc. Networks. **2:** 305–325.
5. Cassell, J. C. 1970. Physical illness in response to stress. *In* Social Stress. S. Levine & N. Scoton, Eds. Aldine. Chicago.
6. Cassell, J. C. 1974. Psychiatric epidemiology. *In* American Handbook of Psychiatry, Vol. II. G. Caplan, Ed.: 401–411. Basic Books. New York.
7. Cohen, C. & J. Sokolovsky. 1979. Health seeking behavior and social networks of the aged living in single-room occupancy hotels. J. Am. Ger. Soc. **27:** 270–278.
8. Hammer, M., S. Makiesky-Barrow & L. Gutwirth. 1978. Social networks and schizophrenia. Schiz. Bull. **4:** 522–545.
9. Weinraub, M. & B. M. Wolf. 1983. Effects of stress and social supports on mother–child interactions in single- and two-parent families. Child Dev. **54:** 1297–1311.
10. Stack, C. 1974. All Our Kin: Strategies for Survival in a Black Community. Harper. New York.
11. Wilcox, B. L. 1981. Social support in adjusting to marital disruption: A network analysis. *In* Social Networks and Social Support. B. H. Gottlieb, Ed.: 97–116. Sage. Beverly Hills, CA.
12. Salzinger, S., S. Kaplan & C. Artemyeff. 1983. Mothers' personal social networks and child maltreatment. J. Abn. Psychol. **92:** 68–76.
13. Granovetter, M. 1973. The strength of weak ties. Am. J. Sociol. **78:** 1360–1380.

14. GARBARINO, J. A. & D. SHERMAN. 1980. High-risk neighborhoods and high-risk families: The human ecology of child maltreatment. Child Dev. **51:** 188-198.
15. COHEN, S. & T. A. WILLS. 1985. Stress, social support, and the buffering hypothesis. Psychol. Bull. **98:** 310–357.
16. BIEGEL, D. E., A. J. NAPARSTEK & M. M. KHAN. 1982. Social support and mental health in urban ethnic neighborhoods. *In* Community Support Systems and Mental Health: Practice, Policy and Research. D. E. Biegel & A. J. Naparstek, Eds.: 21–36. Springer. New York.
17. BANDURA, A. 1971. Social Learning Theory. General Learning Press. New York.
18. WAHLER, R. G. 1980. Parent insularity as a determinant of generalization success in family treatment. *In* The Ecosystem of the "Sick" Child. S. Salzinger, J. Antrobus & J. Glick, Eds.: 187–199. Academic Press. New York.
19. BERKMAN, L. F. & S. L. SYME. 1979. Social networks, host resistance and mortality: A nine year followup study of Alameda Country residents. Am. J. Epidemiol. **109:** 186–204.
20. HOUSE, J. S., C. ROBBINS & H. L. METZNER. 1982. The association of social relationships and activities with mortality: Prospective evidence from the Tecumseh Community Health Study. Am. J. Epidemiol. **116:** 123–140.
21. HOUSE, J. S., K. R. LANDIS & D. UMBERSON. 1988. Social relationships and health. Science **241:** 540–545.
22. BOWLBY, J. 1969. Attachment and Loss, Vol. 1.: Attachment. Penguin. London.
23. BOWLBY, J. 1973. Attachment and Loss, Vol. 2: Separation. Basic Books. New York.
24. BOWLBY, J. 1980. Attachment and Loss, Vol. 3: Loss. Basic Books. New York.
25. SROUFE, L. A. & J. FLEESON. 1986. Attachment and the construction of relationships. *In* Relationships and Development. W. Hartup & Z. Rubin, Eds. Cambridge University Press. New York.
26. MATAS, L., R. A. AREND & L. A. SROUFE. 1978. Continuity of adaptation in the second year: The relationship between quality of attachment and later competence. Child Dev. **49:** 547–556.
27. WATERS, E., J. WIPPMAN & L. A. SROUFE. 1979. Attachment, positive affect, and competence in the peer group: Two studies in construct validation. Child Dev. **50:** 821–829.
28. AINSWORTH, M. & B. WITTIG. 1969. Attachment and exploratory behavior of one-year-olds in a strange situation. *In* Determinants of Infant Behavior, Vol. 4. B. Foss, Ed. Methuen. London.
29. RHEINGOLD, H. L. & C. O. ECKERMAN. 1970. The infant separates himself from his mother. Science **168:** 78–83.
30. ECKERMAN, C. O. & H. L. RHEINGOLD. 1974. Infants' exploratory responses to toys and people. Dev. Psychol. **10:** 225–259.
31. BAUMRIND, D. 1975. The contribution of the family to the development of competence in children. Schiz. Bull. **14:** 12–37.
32. RUTTER, M. 1989. Intergenerational continuities and discontinuities in serious parenting difficulties. *In* Child Maltreatment: Theory and Research on the Causes and Consequences of Child Abuse and Neglect. D. Cicchetti & V. Carlson, Eds.: 317–348. Cambridge University Press. New York.
33. BELL, R. Q. 1966. A reinterpretation of the direction of effects in studies of socialization. Psychol. Rev. **75:** 81–95.
34. CROCKENBERG, S. B. 1981. Infant irritability, mother responsiveness, and social support influences on the security of infant-mother attachment. Child Dev. **52:** 857–865.

35. HOMEL, R., A. BURNS & J. GOODNOW. 1987. Parental social networks and child development. J. Soc. Pers. Rel. **4:** 159–177.
36. BRONFENBRENNER, U. 1979. The Ecology of Human Development: Experiments by Nature and Design. Harvard University Press. Cambridge, MA.
37. BELSKY, J. 1980. Child maltreatment: An ecological integration. Am. Psychol. **35:** 320–335.
38. BELSKY, J. & J. VONDRA. 1989. Parental and contextual influences on maltreatment. *In* Child Maltreatment: Theory and Research on the Causes and Consequences of Child Abuse and Neglect. D. Cicchetti & V. Carlson, Eds.: 153–202. Cambridge University Press. New York.
39. LEWIS, M. & C. FEIRING. 1979. The child's social network: Social object, social functions and their relationship. *In* The Child and its Family: The Genesis of Behavior, Vol. 2. M. Lewis & L. A. Rosenblum, Eds. Plenum. New York.
40. WEINRAUB, M., J. BROOKS & M. LEWIS. 1977. The social network: A reconsideration of the concept of attachment. Hum. Dev. **20:** 31–47.
41. LAMB, M. E., Ed. 1976. The Role of the Father in Child Development. Wiley. New York.
42. LEWIS, M. & M. WEINRAUB. 1976. The father's role in the infant's social network. *In* The Role of the Father in Child Development. M. E. Lamb, Ed. Wiley. New York.
43. LEWIS, M. & L. A. ROSENBLUM, Eds. 1975. Friendship and Peer Relations. Wiley. New York.
44. FINE, G. A. 1980. The natural history of preadolescent male friendship groups. *In* Friendship and Social Relations in Children. H. C. Foot, A. J. Chapman & J. R. Smith, Eds.: 293–320. Wiley. New York.
45. HARTUP, W. W. 1975. Peer interaction and the behavioral development of the individual child. *In* Proceedings of the First International Leo Kanner Colloquium on Child Development, Deviations, and Treatment. E. Schopler, Ed. Plenum. New York.
46. LADD, G. W., C. H. HART, E. M. WADSWORTH & B. S. GOLTER. 1988. The social networks of preschool and school-age children. *In* Social Networks of Children, Adolescents, and College Students. S. Salzinger, J. Antrobus & M. Hammer, Eds.: 59–92. Erlbaum. Hillsdale, NJ.
47. LEWIS, M. & S. SHAEFFER. 1981. Peer behavior and mother infant interaction in maltreated children. *In* The Uncommon Child: The Genesis of Behavior, Vol. 3. M. Lewis & L. A. Rosenblum, Eds. Plenum. New York.
48. FURMAN, W., D. F. RAHE & W. W. HARTUP. 1979. Rehabilitation of socially-withdrawn children through mixed-age and same-age socialization. Child Dev. **50:** 915–922.
49. TIZARD, B. & J. HODGES. 1978. The effect of early institutional rearing on the development of eight-year-old children. J. Child Psychol. Psychiatry **19:** 99–118.
50. SUOMI, S. J. & H. F. HARLOW. 1975. The role and reason of peer relationships in Rhesus monkeys. *In* Friendship and Peer Relations. M. Lewis & L. A. Rosenblum, Eds. Wiley. New York.
51. SALZINGER, S. & J. HAMPSON. 1988. Social networks of mother and child: An examination of their function in developing speech. *In* Social Networks of Children, Adolescents, and College Students. S. Salzinger, J. Antrobus & M. Hammer, Eds.: 19–35. Erlbaum. Hillsdale, NJ.
52. HAMMER, M. & L. GUTWIRTH. 1979. Some preliminary data on the social networks of parents and infants. Paper presented at the American Anthropological Association Meetings. Cincinnati, OH.

53. HAMMER, M., L. GUTWIRTH & S. L. PHILLIPS. 1982. Parenthood and social networks: A preliminary view. Soc. Sci. Med. **16:** 2091–2100.
54. SZALAI, A., Ed. 1972. The Use of Time. Mouton. The Hague.
55. BURGESS, R. L. & R. D. CONGER. 1978. Family interaction in abusive, neglectful, and normal families. Child Dev. **49:** 1163–1173.
56. PATTERSON, G. R. 1980. Mothers: The unacknowledged victims. Monogr. Soc. Res. Child Dev., serial no. 186.

Obesity

A Biobehavioral Point of View[a]

M. KATAHN[b] AND MARK R. McMINN

Department of Psychology
Vanderbilt University
Nashville, Tennessee 37240

If you ask an overweight person, "Why are you fat?", you will, almost invariably, get the answer, "Because I eat too much." You will get this answer in spite of the fact that of thirteen studies, six find no significant differences in the caloric intake of obese versus nonobese subjects, five report that the obese eat significantly less than the nonobese, and only two report that they eat significantly more.

It is hard to overcome this possibly incorrect belief about the cause of obesity when most practicing professionals and certainly every diet book is based on the assumption that excessive caloric intake is at fault. In spite of a failure rate approaching 90 to 95%, we still cling to dietary exhortations in our treatments, and suspect that lack of adherence to our recommendations is responsible for failure.

Recent research in the field of biochemistry suggests that several newly discovered factors, as well as others that have been known for years but generally overlooked, may contribute to obesity in a way that is not easily remedied by dieting. Caloric restriction may lead to an adaptive metabolic response that reduces a person's daily energy needs, and to hormone and enzyme changes that lead to an enhanced rate of fat storage following caloric restriction. Adaptive responses may be associated with initial dispositional tendencies for some individuals to be heavier than others, and, together, these adaptive and dispositional tendencies may provide a basis for the continual frustration experienced by millions of persons who repeatedly diet to lose weight.

We will review evidence for these adaptive and dispositional tendencies that resist weight loss efforts and then suggest an alternative approach to severe caloric restriction based on data from the Vanderbilt University Weight Management Program.

[a] The authors are supported by Grants #MH14757 and #MH08709 administered by the National Institutes of Mental Health.

[b] Address for correspondence: Dr. M. Katahn, Vanderbilt Weight Management Program, New Psychology Bldg., Vanderbilt University, Nashville, Tennessee 37240.

DISPOSITIONAL AND ADAPTIVE TENDENCIES TOWARD OBESITY

Although it is hard to disentangle the effects of learning and the environment from the influence of heredity, the role of genetic influences can be clearly demonstrated in both single- and multiple-gene obesities in animals.[2] The most convincing evidence for a strong genetic component in human obesity is presented by Brook[3] and Brook, Huntley, and Slack,[4] who determined that the correlation between tricep and subscapular skinfolds for monozygotic twins was 0.72 and 0.83, respectively, compared with 0.49 and 0.34 for dizygotic twins. Borjeson[5] compared skinfolds at three sites and found that the average intra-pair differences were three times greater in dizygotic twins than in monozygotic twins. He concluded that the coefficient of heritability was somewhere between 0.50 and 0.88.

A multitude of other studies could be cited to illustrate that there is no longer any argument about the existence of a genetic component that influences the relative ease with which the human body stores fat—the question now becomes, Through what diverse physiological and biochemical mechanisms can it be manifest, and how may these mechanisms be modified, or how can we compensate for them, by changes in our diet and activity habits when it seems desirable to do so for physical or psychological reasons?

Biochemical Mechanisms

Several biochemical mechanisms have been identified that might lead to a between-persons dispositional basis toward obesity. Each of these mechanisms may also respond differentially to overfeeding or underfeeding with respect to an established weight in any given person. Although the boundaries limiting the operation of these biochemical mechanisms are set genetically, there is little doubt that lifestyle differences also affect their operation just as the expression of many genetic potentials depends upon an interaction between an organism and its environment. Thyroid deficiency, operative supposedly in but 5% of the population, is only one of many factors. Variability in other hormones and nerve transmitters that can affect appetite, fat storage, and fat utilization include insulin, the catecholamines, endorphins, serotonin, and dopamine. Enzymatic differences, most strongly verified in animal research, include Na^+,K^+–ATPase, lipoprotein lipase, and various others involved in brown fat thermogenisis, the glycerol phosphate shuttle, and substrate cycling. Central nervous system differences, located especially in the hypothalamus, have been noted in association with these hormonal and enzymatic differences.

All of the biochemical factors are associated with energy utilization. In performing their functions, they can either conserve or waste energy. They provide the biochemical foundation underlying statements such as "all I have to do is look at food and I gain weight" to "he eats everything in sight and never gains an ounce." The first person has a very efficient body—it wastes very little energy performing the work it has to do to stay alive and should that person overeat in the presence of an abundance of food, it will put a large percentage of the overage into its fat banks. The first person is well equipped to withstand the famines that still frequently plague a large percentage of the human race. The second person has an energy-inefficient body. If he overeats, the body simply turns on one of the possible mechanisms to waste the overabundant energy. He is not well equipped to withstand a famine, but he is protected against obesity in times of plenty.

Brown Fat

In an extensive series of studies with rodents, Rothwell and Stock[6,7] and a number of other investigators have established brown fat as a key factor in metabolic functions related to obesity (see McMinn[8] and Morgan & Goldberg[9] for reviews). Brown fat, in contrast with ordinary, "white" fat, is highly vascularized and does not function as a storage depot for excess energy. Instead, brown fat plays a central role in diet-induced thermogenesis and cold adaptation. When normal lean rats and mice are overfed, brown fat can increase in mass and in heat production such that a major portion of excess calories is wasted in heat. The genetically obese varieties lack this adaptive mechanism.[10–12] The fat prone animals gain considerable weight—they can double in fat content, while the lean may gain about one-third the fat that might be expected from the amount of food ingested above energy needs.[13] In addition, in the normal rat, the brown fat remains active when regular feeding is resumed until the extra store of ordinary fat is burned off and normal weight is re-established.

Although the major research has been done with animals, the presence of brown fat in humans has been verified. Of course one cannot assume that it plays an identical role in human predispositions to obesity, but if brown fat is distributed in mass and in function with the great variability that we see in other human attributes, and suitable investigatory techniques can be devised, future studies may reveal at least some role for this tissue in human obesity.

Adipose Tissue Lipoprotein Lipase

Adipose tissue lipoprotein lipase (AT-LPL) has already been implicated in both animal and human dispositions to obesity. AT-LPL resides on the membranes of fat cells and breaks down triglycerides for storage. Elevated levels of lipoprotein lipase activity have been reported in the fatty strains of both rats[14–16] and mice.[17] Cleary, Vasselli and Greenwood[18] have shown that AT-LPL is active without hyperphasia, that is, elevation of AT-LPL activity occurs when genetically obese animals are prevented from overeating. Under these conditions, lean tissue is robbed of nutrients in order to accumulate excess adipose tissue. Schwartz and Brunzell[19] found a correlation of 0.91 between AT-LPL activity and body weight and 0.71 between AT-LPL activity and fat cell size in humans. At least in part, AT-LPL activity is stimulated by insulin, but it can apparently be active independently of that hormone, at least in rodents.

When a person goes on a diet, AT-LPL activity is reduced; the amount of reduction appears to increase over time in all subjects. However, research with humans, notably that of Schwartz and Brunzell[19,20] and Taskinen and Nikkila,[21,22] has demonstrated that AT-LPL activity is less reduced during a period of caloric restriction in obese subjects than in nonobese subjects. Thus, as time goes on, it may become increasingly harder for obese subjects to lose weight. Then, after the termination of a low-calorie diet (e.g., 600 calories in Schwartz & Brunzell[19]), AT-LPL activity will increase many-fold over baseline, three times on the average but as much as six to eight times in some cases. These biochemists use the word "pull"—it is as though the fat cells were pulling the substrate right out of the blood stream. When subjects regain all of their weight (usually even a bit more than they lost to begin with) AT-LPL activity returns to normal or near normal. However, at least for 8 to 14 months after weight loss, it can remain elevated in activity as long as the subject struggles to maintain a lower weight.[19,23]

Na^+,K^+—ATPase

Differences between lean and adipose rodents in the activity of the enzyme responsible for the sodium pump, Na^+,K^+—ATPase, have been reported in a series of studies by Lin *et al.*[24–26] The amount of thermogenesis dependent upon the activity of the sodium pump has been estimated repeatedly, with results ranging up to 40% of the total energy required for basal metabolism. So, if obese mice have less Na^+,K^+—ATPase activity, a thermic mechanism involving sodium pump activity must be considered in understanding the etiology of obesity.

Studies with humans have been less definite than animal studies, however. Consistent with the results of animal studies, DeLuise, Blackburn, and Flier[27] reported less Na^+,K^+—ATPase in the red blood cells of obese humans compared with persons of normal weight. This finding was countered by a later report showing greater enzyme activity in the liver of obese humans than in the nonobese.[28]

Future investigations with human subjects are needed to determine which tissue is most appropriate for measuring Na^+,K^+—ATPase activity. It is of great potential importance in both adaptive and dispositional differences in metabolic activity. It is intriguing to note that Rothwell, Stock, and Wyllie[29] found a remarkably high correlation (0.91) between brown fat activity and Na^+,K^+—ATPase activity within brown fat. However, much more research is needed to determine in what species and within what tissues Na^+,K^+—ATPase activity varies, since the liver tissue of fatty rats does not appear to differ from normal.[30]

Other Enzymes

Other mechanisms that contribute to either adaptive or dispositional weight gain have been suggested but have not been followed up because of various difficulties in pursuing such research. Galton and Bray[31] and Bray[32] reported evidence for the possible role of the glycerol phosphate shuttle in human obesity. One enzyme in the shuttle may be less active in persons with a genetic tendency toward obesity and in persons who have adapted to a diet. The inactivity of this enzyme may lead to greater energy efficiency in the oxidation of NADH and may also lead to greater fat formation since glycerol phosphate is more readily available.

The role of substrate cycling has been implicated, in theory, as a potential contributor to metabolic variation.[33,34] Specifically, an intermediate step in both glycolysis (glucose breakdown) and gluconeogenesis (glucose production) may cycle in a futile manner and thereby waste energy. After dieting (or in persons with a tendency toward obesity) the activity of the substrate cycling may be reduced. The empirical evidence for the role of substrate cycling in obesity is very limited.

ADAPTIVE METABOLIC RESPONSE TO DIET

The exact relationship of changes in metabolic rate to changes in caloric intake is not known with any degree of precision. That is, we cannot predict to what extent metabolism may slow in relationship to increasing amounts of caloric restriction in any individual case. Bray[35] states that adaptation will occur almost invariably when intake is reduced to 800 calories per day, but it is likely that in some persons metabolic changes follow energy intake variations quite closely.

A study by Benedict, Miles, Roth, and Smith[36] revealed a fall in BMR, resting pulse rate, and body weight for a group of healthy, normal weight volunteers placed on a calorie-restricted diet approximately eight weeks before Thanksgiving. The fall partially recovered in two holiday "times out" during Thanksgiving and Christmas. Then, with increasing rapidity, it returned to a lower level when the low-calorie diet was resumed. After losing an average of approximately 7 kg, weight appeared to stabilize at an intake roughly two-thirds of baseline levels, with about a 20% average reduction in BMR.

When the subjects returned to *ad libitum* eating, weight was regained between two and three times faster than the speed with which it was lost.

In a more recent study, DiGirolamo, Smith, and Bjorntorp[37] found that rats fasted for a three-day period in which 10% of body weight was lost required only 60% of their former energy intake to maintain their lowered weight for at least a 13-day period.

Summarizing from the many investigations reported in Bjorntorp, Cairella, and Howard,[38] it appears that the CNS command headquarters in charge of metabolic adaptation lies in the hypothalamus, which organizes

CNS activity to regulate thermogenesis. Upon caloric restriction, CNS activity at various sites, probably including skeletal and heart muscle and brown fat depots, is reduced. For example, CNS activity and norepinephrine turnover is reduced in the heart muscle of rats during caloric restriction.[39] Other signals, relayed through some complex network not as yet entirely understood, result in less fat being incorporated into adipose tissue while following a low-calorie diet.

Metabolic adaptation to a low-calorie diet begins within 72 hours, and proceeds to reach maximum within three to seven weeks. Speed of weight loss slows, both as initial glycogen stores are depleted (along with the large amount of water with which the body's glycogen is stored) and as metabolic adaptation sets in.

When *ad libitum* feeding is resumed, there is a rapid rebound effect, owing in part to the reduced caloric needs relative to intake, the rapid refilling of depleted glycogen storage sites, and the rebuilding of any wasted muscle mass that may have occurred as the body burned some of its own protein stores in order to create needed glucose for energy. For every gram of glycogen restored to the liver and muscles, and for every gram of protein incorporated into muscle tissue, approximately 3 to 4 grams of water are also integrated into the system.

In addition, restoration of additional calories in carbohydrate to the diet appears to turn on a mechanism, apparently related to an increased secretion of insulin necessary to handle the incorporation of increased energy into body cells, that causes sodium retention, and therefore water retention, which for a period of time may actually overcompensate for the previous dehydration and lead to edema.

It is evidence like this, together with the easily observable fact that most people who lose weight by dieting do indeed put it all back in spades within two to five years, that has rekindled interest in what has been called "set-point" theory. As Bennett and Gurin[40] put it, set-point theory claims that physiological/biochemical mechanisms, set by your genes, act to determine what you will weigh "when you are not thinking about it." If you try to change, certainly if by dieting alone, forces are set into motion to counteract your efforts. We have presented only a small fraction of the evidence that has been marshalled to support the set-point notion. However, as will be discussed shortly, set-point theory is best interpreted as a range within which lifestyle factors, such as exercise and diet, work to adjust body weight.

WHAT DOES IT TAKE TO BE A SUCCESSFUL LOSER?

We will focus here on the issue of greatest importance, and that is, not what it takes to lose weight in the first place, but what it takes to keep it off once a person has lost it.

Follow-up research with successful losers—persons who are keeping their weight off after using low-calorie commercial weight loss plans that do not emphasize increasing physical activity—suggests that caloric requirements are reduced as a consequence of such diets. After losing weight on diets of from 330 calories to 800 calories per day, women's' caloric needs, given a sedentary lifestyle, appear to stabilize during the first year of follow-up within the area of 1200 to 1300 calories per day, while men's' stabilize between 1600 and 1800.[41] These caloric intakes, taken from weekly eating diaries of persons who are maintaining their losses and from the maintenance programs prescribed by various diet centers, are between 30 and 40% below the average daily requirements, for persons of average weight, estimated by the Food and Nutrition Board of the National Research Council.

The Vanderbilt Weight Management Program, in contrast with most commercial programs, emphasizes physical activity at least equally with sound nutrition. We have customarily recommended a balanced 1200-calorie reducing diet for women and 1800 for men, together with building up to an average of approximately 45 minutes of extra physical activity per day equivalent to brisk walking. Our emphasis on physical activity as the *key* ingredient necessary for permanent weight management has, until recently (e.g., Bennett and Gurin[40]) been unique in the field. In fact, from a theoretical standpoint, some noted investigators have concluded that exercise is an impractical component to treat.[42–45] They point out that physical activity comprises a very small part of the daily energy expenditure in the Western World—that is, in relation to our basal metabolic energy needs and the energy used during our hours of work, other physical activity plays a minor role. They go on to say that it seems more reasonable to make dietary adjustments than activity adjustments to return to, and to preserve, desirable weight.

We believe this view completely misses the critical role that physical activity plays in weight management. To begin with, health professionals, along with the overweight persons they treat, think first about weight loss because it has to occur first in time and is uppermost in everyone's minds. An increase in activity seems to be a poor way to get that satisfying quick weight loss most overweight persons desire. And health professionals are often just as impatient as the persons they seek to help. They fear that they will lose their clients if weight loss does not proceed rapidly, and sometimes they feel pressure from professional colleagues who review papers submitted for publication to demonstrate large losses in a short period of time.

Because it takes about 35 miles of walking or running to burn enough calories to *lose* a pound of fat, it seems much easier to go on a low-calorie diet and lose that pound overnight (and maybe even two or three) without the need for uncomfortable vigorous exercise. Assuming no change in caloric intake, it would take at least 1750 miles of extra walking, and perhaps more as caloric needs drop with weight reduction, to lose 50 pounds of fat. How many overweight people are ready to start a walking program with that ultimate distance in mind?

This view of exercise in weight control completely misses its singularly important role. Let us examine the apportionment of energy expenditure in a woman about 50 pounds overweight, weighing perhaps 175 pounds, needing approximately 1800 to 2000 calories per day to maintain her weight. Of her basal metabolic needs, perhaps 200 is going toward the maintenance of her excess adipose tissue. Compared with the organs that use the majority of our calories in the resting state—the heart, central nervous system, lungs, liver, kidneys, and skeletal muscle system—fat is relatively inactive tissue, and it may take as little as 200 calories a day to support as much as 50 pounds of fat. During the process of weight loss, this woman can solve the problem of *weight maintenance* if she will learn to expend 200 additional calories a day in her skeletal muscle system. Then, when she reaches desirable weight, if she can continue to burn up 200 additional calories each day, she will be able to return to some approximation of her earlier level of caloric intake, and not put any of her weight back on again. She is now burning the number of calories that previously went to the support of excess fat tissue to the tune of 50 pounds. Just three miles per day of extra walking, or its energy equivalent, can keep her from slowly regaining the weight she has lost. Thinking in terms of just three miles per day for *weight maintenance* is a much different proposition from thinking in terms of *1750* miles of walking to *lose* 50 pounds.

That is the singularly important role of physical activity in weight control.

Of course, metabolic needs and other dispositional factors toward a heavier than average weight, discussed previously in this paper, may require considerable differences in extra energy expenditure on the part of some persons if exercise is to play a major role in permitting food intake to approach the average of persons not predisposed to obesity. The data presented in FIGURE 1 illustrate this variability in persons who have lost significant amounts of weight and maintained their losses for at least five years using physical activity as their key maintenance behavior rather than dietary restriction.

FIGURE 1 presents the complete range of variation in the adult lives of five persons whose biological predispositions, given their previously sedentary lives, established what Bennet and Gurin[40] refer to as a "set-point" at the top of the depicted range when eating without restraint. Present weight is indicated by the cross bars at the lower end of the ranges.

The first woman (over 40 pounds lighter than her highest weight six years ago) averages approximately 1860 calories per day, adding about four miles of either walking or jogging to the baseline requirements of about two miles of movement in her work and other responsibilities.

The second woman (over 50 pounds lighter) maintains her weight at about 1915 calories, provided she adds 20 minutes every day of continuous free-style swimming to an otherwise sedentary existence.

The third woman maintains herself at about 1905 calories averaging about seven miles of walking every day.

These data are obtained from eating and activity diaries kept as part of our follow-up research from a select cadre of former participants each year.

Today, these three women all fall within normal limits of energy needs, *provided* they add the amount of activity that might have been required of

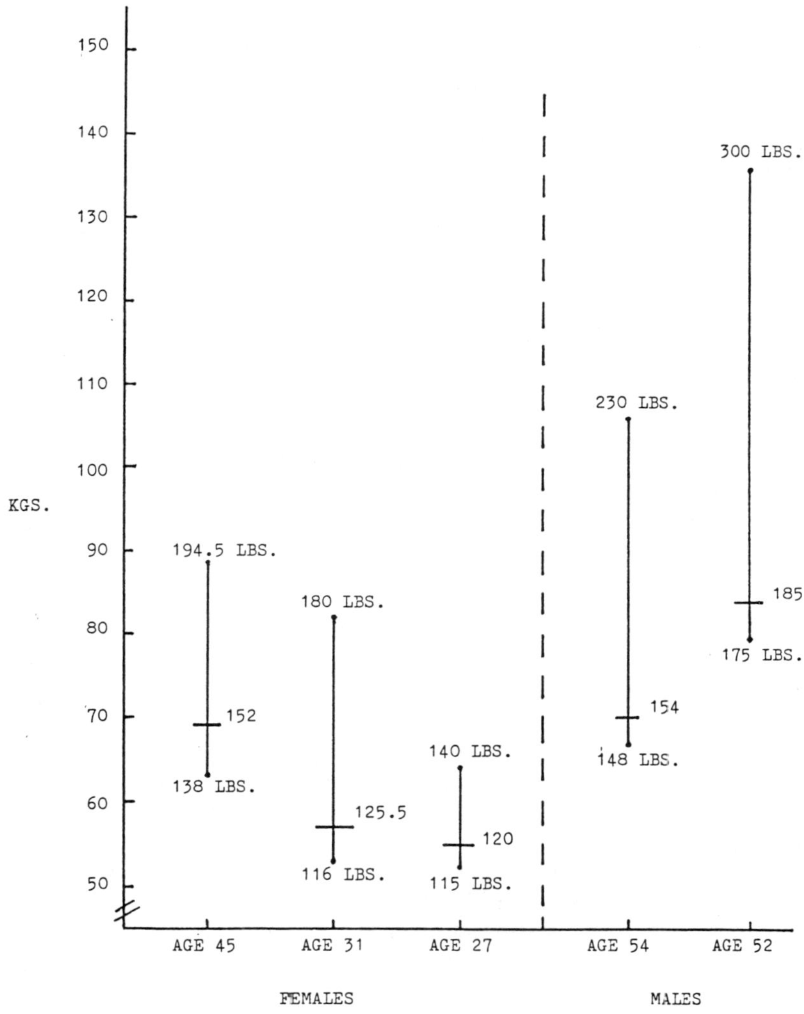

FIGURE 1. Weight ranges in their adult years of five formerly obese persons who have maintained significant weight losses for at least five years (present weight indicated by cross-bars).

them in their daily lives a few generations ago. Without that level of activity there is no doubt that their caloric needs at desirable weight would be reduced to the levels (1200 to 1300) reported earlier in this paper for persons who have used low-calorie diets and who are presently relying on dietary restriction for weight control.

The first man illustrated in the figure once weighed 230 pounds. He now maintains himself at 2960 calories per day with 35 to 40 miles of jogging, and tennis once or twice a week. He has a sedentary job, and without extra physical activity his total amount of walking would rarely exceed two miles per day. However, his physical activity level puts his daily caloric requirements several hundred calories higher than the average inactive male of his age.

The second man provides an example of what it might take in the way of physical activity for a person with extreme tendencies toward obesity. His is a "high set-point" range. He lost 125 pounds on an 1800-calorie diet combined with what most overweight persons would consider an unbelievable increase in physical activity. He maintains his present weight on approximately 2600 calories per day and a weekly average of 35 miles of jogging, four hours of racquet ball, five hours on an exercise bicycle, and one and one-half hours of weight training. He no longer drives to work or to appointments near his office and averages about five miles per day of additional walking. His is the sort of genetic predisposition toward obesity that normal amounts of food would return to a grossly overweight condition; without his present amount of activity, the maintenance of desirable weight might require a daily intake of perhaps 1600 calories, just as we have observed in men who are relying on caloric restriction to maintain their weights after low-calorie diets. In such "high set-point" cases, we should not deceive ourselves—it will take a heroic effort in the way of physical activity to compensate and permit such persons to approach the food intake characteristic of the average.

Our files contain follow-up data on weight changes and level of physical activity for two years on 330 persons (87% women) who have participated in the Vanderbilt Program. Groups have been led by various persons, including professional staff, graduate students, and weight management specialists (paraprofessionals, all formerly overweight, who have been trained in sound nutrition, physical fitness, and group leadership skills). Among all groups, the correlation between weight loss from the date of entry in the program to follow-up ranges from 0.15 to 0.40 with amount of increase in physical activity, as determined from ratings obtained from interviews and follow-up questionnaires. Leaders who emphasized physical activity to a greater degree in treatment seem to have the groups in which the correlation between long-term weight loss with physical activity is highest.

However, in spite of what we feel is the proven value of physical activity in weight control, we are still failures when it comes to getting morbidly overweight persons permanently committed to the level of activity that is required. For example, in one group of severely obese participants (mean = 108 pounds above desirable weight, $n = 44$) that was led by one of the authors (MK) together with Dr. John Please, codirector of the program, only 39% were active at the recommended extra 200 calories a day at a 15-month follow-up, and only 15% had stayed consistently active at that level throughout 27 months of follow-up. Indeed, weight loss was highly related to activity level, with those persons equalling or exceeding 200 calories a day of extra activity (usually 45 minutes of walking) maintaining a mean loss of 46.7 pounds, compared with only 18.5 pounds for the less active persons (see Katahn, Please, Thackrey, and Wallston[46] for a more complete description of this research).

In the larger sample of 330 persons who averaged in the vicinity of 50 pounds overweight on entry to the program, we find 20% consistently active over two years of follow-up. They are maintaining over twice the mean weight loss (13.37 pounds vs. 6.05 pounds) compared with those persons who do not meet the 45 minutes per day of movement that we so strongly encourage.

Because of the adherence problem, we now (since fall, 1982) approach weight management from a maintenance perspective, rather than a weight loss perspective. At the onset of the program, participants are helped to set up a program of physical activity that they feel they can stick with for life before we encourage any caloric restriction to speed weight loss itself. While we are working on the activity component, we also present sound nutritional information and use eating diaries to illustrate what it will take to lose weight and then to maintain desirable weight once it is reached. A large percentage of persons begin to lose weight "without dieting" at a satisfactory rate. Those who do not are helped to design a balanced, calorie-restricted diet that will achieve a loss of at least one pound per week. While a full year follow-up on our 1982–1983 participants is not yet available, a check on eating and activity records from our groups indicates that at least half are sustaining the recommended energy expenditure of 200 calories a day, or more, of physical activity after seven months.

In summary, we have reviewed a number of the biochemical mechanisms that help explain why obesity cannot be easily remedied by dieting. Short of surgical intervention, and possible discoveries in the way of acceptable long-term pharmacological interventions, an increase in physical activity seems to be the only way to maintain desirable weight after weight loss has been achieved through a combination of a temporary, sound calorie-restricted diet and exercise. Adherence remains a major problem, as well as designing schemes to help more people remain motivated to reach desirable weight, after which extra physical activity can play its key role in maintenance.

Furthermore, at the present time it is not known to what extent physical activity can alter the action of the predisposing biochemical factors that we have discussed. Past research indicates that certain changes do occur with activity that may reduce fat storage potential. For example, insulin levels are lowered, oxidative capacity of muscle tissue and myoglobin content increase, muscle cell mitochondria increase in number and larger amounts of glycogen are stored in active muscles, serum lipids and cholesterol levels may be reduced, and sensitivity to fat-mobilizing hormones increases.[47,48]

But optimism over the ultimate potential of increased physical activity must be tempered with caution, especially and unfortunately in the case of obese women who seem to be under the greatest social pressure of all to lose weight. As Després *et al.*[43] report in their study of body composition and lipolysis, exercise may not achieve similar fat loss, and fat-mobilizing hormone changes in women as it does in men. The male body appears genetically programmed to respond with adaptive fat-burning and fat loss changes to physical activity, while the female body may resist changes in its fat storage capacity in the face of exercise just as it resists changes to diet more "successfully" than the male.

The overall paradigm for future research in the area should include investigations of various levels of caloric restriction and physical activity on the rate of loss, future weight maintenance, and the biochemical reactions to such combinations. We are making a start in this direction in our own laboratory, using animal analogues of human methods of weight control, that is, varying the nature of the diet and amount of exercise, and then examining the activity of AT-LPL, the enzyme that may be responsible for the accelerated storage of fat after a low-calorie diet.

We look forward to making a report on this research in the near future.

ADDENDUM

In the time intervening between the presentation on which this article is based and its final preparation for publication, the authors have become aware of additional research that sheds further light on dietary and biochemical factors that may help us in our understanding and treatment of obesity.

One series of studies[49-53] suggests that (1) under normal conditions very little dietary carbohydrate is converted to body fat, (2) short bouts of carbohydrate overfeeding lead to increased glycogen (not fat) storage and an increase in metabolic rate, (3) one must remain in positive energy balance for a considerable period of time before significant amounts of carbohydrate are converted to fat for storage, (4) holding genetic influences constant, body fat is closely adjusted to the amount of fat in the diet, and (5) considering that the body burns a blend of glucose and fat in its fuel mixture, perhaps the best way to lose weight is to eat less fat in your daily diet than the body burns in its fuel mix. Weight loss will be gradual and level off when the body makes a new adjustment in its fuel mix to match the change in diet. An additional benefit of lowering fat intake and increasing carbohydrates (in the form of more fruit, vegetables, and grain foods) is that total caloric intake tends to decrease automatically, facilitating weight loss. Because of the difference in caloric density (4 calories per gram of carbohydrate, 9 per gram of fat) and the much greater bulk of carbohydrate foods compared with fat due to their water, air and fiber content, one cannot easily consume as many calories on a high-carbohydrate diet as on a high-fat diet.

Whereas little or no carbohydrate is converted for fat storage with a short-term bout of carbohydrate overfeeding, and such overfeeding is met with an increase in metabolic rate, overfeeding with fat leads to immediate incorporation of the excess energy and no change in energy expenditure.[54] Approximately 97% of the energy contained in any overconsumption of dietary fat will be available for storage while a maximum of between 65 and

75 percent of the caloric content of carbohydrate will ultimately be available for storage, but only with prolonged overfeeding.[50]

Finally, further work confirms the rebound elevation in AT-LPL after large amounts of weight loss and the continuing long-term influence of this enzyme in facilitating the regaining of weight, which was discussed earlier in this paper.[55] In addition, this recent work points to the activation of a gene inside fat cells that triggers the extreme elevation of AT-LPL. The fatter the person to begin with, and the more weight lost, the greater the elevation of AT-LPL, which seems to indicate that the more you lose, the harder your body will fight to regain its weight.

There is, however, considerable inconsistency in the research on the effects of dieting on AT-LPL. Studies that show the rebound elevation use massively obese subjects who follow very low calorie diets for prolonged periods of time. It is not clear whether the activity of this enzyme depends upon the initial weight of the person, the amount of previous overeating, the initial level of enzymatic activity, the degree of caloric restriction and speed of loss, the amount of weight lost, and the period of time during which a person follows any particular level of caloric restriction. There is some indication that a certain threshold of weight loss must be reached in the context of very low-calorie dieting before super-reactivity is triggered. It is also not clear whether the nutrient mixture of the diet can affect AT-LPL activity, that is, a low-fat diet without carbohydrate restriction versus various degrees of caloric restriction.

In conclusion, the two lines of research discussed above suggest that it is primarily the fat in the diet that leads to endogenous obesity and that the use of very low calorie diets by the massively obese for a prolonged period can have self-defeating aftereffects.

REFERENCES

1. Thompson, J. K., G. J. Jarvie, B. B. Lahey & K. J. Cureton. 1982. Exercise and obesity: Etiology, physiology, and intervention. Psychol. Bull. **91:** 55–79.
2. Festing, M. F. W. 1979. Animal Models of Obesity. Oxford University Press. New York.
3. Brook, C. G. D. 1975. Genetic aspects of obesity. Postgrad. Med. J. **2:** 719–721.
4. Brook, C. D. G., Huntley & Slack. 1975. Influence of heredity and environment in determination of skinfold thickness in children. Br. J. Med. **2:** 719–721.
5. Borjeson, M. 1976. The aetiology of obesity in children. Acta Paediatr. Scand. **65:** 279–287.
6. Rothwell, N. J. & M. J. Stock. 1981. Influence of noradrenaline on blood flow to brown adipose tissue in rats exhibiting diet-induced thermogenesis. Pfluegers Arch. **389:** 237–242.
7. Rothwell, N. J. & M. J. Stock. 1981. Hyperphagia, thermogenesis, and leanness. *In* Recent Advances in Obesity Research: III. P. Bjorntorp, M. Cairella & A. N. Howard, Eds. John Libbey. London.

8. McMinn, M. R. 1981. A third variable in obesity: The effects of brown adipose tissue on thermogenesis. Obesity Metab. **1:** 198–208.
9. Morgan, B. L. G. & J. C. Goldberg, 1981. Brown adipose tissue. Obesity Metab. **1:** 198–208.
10. Himms-Hagen, J. & M. A. Desautels. 1978. Mitochondrial defect in binding of purine nucleotides and a failure to respond to cold by an increase in binding. Biochem. Biophys. Res. Commun. **83:** 628–634.
11. Hogan, S. & J. Himms-Hagen. 1980. Abnormal brown adipose tissue in obese (ob/ob) mice: Response to acclimation of cold. Am. J. Physiol. **239:** E301–E309.
12. Thurlby, P. L. & P. Trayhurn. 1980. Regional blood flow in genetically obese (ob/ob) mice. Pfluegers Arch. **385:** 193–201.
13. Rothwell, N. J. & M. J. Stock. 1979. A role for brown adipose tissue in diet-induced thermogenesis. Nature **28:** 31–35.
14. de Gasquet, P., E. Pequignot, D. Lemonnier & A. Alexiu. 1973. Adipose-tissue lipoprotein lipase activity and cellularity in the genetically obese Zucker rat (*fa/fa*). Biochem. J. **132:** 633–635.
15. Gruen, R. K. & M. R. C. Greenwood. 1981. Adipose tissue lipoprotein lipase and glycerol release in fasted Zucker (*fa/fa*) rats. Am. J. Physiol. **24:** E76–E83.
16. Gruen, R., F. Hietanen & M. R. C. Greenwood. 1973. Increased adipose tissue lipoprotein lipase activity during the development of the genetically obese rat (*fa/fa*). Metabolism **27:** 1955–1966.
17. Rath, E. A., D. A. Hems & A. Beloff-Chain. 1974. Lipoprotein lipase activities in tissues of normal and genetically obese (ob/ob) mice. Diabetologia **10:** 261–265.
18. Cleary, M. P., J. R. Vasselli & M. R. C. Greenwood. 1980. Development of obesity in the Zucker obese (*fa/fa*) rat in the absence of hypergagia. (Am. J. Physiol. **238:** E284–E292.
19. Schwartz, R. S. & J. D. Brunzell. 1981. Adipose tissue lipoprotein lipase and obesity. *In* Recent Advances in Obesity Research: III. P. Bjorntorp, M. Cairella & A. N. Howard, Eds. John Libbey. London.
20. Schwartz, R. S. & J. D. Brunzell. 1981. Increase of adipose tissue lipoprotein lipase activity with weight loss. J. Clin. Invest. **67:** 1425–1430.
21. Taskinen, M-R. & E. A. Nikkila. 1979. Effects of caloric restriction on lipid metabolism in man. Atherosclerosis **32:** 289–299.
22. Taskinen, M-R. & E. A. Nikkila. 1981. Lipoprotein lipase of adipose tissue and skeletal muscle in human obesity: Response to glucose and semistarvation. Metabolism **30:** 810–817.
23. Schwartz, R. S. & J. D. Brunzell. 1978. Increased adipose tissue lipoprotein lipase in moderately obese men after weight reduction. Lancet **1:** 1230–1231.
24. Lin, M. H., D. R. Romsos, T. Akera & G. A. Leveille. 1978. Na^+, K^+—ATPase enzyme units in skeletal muscle from lean and obese mice. Biochem. Biophys. Res. Commun. **80:** 398–404.
25. Lin, M. H., D. R. Romsos, T. Akera & G. A. Leveille. 1979. NA^+, K^+—ATPase enzyme units in skeletal muscle and liver of 14-day-old lean and obese (ob/ob) mice. Proc. Soc. Exp. Biol. Med. **161:** 235–238.
26. Lin, M. H., D. R. Romsos, T. Akera & G. A. Leveille. 1981. Functional correlates of Na^+, K^+—ATPase in lean and obese (ob/ob) mice. Metabolism **30:** 431–438.
27. DeLuise, M., G. L. Blackburn & J. S. Flier. 1980. Reduced activity of the red-cell sodium–potassium pump in human obesity. N. Engl. J. Med. **303:** 1017–1022.

28. BRAY, G. A., J. G. KRAL & P. BJORNTORP. 1981. Hepatic sodium potassium-dependent ATPase in obesity. N. Engl. J. Med. **304:** 1580–1585.
29. ROTHWELL, N. J., M. J. STOCK & M. G. WYLLIE. 1981. NA^+, K^+—ATPase activity and noradrenaline in brown adipose tissue of rats exhibiting diet-induced thermogenesis. Biochem. Pharmacol. **30:** 1709–1712.
30. BRAY, G. A., D. A. YORK & Y. YUKUMURA. 1978. Activity of (Na^+ + K^+)—ATPase in the liver of animals with experimental obesity. Life Sci. **22:** 1637–1642.
31. GALTON, D. J. & G. A. BRAY. 1967. Metabolism of alpha-glycerol phosphate in human adipose tissue in obesity. J. Clin. Endocrinol. Metab. **27:** 1573–1580.
32. BRAY, G. A. 1969. Effect of caloric restriction on energy expenditure in obese patients. Lancet **2:** 397–398.
33. JAMES, W. P. T. & P. TRAYHURN. 1976. An integrated view of the metabolic and genetic basis for obesity. Lancet **2:** 770–773.
34. NEWSHOLME, E. A. 1980. A possible metabolic basis for the control of body weight. N. Engl. J. Med. **302:** 400–405.
35. BRAY, G. A. 1983. The energetics of obesity. Med. Sci. Sports Exercise **15:** 32–40.
36. BENEDICT, F. G., W. R. MILES, P. ROTH & M. SMITH. Human Vitality and Efficiency under Prolonged Restricted Diet. Carnegie Institutes of Washington, Washington, D. C., Publication 280. (Quoted from Garrow, J. S. 1978. Energy Balance and Obesity in Man.: 89. Elsevier/North-Holland Biomedical Press. New York.)
37. DIGIROLAMO, M., U. SMITH & P. BJORNTORP. 1981. Refeeding effects on adipocyte metabolism. *In* Recent Advances in Obesity Research: III. P. Bjorntorp, M. Cairella & A. N. Howard, Eds. John Libbey. London.
38. BJORNTORP, P., M. CAIRELLA & A. N. HOWARD. 1981. Recent Advances in Obesity Research: III. John Libbey. London.
39. LANDSBERG, L. & J. B. YOUNG. 1981. The sympathetic nervous system and carbohydrate metabolism. *In* Recent Advances in Obesity Research: III. P. Bjorntorp, M. Cairella & A. N. Howard, Eds. John Libbey. London.
40. BENNETT, W. & J. GURIN, 1982. The Dieter's Dilemma. Basic Books. New York.
41. KATAHN, M. 1982. Follow-up maintenance plans of three commercial weight loss programs. Unpublished research, Vanderbilt University.
42. GARROW, J. S. 1978. Energy Balance and Obesity in Man. Elsevier/North Holland Biomedical Press. New York.
43. RODIN, J. 1980. Pathogenesis of obesity: Energy intake and expenditure. *In* Obesity in America. G. A. Bray, Ed. U.S. Department of Health, Education and Welfare. Washington, D.C.
44. VAN ITALLIE, T. B. 1979. Obesity: Adverse effects on health and longevity. Am. J. Clin. Nut. **32:** 2723–2733.
45. VAN ITALLIE, T. B. 1980. Conservative approaches to treatment. *In* Obesity in America. G. A. Bray, Ed. U.S. Department of Health, Education, and Welfare. Washington, D.C.
46. KATAHN, M., J. PLEASE, M. THACKREY & K. A. WALLSTON. 1982. Relationship of eating and activity self-reports to follow-up weight maintenance in the massively obese. Behav. Ther. **13:** 521–528.
47. HENSEL, H. & G. HILDEBRANDT. 1964. Organ systems in adaptation: The muscular system. *In* Handbook of Physiology. Section 4. D. B. Dill, Ed.: 73–90.

48. DESPRÉS, J. P., C. BOUCHARD, R. SAVARD, M. MARCOTTE & G. THERIAULT. 1983. Effect of a twenty-week endurance training program on adipose tissue morphology and lipolysis in men and women (abstract). Med. Sci. Sports Exercise **15:** 138.
49. ACHESON, K. J., J. P. FLATT & E. JEQUIRE. 1982. Glycogen synthesis versus lipogenisis after a 500 gram carbohydrate meal in man. Metabolism **31:** 1234–1240.
50. ACHESON, K. J., Y. SCHUTZ, T. BESSARD, K. ANANTHARAMAN, J. P. FLATT & E. JEQUIRE. 1988. Glycogen storage capacity and *de novo* lipogenisis during massive carbohydrate overfeeding in man. Am. J. Clin. Nutr. **48:** 240–247.
51. ACHESON, K. J., Y. SCHUTZ, T. BESSARD, E. RAVUSSIN & E. JEQUIRE. 1984. Nutritional influences on lipogenisis and thermogenisis after a carbohydrate meal. Am. J. Physiol. **246:** E62–70.
52. FLATT, J. P. 1987. Dietary fat, carbohydrate balance, and weight maintenance: Effects of exercise. Am. J. Clin. Nutr. **45:** 296–306.
53. FLATT, J. P., E. RAVUSSIN, K. J. ACHESON & E. JEQUIER. 1985. Effects of dietary fat on post-prandial substrate oxidation and on carbohydrate and fat balances. J. Clin. Invest. **76:** 1019–1024.
54. SCHUTZ, Y., J. P. FLATT & E. JEQUIER. 1989. Failure of dietary fat intake to promote fat oxidation: A factor favoring the development of obesity. Am. J. Clin. Nutr. **50:** 307–314.
55. KERN, P. A., J. M. ONG, B. SAFFARI & J. CARTY. 1990. The effects of weight loss on the activity and expression of adipose-tissue lipoprotein lipase in very obese humans. N. Engl. J. Med. **322:** 1053–1059.

Addiction as a Cultural Concept

STANTON PEELE[a]

Mathematica Policy Research, Inc.
Princeton, New Jersey 08543

Our current conception of addiction is a historical anomaly, one that has arisen independent of laboratory or epidemiological data about drug use. This concept has never reflected actual patterns of heroin use, and it currently does no better at describing cocaine use. Neither this vision of heroin addiction nor an equally popular, complimentary model of alcoholism accurately reflects data on the cause, epidemiology, life history, or consistency of addictive behavior. Nonetheless, versions of addictions based on these images of narcotic addiction and alcoholism have become increasingly popular in the second half of the twentieth century and have been generalized to whole new areas of behavior, where they succeed no better at explaining the data. These concepts, moreover, have considerable potential for doing harm.

INTRODUCTION

In 1929, two Philadelphia physicians—Arthur Light and Edward Torrance—attempted to identify physiological correlates of the withdrawal experienced by hospitalized addicts suddenly withdrawn from morphine.[1] The range and care of their measures, including detailed analysis of the blood, blood pressure, respiratory data, cardiovascular recovery rates, and urinalysis, has hardly been matched since. The research turned up no reliable biological index for withdrawal: The variability among the addicts on all the measures was too great.

Beyond these measures, the researchers reported the connection between actual administration of the drug and craving as described by the addicts was highly unreliable and subjective. The most recalcitrant subject refused to continue the experiment at 36 hours after withdrawal unless he was given more morphine, at which time the experimenters injected him with sterile water. This addict "promptly went to sleep for a period of eight hours" and "never became aware of the fact that he was given nothing but sterile water" (p. 12).[1] Noting their own failure to "find any marked changes" in circulation, metabolism, respiration, or blood composition, the researchers anticipated other investigators might criticize the research regimen in the experiment. They cautioned any such critics, who might have observed

[a] Address for correspondence: Stanton Peele, 27 West Lake Blvd., Morristown, NJ 07960.

addict behavior during withdrawal, that "the incessant begging and annoying behavior of the addict during the withdrawal period becomes at times almost unbearable," thereby "warping" the judgment of observers and leading them "to conclusions that would not have been reached except for the behavior of the addict" (p. 14).[1]

Light and Torrance did observe a withdrawal syndrome composed of restlessness, vomiting, diarrhea, perspiration, and enervation. However, they considered those reactions that supposedly defined narcotic withdrawal not to be particularly singular or noteworthy; for example, they reported observing a similar syndrome among "a university football team just prior to the playing of a so-called 'important game' . . . yet, when the whistle starting the game is blown, all fatigue quickly disappears" (pp. 14–15).[1] Observations such as these led subsequent observers to accuse Light and Torrance of naiveté about the biological reality of withdrawal, and of mistaking withdrawal for a form of malingering.

Light and Torrance's addicts were maintained on high levels of morphine, and yet their withdrawal could be overcome by admonition, forced labor, or H_2O injection. Unlike the high-dosage levels these 1920s addicts were accustomed to, addicts on the streets of major North American cities today often report to clinics with pronounced addictive symptoms but are not found to have any narcotics in their systems. This phenomenon has prompted the coining of phrases like "pseudo-junkie" and "pseudoheroinism" and speculation about "psychologic vs. pharmacologic heroin dependence."[2–4] In other words, a substantial number of patients who report potent addictive symptoms have taken little or no heroin, while regularly maintained narcotics users often express feeble or inconsistent withdrawal. Our reaction to these phenomena does not conform to the supposedly empirical basis of science: We deny the former is "real" and ignore the latter in order to maintain our existing preconceptions of addiction.

Since the 1929 Light and Torrance research, we have observed a hardening of ideas about the reality of addiction and its invariant relationship to narcotics use. Yet we are less able actually to account for observations either about clinical addicts, or about the millions of people who take considerable amounts of narcotics (in the hospital, for example) without becoming addicted. The formalization of the addiction concept and of notions of addictive symptoms does not represent a scientific advance, and instead is better understood as a cultural phenomenon that fulfills functional and symbolic needs. If we actually wished to create a scientifically well-defined concept of addiction, we would need to wean ourselves from our preoccupation with narcotics and several other illicit drugs and to think about why people form overwhelming attachments of all kinds.[5]

A HISTORY OF THE ADDICTION CONCEPT

Light and Torrance's research took place in a historical epoch when the addiction syndrome was newly formalized as a specific entity traceable to habitual narcotics use and cessation of use. Ten to 20 years earlier, Light and Torrance would not have been able to *find* hospitalized, long-term narcotics addicts who would manifest such ready indications of the addiction and withdrawal syndromes as their subjects presented. In other words, even the somewhat pale list of symptoms these addicts manifested—considered as a specific, chemically induced syndrome—was of recent historical origin. The narcotic addiction syndrome had not been widely identified in the public mind or by physicians in the nineteenth century or in any other previous era, *although narcotics had been known and used since antiquity.*

The German physician Levinstein was the first to describe narcotic addiction in detail, in 1877. Even so, at this early date Levinstein "still saw addiction as a human passion 'such as smoking, gambling, greediness for profit, sexual excesses, etc.' " (Berridge & Edwards,[6] pp. 142–143). Further, "from 1870 to 1900, most physicians regarded addiction as a morbid appetite, a habit, or a vice" (Isbell,[7] p. 115). At the same time, "acetanilide, bromide, and caffeine attracted almost comparable concern to that drawn by opium," and "the analogy so easily drawn with tobacco and particularly alcohol habituation" confused notions of narcotic addiction and "tangled efforts at control" (Sonnedecker,[8] p. 21). Earlier, although some theorists described narcotic addiction, "this does not mean [they] . . . held any concept distinguishing addiction to opium from addiction to, say, sugar plums . . . . In this period between the late 16th and the early 19th centuries . . . 'to addict' commonly meant 'to devote, give up, or apply habitually to a practice' such as to a vice . . . . [those using the term] meant: It's a bad habit" (Sonnedecker,[8] p. 18).

The modern form of the concept of addiction as an uncontrollable disease did not appear originally with narcotics, however, but with alcohol. Levine[9] has described "The Discovery of Addiction" in his article of that title: "The idea that alcoholism is a progressive disease—the chief symptom of which is loss of control over drinking behavior and whose only remedy is abstinence from all alcoholic beverages—is now about 175 or 200 years old, but no older" (p. 143). Previously, in colonial America and before, habitual drunkenness was considered a vice or moral failing or lack of self-control. Only very near the end of the eighteenth century was alcohol first recognized, even by drunkards themselves, as having the power to cause people to drink uncontrollably.

In the nineteenth century the temperance movement argued that alcohol *inevitably* provoked loss of control. That is, the nineteenth-century view of alcohol addiction is exactly that which in the twentieth century has been connected to narcotics: that the drug is inherently addictive so that regular use guarantees an enslavement of the individual that leads progressively to moral collapse and death. This idea of progressive, irreversible, inevitable exacerbation of the habit, causing loss of control of personal behavior and of the ability to make moral discriminations, actually retains strong elements of both colonial and temperance moralism. It is therefore not correct to say simply that modern disease notions have replaced outdated "moral" models of drug use. Rather, relabeling misbehavior as a medical consequence of drug use locates the source of evil in the drug and dictates that the addict's moral responsibility is to avoid the substance entirely—that is, to abstain.

Essential redefinitions of both alcohol and narcotic addiction occurred at the turn of the twentieth century. The term "alcoholic" was accepted as a popular designation for the chronic inebriate only in this century, after the founding of Alcoholics Anonymous. Before that time, "drunkard" was the standard designation and dipsomaniac was for a long time the preferred psychiatric term. After World War I, Dr. William Silkworth became the first to treat alcoholics based on the idea that they suffered from an inbred allergy to alcohol that caused them to lose control of their drinking. One of his patients, William Wilson, cofounded Alcoholics Anonymous in 1935. The Silkworth/Wilson model of alcoholism has continued to grow steadily, aided by an effective campaign led by Marty Mann and the National Committee for Education on Alcoholism (later to become the National Council on Alcoholism) she helped organize in 1944.[10]

This modern version of the disease theory of alcoholism thus conceived of alcoholism as a danger for only a small group of afflicted, biologically predestined individuals. Only *this* group had to abstain, or else they would progress to the same self-destruction that the temperance movement had outlined for all drinkers. Such a revised disease theory was required (after Prohibition was repealed in 1933) to fit a world in which drinking was ubiquitous, popular, and largely benign. Today, the AA-modified disease model represents the dominant American conception of alcoholism, and public opinion polls indicate that about 90% of Americans accept the view that alcoholism is an illness that must be treated medically.

Changes in views of drug addiction were in almost an exactly opposite direction. In the case of narcotics and (and, along with it, cocaine), the entire thrust was to redefine previously accepted substances as dangerous and to proscribe their use for ordinary, law-abiding citizens. The campaign against narcotics under the leadership of Harry Anslinger (founder of the Federal Bureau of Narcotics) began by imposing increasingly stern legislation on labeling, importation, and administration of the opiates. Heroin was introduced in the United States in 1898; by the 1920s it had become the principal object of addiction control efforts, while its use had been relegated to a small group of inner-city addicts. What is most important about these political, economic, medical, and public-relations developments is that narcotics, especially in the form of heroin, came to be seen in American society as the nonpareil drug of addiction—as leading inescapably from even the most casual contact to an intractable dependence, the withdrawal from which was traumatic and unthinkable for the addict.

That addiction and alcoholism had to be discovered seems bizarre and unnecessary to us, owing to the thoroughness of our indoctrination in the idea that these things are biological entities that have been independently established through clear scientific discovery and practical experience. How, then, have they been missed by so many of the world's cultures for so many centuries? After all, both alcohol and narcotics have been used widely throughout history. Yet only relatively recently, and then primarily in a few Western societies, did addiction and alcoholism come to be perceived as biological phenomena, a part of the natural landscape. How have so many societies and individuals misunderstood, ignored, or failed to perceive such obvious consequences of alcohol and narcotic consumption?

This issue so fundamentally undermines the basis of what we assume today to be objective reality that addictionologists regularly seek to explain away data such as American and British opiate use in the nineteenth century. For in the last century, opiate and other drug use in the United States and Britain was massive and indiscriminate and yet, only near the very end of this era—paradoxically when both societies had substantially reduced their use of opiates—was addictive symptomatology first recognized as a specific byproduct of narcotics use and the addiction concept invented.

Historical works generally maintain that widespread narcotics use failed to create an awareness of addictive symptomatology in nineteenth-century societies because ignorance prevented people from drawing the appropriate connections between usage and addiction symptoms such as withdrawal. These explanations manage to be at the same time tautologous (addiction was not recognized because it was unrecognized) and preposterous (people far more familiar than we are with self-administration of narcotics were not as aware as we are of their inevitable effects). For example, Lindesmith[11] argued addiction was not common in the last century because addiction can only occur when the narcotics user understands that narcotics produce withdrawal effects and that renewed use relieves withdrawal distress. In other words, for Lindesmith, the genuine addict could exist only in an era that has an understanding of addiction identical to that which currently dominates our society!

Berridge (a historian) and Edwards (a psychiatrist) examined the social and medical history of the addiction concept as it developed in England. These authors described the massive use of opiates by working-class Britons through the middle of the nineteenth century: In one region (the Fens), per capita consumption was the equivalent of 137 therapeutic doses of opiates per annum. The commonplace use of narcotics did not arouse special public concern about addiction, and only late in the century did medical authorities label and treat addiction as a specific medical syndrome in connection with the popularity of injectable morphine among the middle classes. Even at this point, however, the medical image of the specificity and frequency of the narcotic addiction syndrome seems to have been tremendously overstated:

> There is little evidence that there were large numbers of morphine addicts in the late nineteenth century . . . . The quite small number . . . who happened to be obvious to the medical profession assumed the dimensions of a pressing problem—at a time when, as general consumption and mortality data indicate, usage and addiction to opium in general was [*sic*] tending to decline, not increase. Morphine use and the problem, as medically defined, of hypodermic

self-administration were closely connected with the medical elaboration of a disease view of addiction (pp. 147–150).[6]

This description actually allows for two separate interpretations (both of which these authors make). Either there was a great deal of addiction in the mid-nineteenth century when opiate consumption was greater, but physicians only began to recognize addiction as it actually was on the wane; or else addiction actually did increase at the end of the century, even though consumption was declining, because "the profession, by its enthusiastic advocacy of a new and more 'scientific' remedy and method, had itself contributed to an increase in addiction" (p. 149). In the latter case, the very medical imagery of addiction contributed to compulsive drug use.

Berridge and Edwards' potentially radical, revisionist work suggests "Addiction is now defined as an illness because doctors have categorized it thus" (p. 150). At exactly this point, the reader is referred to an appendix in which Edwards announces: "The opiates are drugs of addiction . . . anyone who takes an opiate for a long enough period and in sufficient dose will become addicted" (p. 278). Edwards is so confident of this assertion that he does not feel an obligation to reference it. What then are we to make of his own historical analysis with Berridge indicating that addiction has only recently been invented by the medical profession—and that this invention has had counterproductive effects? Apparently, despite their own data, these authors (particularly Edwards) are absolutely incapable of reconceptualizing addiction as something other than an inevitable physiological consequence of continued narcotics use.

The cross-cultural literature on drinking styles and the effects of alcohol presents a similar dilemma. In the words of several prominent ethnographers in the alcoholism field: "Drinking problems are virtually unknown in most of the world's cultures" (Heath,[12] p. 436), and "solitary, addictive, pathological drinking behavior does not occur to any significant extent in small-scale, traditional, preindustrial societies" (Marshall,[13] p. 451). Finally, "beverage alcohol usually is not a problem in a society unless . . . it is defined as such" (Marshall,[13] p. 452). Heath[14] investigated the Bolivian Camba—a group with among the highest recorded rates of alcohol consumption in the world. People in this culture drink an 89% ethanol beverage. They only drink at social gatherings, held several times a month, in which all those present over 12 years old drink throughout the day and night. Although these drinkers typically blacked out, Heath observed no cases of antisocial aggression, alcohol withdrawal, or solitary or loss-of-control drinking. One such contradictory instance as this is sufficient to disprove any biologically determined formula about the natural relationship between heavy drinking and alcoholism.

WHAT IS THE EMPIRICAL GROUNDING FOR OUR BELIEFS ABOUT ADDICTION?

Although historical and cross-cultural cases reveal that addiction is neither a universal concept nor a universal phenomenon, it is commonly held that a host of solid scientific evidence underlies our beliefs about the special addictiveness of narcotics. This supposed scientific validation allows us to claim most of the world's population has been wrong about narcotics and alcohol, and instead ought to think like we do now about addiction. Because the United States is the world's leading exporter of scientific ideas, a realignment of attitudes about alcoholism and addiction is occurring today in many countries worldwide.

Let us outline briefly what type of evidence would either support or disprove the idea that narcotics are drugs of addiction. If narcotics are addictive, people who take them should be inclined to take them more frequently, compulsively, and unvaryingly than do users of other, nonaddictive drugs, or to have fewer degrees of freedom than people reveal in ordinary (that is, nonaddicted) habitual behavior. It is perhaps not surprising that research testing these notions has rarely been carried out; after all, we *know* that narcotics are addictive. Thousands of people have reported for treatment for such addiction over the decades since the 1920s; laboratory animals can be made to welcome injections of narcotics; and so on.

On the other hand, evidence and unbiased observation regularly find that street narcotics use, even regular use, does *not* lead to addiction. This evidence is too extensive to review here, beyond a quote from one typical, recent study of black heroin users in four American cities: "The heroin users and the lifestyles presented reveal men who, despite regular heroin use, engage in many conventional activities and are able to control their heroin use, taking on the average only one shot of heroin a day. This lifestyle challenges the current media and popular image of . . . inner-city heroin users as . . . [being] enslaved by an uncontrollably escalating heroin habit" (from the book jacket of Hanson *et al.*[15]). This statement is wrong, however, in limiting mistaken images to the media and popular opinion. These images are accepted and propagated by leading scientific researchers, including those whose results most thoroughly disprove the notions of addiction they defend.

One event and the research that accompanied it not only presents conclusive evidence that popular *and* scientific images of addiction are wrong, but also indicates how mistaken images remain unshaken despite thoroughgoing assaults on their fundamental assumptions. The research in question is that conducted by Robins, Helzer, and others of the use of narcotics by G.I.s who returned from Vietnam. Narcotics users were identified and interviewed on their return home and three years afterwards; the researchers in addition analyzed urine samples from subjects. The most significant aspect of this research was that it identified addicted heroin users in a nonclinical setting. The results of the study, in the words of the investigators, "changed our view of heroin."[16] The questions they posed in their research and the answers they obtained are as follows:

1. Does the use of heroin rapidly progress to regular use and addiction?

> Use of heroin purchased on the streets of the United States in 1974 did not lead rapidly to daily or compulsive use, no more so than did use of amphetamines or marijuana.

2. Does heroin use supplant the use of other drugs?

> Heroin does *not* seem to supplant the use of other drugs . . . . The stereotype of the heroin addict as someone with a monomaniacal craving for a single drug seems hardly to exist in this sample. Heroin addicts use many other drugs, and not only casually or in desperation.

3. Is addiction to heroin more or less permanent without prolonged treatment?

> Of all the men addicted in Vietnam [defined as prolonged heavy use and severe withdrawal symptoms lasting more than two days], only 12% have relapsed to addiction at any time since their return . . . . Of those men who were addicted in the first year back, half were treated and half were not . . . . Of those treated, 47 percent were addicted in the second period; of those not treated, 17 percent were addicted . . . . Treatment is certainly not always necessary for remission.

4. Does recovery from addiction require abstinence?

> Perhaps an even more surprising finding than the high proportion of men who recovered from addiction after Vietnam was the number who went back to heroin without becoming readdicted . . . . Half of the men who had been addicted in Vietnam used heroin on their return home, but only one-eighth became readdicted to heroin. Even when heroin was used frequently . . . , only one-half . . . became readdicted (pp. 217–223).

The findings that heroin use no more often led to addiction (or regular or compulsive use) than did amphetamines or marijuana; that those addicted to heroin often used other drugs, sometimes in preference to heroin; that spontaneous recovery was more common than not; and that many of those who gave up their addictions after returning home did not relapse to addiction when they used heroin stateside attack the foundations of the claim that the opiates are, in Edwards' words above, special "drugs of addiction." What may be more remarkable than the findings themselves, however, is the total lack of impact they have had on addiction research and theory. Few researchers today would be inclined to challenge the claims Edwards makes which, after all, appeared after the Vietnam data were published.

Indeed, even the investigators who revealed the startling findings about Vietnam veterans could not accept the implications of their own research. In their report of their results, these authors remarked that "Heroin is 'worse' than amphetamines or barbiturates only because 'worse' people use it" (p. 229). Nonetheless, the investigators, who titled their work "Vietnam Veterans Three Years After Vietnam: How Our Study Changed Our View of Heroin," indicated amazement that heroin users acted in no more addicted a way than users of other drugs even though "laboratory experiments have shown it to be a highly addicting drug" (p. 216). Typically, this last statement was unreferenced.

Actually, according to Charles Schuster[17] (currently director of the National Institute on Drug Abuse and a leading animal researcher), "compulsive drug-seeking behavior is often attributed to the seductive reinforcing effects of certain insidious drug molecules." Instead, his research indicates, "behavioral variables are as important as pharmacologic ones in the development of compulsive drug-seeking behavior" (p. 358). Another behavioral psychopharmacologist concluded after several decades of animal research, "any intrinsic, pharmacological reinforcing functions [of drugs] are altered radically by seemingly small changes in behavioral context"[18] (p. 389).

These conclusions are based on studies finding that animal drug self-administration requires a specific experimental environment and can be "turned off" by such minor modifications as increasing the amount of bar pressing required to obtain the drug. In other circumstances, animals can hardly be forced to take a drug. Alexander and his colleagues[19] noted that animals in spacious cages they shared with other rats overwhelmingly preferred drinking water to a narcotic solution, even after having drunk the solution exclusively for several weeks. Falk[18] similarly noted animals that consume drugs and alcohol excessively when under extremely uncomfortable experimental inductions cease to do so as soon as normal laboratory conditions are reinstated. Findings like these led Dole[20] (1980) to note: "Most animals cannot be made into addicts." In response to drugs reported regularly to addict human beings, "animals generally avoid such drugs when they are given a choice" (p. 142).

Robins *et al.*'s faith that, while their own research contradicts such a notion, other research demonstrates the genuine nature of heroin addiction presents a kind of "Catch 22" in addictionology. No amount of data disproving the most basic assumptions of the current model is sufficient to undermine this model, since the model is already beyond questioning. In a related analysis, Peele[21] analyzed shifting, sometime radically divergent findings about the likelihood of former alcoholics or other addicts moderating their consumption. Sometimes the same groups present diametrically opposed results. For example, we saw above that Robins, Helzer *et al.*[16] found that the large majority of returned Vietnam narcotic addicts who used heroin in the States did not relapse into readdiction. Five years later, the same group reported that 1.6% of alcoholic patients achieved genuine moderate drinking, leading to the conclusion that "The evolution to stable moderate drinking appears to be a rare outcome among alcoholics"[22] (p. 1678).

What accounts for these remarkably disparate images of the possibility of attenuating addictive substance use? One might posit that narcotics addiction is the easier habit to moderate, although this is certainly not a popular point of view or one that researchers such as Robins and her colleagues would be likely to endorse. Alternately, perhaps the earlier narcotics research was severely flawed, while the later alcoholism research was not; indeed, the Helzer *et al.*[22] team (while not discussing their own earlier strongly contradictory findings with narcotic addiction) discounted the discovery of substantial controlled-drinking outcomes by other investigators on these grounds. An alternate explanation offered by Peele[21] is that the explanatory culture changed: that growing medicalization of alcoholism treatment, rapid growth in the acceptance of the disease view of alcoholism, and other background and professional factors in the lives of researchers and the scientific (as well as popular) culture accounted for changes in reported findings.

THE CULTURAL CONCEPT OF ADDICTION

Room[23] attempted to explain the "culture-bound" appearance of addiction "as depending for its existence and meaningfulness on sociocultural characteristics specific to particular times and places" (p. 133). Room's concern was especially with "loss-of-control" models, which Levine's[9] analysis—in the case of American attitudes towards alcohol and habitual drunkenness—showed clearly to be a cultural invention. For Room, such an idea of loss of control is the mirror image of the Calvinistic notion of control, thereby explaining its appearance most prominently in advanced industrial societies. Room expresses here, in common with many clinicians and liberal commentators, a neutrality, if not negativity, toward self-conscious Western ideas of self-control.

Nonetheless, the occurrence of addiction is not clearly linked to Protestantism or to the achievement ethos. Within the United States and worldwide, for example, alcoholism is prominent among the Irish Catholic and non-Protestant Eastern European groups.[24] Moreover, as Room[23] noted, Native American cultures do *not* share the Calvinistic value of constant self-control, and yet they display the most severe alcoholism problems in the United States. Jews and Chinese Americans, on the other hand, consistently display the fewest alcohol problems among American ethnic groups, including very few observed cases of clinical alcoholism. Yet, the Jews and Chinese Americans are distinguished by their high levels of achievement motivation, values toward self-control, and community disapproval of antisocial acting out.[25]

MacAndrew and Edgerton's[26] analysis, *Drunken Comportment,* described how various cultures create a social compact about exactly what behavior—or misbehavior—will be tolerated on drinking occasions, even those involving drunken excess. Remarkably, nearly all drunken behavior occurs within these cultural guidelines. For example, the researchers described cultures that practice drunken sexual orgies in which incest taboos are observed by culture members who are apparently uncontrollably intoxicated. These taboos apply to intricate familial relationships that observers outside the culture are unable even to comprehend.

The question of whether certain involvements thought to be addictive excuse certain types of behavior is central to current legal, political, economic, and therapeutic debates. The rapidly expanding reliance on loss-of-control models of addiction has generalized images originally proposed for disease views of alcoholism and heroin use to wholly new areas of behavior. The expanded application of these addictive models has profound implications for psychological experience, personal responsibility, and addictive phenomenology in our society.[27]

MORALISM, POLITICS, ECONOMICS AND THE ADDICTION CONCEPT

While addiction models such as the disease theory of alcoholism purport to be value free, they actually convey distinct values about human responsibility and about the desirability of certain kinds of behavior. For example, the application of addiction and dependence models to different drugs has always projected the dominant moral views of our society (see, for example, the drug tables popular in the 1960s that labeled all disapproved drugs—but no legal drugs other than alcohol—capable of producing psychic or physical dependence; Peele,[5] p. 22). In the case of drugs in the United States, the moral message is of the evil and allure of the illicit drug experience, and of the need totally to avoid such experience.

The moral lesson that drugs control and corrupt users was graphically depicted in the classic drug film, "Reefer Madness." This lesson is regularly repeated with whichever new drugs become popular for recreational use. Often, this message is presented in the guise of scientific discovery. For example, in the NIDA publication, *Cocaine Use in America,* Cohen[28] wrote:

> Cocaine-dependent humans prefer it to all other activities. They will continue using it until they are exhausted or the cocaine is depleted. They will exhibit behaviors markedly different from their precocaine lifestyle. Cocaine-driven humans will relegate all other drives and pleasures to a minor role in their lives. [p. 152]

This quote supports the imagery of "Reefer Madness" and "Demon Rum" with claims to have scientifically linked certain kinds of uncontrolled, immoral behavior to a specific chemical structure:

> If we were to design deliberately a chemical that would lock people into perpetual usage, it would probably resemble the neuropsychological properties of cocaine . . . . It is likely that anyone with access to cocaine in quantity is at risk . . . . The primary deterrent [to cocaine dependence] is the inability to sustain the practice because supplies become unavailable. The user is then driven to obtain additional cocaine without particular regard for social constraints. A variety of paranoid, manic and depressive psychotic states result with accidental, homicidal or suicidal potentials. [pp. 151–153]

Despite decades of experience with this drug, including much laboratory experimentation and growing recreational use in the 1970s, cocaine was designated as a nonaddictive (or non-physical-dependence-producing) agent well into the 1970s. As cocaine became a major recreational drug in the 1980s, pharmacologists began claiming cocaine produced a condition indistinguishable from addiction because of cocaine's extreme "psychological addictiveness" (cf. Peele[5]). It is evident now from Cohen's quote above that the line separating cocaine from "genuine" addictiveness has now been discovered to have been exceeded. What epidemiological data have prompted the discovery of cocaine's inherent addictiveness?

Preliminary results from the 1988 NIDA National Household Survey of Drug Abuse indicate very few cocaine users become addicted. The survey found that 21 million Americans had used cocaine in their lives, 8 million had used it in the last year, 3 million were current users, but that only 300,000 used cocaine daily or nearly every day. Government statistics thus show that 10% of all current users and about 1% of lifetime users use the drug close to daily. Siegel[29] followed a group of regular cocaine users for nine years. Of this group, four-fifths remained social, situational, or recreational users. Moreover, even those in this study who abused the drug did so intermittently and thus did not resemble the addicted cocaine hotline callers who typify cocaine use for numerous television programs about cocaine. These findings agree with the results of other field studies of cocaine use.[30]

As for crack, a front-page story on crack addiction in the *New York Times*[31] trumpeted the headline, "Importance of User's Environment is Stressed Over the Drug's Attributes." The first paragraph of the article stated[6]: "Drug experts now believe that the extreme difficulties they face in treating crack addiction stem far more from the setting and circumstances of the users than the biochemical reaction the drug produces." The *Times* article reported that addicts in surveys conducted in the United States, Britain, and Canada reported they found it easier to quit cocaine—"either injected, sniffed or smoked"—than alcohol, heroin, or cigarettes. By the other key measure of addiction in addition to difficulty in ceasing use, that is, the frequency with which use leads to compulsive use, cocaine also seems considerably less addictive than some other familiar substances. The *Times* cited figures from NIDA researchers indicating that five times as many cigarette smokers become addicted as crack users. In all of these data, we see that a new drug presented as the penultimate addictive substance falls into place as being no more or less addictive than other popular illicit and recreational drugs and that, moreover, situational and social factors remain crucial in determining the drug's addictive usage patterns.

Nonetheless, it appears to be obligatory to begin not only popular but scientific discussions of cocaine use with lurid descriptions of the addictive nature of the drug and of clinical or historical accounts of hopelessly self-destructive drug users. Perhaps most scientists fear that to do otherwise might encourage cocaine experimentation, including that small minority for whom such use becomes compulsive and self-destructive. The rewards and punishments are so fundamentally opposed to any announcements of controlled use of illicit substances that they are guaranteed not to appear, thus confirming the worst expectations about any drug that society and its scientists focus their attention on. The controlled-drinking dispute in the United States is another example of this trend; no one can afford to endorse the possibility of controlled drinking by alcoholics, and, indeed, not even those who discover it accept controlled drinking as a possible therapy outcome.

Pokorny, Miller, and Cleveland,[32] for example, examined outcomes among a group of alcoholics treated in a hospital alcoholism program. The study revealed 23% of patients were drinking in a mild, social way, and 25% were abstinent one year after discharge from the hospital; in this study, abstinence was the *less* stable pattern, with abstinence decreasing over time while moderate drinking *increased* over the course of the study. This occurred although the study reported hospital treatment insisted that "life-long abstinence is a necessity in the rehabilitation of alcoholics." Results for a highly unstable group of alcoholics who varied between abstinence and excessive drinking were so poor that the investigators concluded hospital treatment was hardly worthwhile for them. The chief investigator wrote me about this study:

> We did not have controlled drinking as a goal, and this was nowhere advocated or taught to patients, even any subgroup of patients. We simply reported the findings at follow-up, which included a substantial group of patients who were not totally abstinent but whose behavior could fairly be classed as improved, perhaps even "controlled" . . . . My personal views were then and have remained that abstinence is the only reasonable goal for clearcut alcoholics, but I try to keep an open mind on the subject. [A.D. Pokorny, personal communication, July 16, 1987]

This study and its principal author's response raise the question, "Why bother to conduct research?" Clearly, we are dealing in the case of addiction with areas in which scientific investigators do not simply ask questions, get answers, and apply results.

The model of addiction as a distinct malady requiring treatment that substantially enhances prognosis has a strong economic basis. Miller and Hester[33] noted in reference to comparisons between inpatient and outpatient care for alcoholism: "Every study has reported either no statistically significant differences between treatment settings or differences favoring less intensive settings" (p. 802). Nonetheless, hospital treatment for alcohol and drug dependence has increased several-fold during the 1980s; it has also become increasingly coercive and most patients are now forced into treatment by the courts and businesses.[27] The principal advantages to expensive, inpatient care seem to be financial ones for providers and a sense of neat categorization and hoped-for benefits for society at large.

Berridge and Edwards[6] explain that "images of addiction are in fact consistently and relentlessly marketed—in the nineteenth century to make opium the property of the medical profession . . . . The nineteenth-century discovery that the addict is a suitable case for treatment is today an entrenched and unquestionable premise, with society unaware of the arbitrariness of this come-lately assumption . . . . [However] any suggestion that the current model is fundamentally mistaken in its assumption [*sic*], that the treatment enterprise should be closed down and people with bad habits left to their own devices, would be dismissed only as outrageous and bizarre" (pp. 250–251). Edwards may have been jaundiced by his own research experience, in which a well-controlled study of hospital treatment for alcoholism revealed just as much improvement among one group given a single session of advice as occurred in a comparable group receiving the full complement of inpatient and outpatient hospital services.[34]

The extent of the solidifying and broadening of the addiction concept goes beyond deciding that cocaine was previously wrongly thought to produce "psychic dependence" and is actually capable of producing "physical dependence," that alcoholism is a treatable disease so that those with a drinking problem who deny they require alcoholism treatment ought to be threatened with jail or loss of job, or, alternately, that those who commit crimes and who also drink heavily should be offered treatment in place of jail sentences. Entirely new areas have been opened to disease imagery, understanding, and treatment. Children and other relatives of alcoholics who do not themselves have drinking problems are now treated as though they have a disease, as are those who compulsively gamble, shop, overeat, fornicate, or participate in abusive relationships. Any and all of these compulsions and others (like PMS), reconceived according to the model of misbehavior as uncontrollable addiction, dominate contemporary psychological thought.[27]

Actually, the tail is now wagging the dog. We are not so much misconceiving addiction as we are living in a culture increasingly controlled by a new notion of individual responsibility based on the addictive model. To argue today that people—even those who drink a good deal or take drugs or have premenstrual mood swings—ought to be held liable for their conduct, particularly when they harm others, is to wage an increasingly uphill battle. The person who says people who drink too much or who misbehave when they drink are the primary agents of their actions and should be held accountable for them is actually the one least likely to become alcoholic.[25] Nonetheless, one who declares such a view today is considered ignorant of modern scientific advances in the field of alcoholism and addiction.

The scientific data are a far cry from providing support for this view. Actually, the modern, so-called "scientific" disease model of alcoholism comprises a mass of prejudices and misinformation. It is certainly not the "value-free" view its supporters contend it to be, at the same time that alternative views are either accused of amorality (because they maintain that people often take drugs or drink without losing control of their lives) or moralism (because they insist that alcoholics are, like everyone else, purposive actors, even while they are drinking). In fact, the modern, broadened concept of addiction represents a new moral vision, one that unfortunately will not reduce addictive behavior. It cannot treat away addiction, while it *does* encourage more misbehavior under the guise of addictive symptoms.[27]

Issues of drug use and other excessive behavior have *always* been morally tinged, just as models about these things have *from the beginning* of scientific theorizing about them been heavily influenced by politics and social conceptions. Now, as much as or more than ever, the science of addictionology has become a political, economic, and religious tool. We feel confident that we long ago left behind the era where Galileo could be persecuted for maintaining empirically based but unpopular conceptions of the universe. Yet, we have progressed in some ways remarkably little from Galileo's time in the sense that what is declared scientifically "true" depends primarily on popular opinion. Nowhere is this more evident than in the case of addiction, an area that touches our deepest fears about our ability to manage our selves, our children, and our society.

REFERENCES

1. LIGHT, A. B. & E. G. TORRANCE. 1929. Opiate addiction. VI: The effects of abrupt withdrawal followed by readministration of morphine in human addicts, with special reference to the composition of the blood, the circulation and the metabolism. Arch. Intern. Med. **44:** 1–16.
2. GAY, G. R., E. C. SENAY & J. A. NEWMEYER. 1973. The pseudo-junkie: Evolution of the heroin lifestyle in the nonaddicted individual. Drug Forum **2:** 279–290.
3. GLASER, F. B. 1974. Psychologic vs. pharmacologic heroin dependence. N. Engl. J. Med. **290:** 231.
4. PRIMM, P. J. 1977. Pseudoheroinism. *In* Drug Abuse: Clinical and Basic Aspects. S. N. Pradham & S. N. Dutta, Eds.: 313–318. Mosby. St. Louis, MO.
5. PEELE, S. 1985. The Meaning of Addiction: Compulsive Experience and Its Interpretation. Lexington. Lexington, MA.
6. BERRIDGE, V. & G. EDWARDS. 1987. Opium and the People: Opiate Use in Nineteenth-Century England. Yale University. New Haven, CT.
7. ISBELL, H. 1958. Clinical research on addiction in the United States. *In* Narcotic Drug Addiction Problems. R. B. Livingston, Ed.: 114–130. Public Health Service. Bethesda, MD.
8. SONNEDECKER, G. 1958. Emergence and concept of the addiction problem. *In* Narcotic Drug Addiction Problems, R. B. Livingston, Ed.: 14–22. Public Health Service. Bethesda, MD.
9. LEVINE, H. G. 1978. The discovery of addiction: Changing conceptions of habitual drunkenness in America. J. Stud. Alcohol **39:** 143–174.
10. PEELE, S. 1988. Can we treat away our alcohol and drug problems or is the current treatment binge doing more harm than good? J. Psychoactive Drugs **20:** 375–383.
11. LINDESMITH, A. R. 1968. Addiction and Opiates. Aldine. Chicago.
12. HEATH, D. B. 1982. Sociocultural variants in alcoholism. *In* Encyclopedic Handbook of Alcoholism. E. M. Pattison & E. Kaufman, Eds.: 426–440. Gardner Press. New York.
13. MARSHALL, M. 1979. Conclusions. *In* Beliefs, Behaviors, and Alcoholic Beverages: A Cross-Cultural Survey. M. Marshall Ed.: 451–457. University of Michigan. Ann Arbor, MI.
14. HEATH, D. B. 1958. Drinking patterns of the Bolivian Camba. J. Stud. Alcohol **19:** 491–508.
15. HANSON, B., G. BESCHNER, J. M. WALTERS & E. BOVELLE. 1985. Life with Heroin: Voices from the Inner City. Lexington. Lexington, MA.
16. ROBINS, L. N., J. E. HELZER, M. HESSELBROCK & E. WISH. 1980. Vietnam veterans three years after Vietnam: How our study changed our view of heroin. *In* The Yearbook of Substance Use and Abuse. L. Brill & C. Winick, Eds. Vol. **2:** 213–230. Human Sciences Press. New York.

17. SCHUSTER, C. R. 1986. Implications of laboratory research for the treatment of drug dependence. *In* Behavioral Analysis of Drug Dependence. S. R. Goldberg & I. P. Stolerman, Eds.: 357–385. Academic Press. New York.
18. FALK, J. L. 1983. Drug dependence: Myth or motive? Pharmacol. Biochem. Behav. **19:** 385–391.
19. ALEXANDER, B. K., S. PEELE, P. F. HADAWAY, S. J. MORSE, A. BRODSKY & B. L. BEYERSTEIN. 1985. Adult, infant, and animal addiction. *In* The Meaning of Addiction. S. Peele, Ed.: 73–96. Lexington. Lexington, MA.
20. DOLE, V. P. 1980. Addictive behavior. Sci. Am. **June:** 138–154.
21. PEELE, S. 1987. Why do controlled-drinking outcomes vary by country, by investigator and by era?: Cultural conceptions of relapse and remission in alcoholism. Drug Alcohol Dep. **20:** 173–201.
22. HELZER, J. E., L. N. ROBINS, J. R. TAYLOR, K. CAREY, R. H. MILLER, T. COMBS-ORME & A. FARMER. 1985. The extent of long-term moderate drinking among alcoholics discharged from medical and psychiatric treatment facilities. N. Engl. J. Med. **312:** 1678–1682.
23. ROOM, R. 1985. Dependence and society. Br. J. Addict. **80:** 133-139.
24. GREELEY, A. M., W. C. MCCREADY & G. THEISEN. 1980. Ethnic Drinking Subcultures. Praeger. New York.
25. PEELE, S. 1987. A moral vision of addiction: How people's values determine whether they become and remain addicts. *In* Visions of Addiction: Major Contemporary Perspectives on Alcoholism and Addiction. S. Peele, Ed.: 201–233. Lexington. Lexington, MA.
26. MACANDREW, C. & R. B. EDGERTON. 1969. Drunken Comportment: A Social Explanation. Aldine. Chicago.
27. PEELE, S. 1989. Diseasing of America: Addiction Treatment Out of Control. Lexington. Lexington, MA.
28. COHEN, S. 1985. Reinforcement and rapid delivery systems: Understanding adverse consequences of cocaine. *In* Cocaine Use in America: Epidemiological and Clinical Perspectives. DHHS Publication No. ADM 85-1414. N. J. Kozel & E. H. Adams, Eds.: 151–157. U.S. Government Printing Office. Washington, DC.
29. SIEGEL, R. K. 1984. Changing patterns of cocaine use: Longitudinal observations, consequences, and treatment. *In* Cocaine: Pharmacology, Effects, and Treatment of Abuse. DHHS Publication No. ADM 84-1326. J. Grabowski, Ed.: 92–110. U.S. Government Printing Office. Washington, DC.
30. ERICKSON, P. G., E. M. ADLAF, G. F. MURRAY & R. G. SMART. 1987. The Steel Drug: Cocaine in Perspective. Lexington. Lexington, MA.
31. KOLATA, G. 1989. Experts finding new hope on treating crack addicts. N. Y. Times. **August 24:** A1, B7.
32. POKORNY, A. D., B. A. MILLER & S. E. CLEVELAND. 1968. Response to treatment of alcoholism: A follow-up study. J. Stud. Alcohol **29:** 364–381.
33. MILLER, W. R. & R. K. HESTER. 1986. Inpatient alcoholism treatment: Who benefits? Am. Psychol. **41:** 794–805.
34. ORFORD, J. & G. EDWARDS. 1977. Alcoholism. Oxford University Press. New York.

The Use of Biofeedback in the Treatment of Disorders of Childhood

ELLIS BAROWSKY

Department of Special Education
Hunter College
City University of New York
New York, New York 10021

The behavioral techniques for the management and treatment of disorders of childhood are not new to the literature. Guided imagery,[1] hypnotic suggestions,[2] and behavioral relaxation training[3] have all proven effective in treatment of the symptoms of psychosomatic illness as well as with acute and chronically ill children. Biofeedback techniques, however, which have been proven successful in adult populations, are conspicuously absent from the pediatric literature. A recent Medline literature search sites 1565 biofeedback studies. Of these only 174 or 11% refer to the use of biofeedback with children. Greater scrutiny of these citations indicate that 130 pertain to the specific application of biofeedback principles in specific childhood disorders while the remaining 44 studies make only brief reference to the possible applications of biofeedback to children.

TABLE 1 identifies the relative frequencies in which biofeedback has been applied to the management of disorders in children. In reviewing the incidence of biofeedback application, we notice the lack of its use in anxiety reduction and relaxation training per se. This indication may be a barometer of how acceptable biofeedback has been to the practicing clinician.

The use of biofeedback as a relatively noninvasive behavioral technique has gained attention in the acquisition of adaptive skills with the developmentally disabled. While once regarded as an experimental technique, its application to rehabilitation has been acknowledged in more recent years for use with persons whose motor skills and sensory feedback channels have become impaired as a result of central nervous system (CNS) insult. This is particularly true when "deficient motor control may be secondary to inadequate proprioceptive input or to adequate inhibition of muscular contraction" (p. 546).[4]

The reluctance to use biofeedback may be attributed to (1) the argument that it is often not the treatment of choice,[5] (2) parents are resistant or often refuse consent, and (3) young children often require intrinsic reinforcement to cooperate and therefore the application of biofeedback becomes a more

TABLE 1. Biofeedback with Disorders Found in Children

Dysfunction	Number of Studies	Percent of Total
Bowel/Bladder	40	31
Learning disability (hyperactivity)	25 (17)	19.2 (13.6)
Pain syndrome	18	13.8
Orofacial	14	10.8
Postural	13	10.0
Chronic illness	8	6.1
Visuomotor	3	2.3
Other	11	8.5

NOTE: Biofeedback intervention with children has been reported infrequently in the professional literature. The relative frequency with which it has been applied to different disorders of childhood is indicated.

complex procedure than with adults. Miller[6] has indicated that biofeedback is useful when certain conditions are met. These conditions include: (1) the medically desirable direction of change is clear, (2) a learnable response that can produce change is available, (3) the desired learning has been impeded by poor or inaccurate perception, (4) instrumentation can be used for better feedback, and (5) no motivation for maintaining the medically undesirable condition exists. Under these conditions, the approach to modify a behavior or link in a chain of behaviors can better be defined. The first need is to identify the disorder and the components of the behavioral change that are targeted for modification (TABLE 2). Underlying the behavior is a psychophysiological system that maintains the symptoms of the disorder. Upon the basis of the physiological symptom, the biofeedback procedure is chosen. Four common responses underlie most symptoms and are related to the patient's psychological response.

RESPONSES MEASURED

The use of the electroencephalograph (EEG) measures the changing electrical potential of the neural cells. The change in neural activity or potential reflected in the EEG signal is an average of many cells with specific patterns indicating levels of arousal. EEG recordings have been used by a number of researchers to reduce seizure behavior. Sterman and Friar[7] reduced epileptic seizures in a twenty-three-year-old woman by increasing the period of time during which the subject was able to maintain a frequency of 12–14 Hz in the sensory motor cortex. Similarly, Finley and associates[8] treated a thirteen-year-old boy who had been observed to have up to seventy seizures a day. EEG was used to provide feedback by means of a blue light and tone to signal the presence of a 12-Hz EEG. An operant paradigm was established whereby the accumulation of five-second periods of 12-Hz responses were convertible to points which were then exchanged for money. Contingent reinforcement resulted in a sixfold increase in 12-Hz activity and a concomitant decrease in seizure behavior. Seizures were reduced from seventy a day to about one per hour. After two months of training, a discrimination paradigm was enlisted. Seizure behavior was marked by an EEG pattern of 4–7 Hz. When a pattern of 4–7 Hz was present, a red training light was illuminated and the boy was instructed to say "red light off." During this time no points were accumulated. The red light was cued by the EEG activity and driven by the electroencephalograph. With the interruption of the 4–7-Hz pattern and an increase in the 12-Hz pattern, seizures were eliminated and a more normative EEG was attained with this reduced seizure frequency.

Electromyogram biofeedback is used more frequently with clinical symptoms associated with tension responses. Electromyogram and electromyometer recordings indicate the change in potential along the motor neurons and muscle fiber. The greater the number of the units activated, the higher the amplitude or the strength of the EMG signal. EMG recordings of muscle activity are often employed along with relaxation training to treat stress disorders and disorders resulting in heightened muscle activity, such as in tension headaches.

A third response used in treating children is the galvanic skin response (GSR). The GSR is one mechanism that measures skin resistance or

TABLE 2. Intervention Strategy

I. Disorder
 a. Target behavior
 b. Underlying physiological system
 c. Biofeedback method
 d. Baseline
II. Feedback stimulus
 a. Visual
 b. Auditory
 c. Tactile
III. Stimulus threshold
 a. Binary
 b. Analogue
IV. Reinforcement
 a. Intrinsic (symptom reduction)
 b. Extrinsic (primary or conditioned S^r)

NOTE: To develop an effective intervention strategy, the physiological response mechanism underlying the disordered behavior must be identified. On the basis of the mechanism, the biofeedback technique for monitoring the response must be chosen and stimulus and reinforcement features specified.

electrodermal activity. A small current is run across the skin, and with increased sympathetic activity, sweat gland activity increases, resulting in reduced skin resistance. GSR patterns can be found to be greatly variable and dependent upon climatic conditions of the biofeedback setting. While a baseline can be established during each biofeedback session in order to establish changes in skin resistance, it appears more difficult to compare sympathetic nervous system activity from one session to the next. Reductions in skin resistance often occur in response to anxiety states.

A fourth type of biofeedback training involves a thermal response. The thermal response is a record of changes in skin temperature as a result of changes in vascular supply to the periphery of the body. Decreased sympathetic activity results in vasodilation, whereas increased sympathetic activity results in vasoconstriction and reduced flow. The use of thermal biofeedback has been helpful in disorders where an increase in peripheral blood flow is desirable and as a method of shunting blood away from other areas of the body. The latter is found in the treatment of migraine headaches where pain is the result of increased blood volume to the cerebral cortex. Diverting the blood flow to peripheral areas of the body, as occurs in hand warming, results in reduced volume to the brain. Similar approaches have been used with Raynaud's syndrome and reflex sympathetic dystrophy.[9]

Returning to TABLE 2 we find that a baseline and the responsiveness of the psychological system is determined before intervention is begun.

FEEDBACK STIMULUS

The stimulus that is being "fed back" as part of the cybernetic loop is an important component in biofeedback training. The stimulus should maintain an instructional quality as it allows the person to associate the psychophysiological response to a sensation they are having at the time. Using Sherington's model, the feedback is generally the result of interoceptive stimulation or proprioceptive stimulation arising from the activity of the body. An external or exteroceptive stimulus now becomes paired with the physiological change or proprioceptive feedback. This helps to cue the child to the change that is occurring in the bodily function being monitored. Whether this is a result of changes in the activity of the skeletal, circulatory, or electrodermal system of the body, feedback is essential. The paired stimulus can be visual, auditory, tactile, or any external source that can be driven by the biofeedback system, as long as it meets the processing capacities of the patients. One of the problems we have encountered with adults and generally have not encountered with children is the preference for auditory feedback. Adults prefer to perform the prescribed activities for EMG relaxation with their eyes closed, believing that they cannot relax when their eyes are open. For this reason we often use auditory feedback for training involving EMG reduction. Auditory feedback may be used with children although visual feedback is as effective a feedback stimulus.

The threshold at which feedback is presented to the child is another important variable. The stimulus feedback may be presented in either binary or analogue form. Binary feedback refers to an "on-off" pattern in which the feedback is either presented or removed, contingent upon a response. This "all or none" phenomenon serves to orient the child but is found to provide only limited additional instruction. Providing feedback in analogue form allows for a more instructional presentation, corresponding with graded increases or decreases in the responsiveness of the person. For example, if the goal of a biofeedback session is to increase muscle tone, a concomitant increase in signal intensity may be provided to the subject as muscle tone increases.

The value of feedback has been demonstrated by Talbot[10] in a study involving augmented feedback in the eye-hand coordination of students with cerebral palsy. The researcher divided 59 students with cerebral palsy into three groups. The Southern California Motor Accuracy Test (SCMAT) was used and the students were required to trace lines. One group traced lines with auditory feedback while a second group traced lines without feedback. A third, control group refrained from any motor activity. The first group used a light-pen-like device, and deviation from the specified line resulted in feedback by an auditory signal. The subject thus had immediate feedback of any deviation from the line. Each subject took a pre- and post-test after 40 training sessions. The second group did not receive feedback while involved in line tracing, and the control group received neither training nor feedback. After an evaluation of performance, the group that received feedback excelled in motor accuracy and maintained this motor accuracy throughout a three-month interval after which a second post-test was administered.

REINFORCEMENT

One of the objections to the use of biofeedback with children results from the contention that because biofeedback developed in the operant laboratory, a program involving extrinsic reinforcement is necessary for its success. Finley and associates[11] used an operant paradigm with reinforcement delivered through use of an automatic food dispenser and driven by EMG instrumentation. The purpose was to modify muscle tone in 15 subjects with cerebral palsy. The persons ranged from 4 years to 22 years of age with a diagnosis of mild to severe cerebral palsy. Subjects possessed a range of intellectual abilities from severely retarded to gifted, and the functional abilities of the subjects, including walking and talking, also varied. The subjects were divided into two groups. A group of ten constituted "the on-line group" for reward dispensing and the second group of five subjects served as the "off-line group." The two groups were matched on the basis of functional level. The universal feeder was loaded with toys, tokens, and candy. Each complement of "reinforcers" was chosen by the children in conjunction with their parents. All children were trained for frontal EMG and forearm flexor EMG, and response threshold was set individually with each subject. This was done so that reduction in EMG could be achieved through training and was neither too easy nor too difficult to attain. All children received auditory feedback, which consisted of a clicking sound when threshold was attained. The on-line group also received reinforcers delivered by a universal feeder contingent upon their EMG reduction. An analysis of variance across the two conditions was significant for EMG reduction among children receiving on-line reinforcement. A greater evaluation of the research data demonstrated that while EMG reduction was enhanced by the use of on-line reinforcement, those children serving in the control group also demonstrated a learning curve. Thus, while an operant paradigm was employed, it only served to enhance the response change. Other studies seem to suggest that while intrinsic reinforcement or the "benefits of symptom reduction" can be used with older children, a primary reinforcement or extrinsic supplement has been shown to be more effective in obtaining changes in the desired direction with young children.

GENERALIZATION

The laboratory or therapeutic setting occupies only a small part of the child's life. Often, activities arranged within the training setting represent the child's only experience with the behavior that we hope will become part of their repertoire. As a result, activities for reinforcing these behaviors should accompany biofeedback training and should take place in the environment in which we hope to generalize the learned response. This setting will most often be the child's home or school. The time spent in therapeutic activity even with these exercises is minimal compared with the overall activity pattern of the child. Reinforcing desired patterns becomes even more important when dealing with a child who has significant developmental disabilities. Response patterns of adaptive behavior are more difficult to achieve and the limited cognitive ability of the more severely disabled demand efficiency in learning and teaching these tasks. For the child with cerebral dysfunction, and more specifically the physically disabled child, learning the concepts that the nondisabled learn are often more difficult. The effects of posture and difficulties in maintaining an upright vertical orientation to the world around them interferes with concept formation. The presence of obligatory reflex patterns may preclude orientation to the midline, sound vocalization, and the development of bimanual skills. The asymmetrical tonic neck reflex (ATNR), which is often observed in babies, may become a persistent pattern as a result of central nervous system disturbance. This pattern, which involves both upper and lower extremities and head position, can be triggered by difficulty in head control. The Moro or startle reflex which triggers a full-body response and abrupt change in posture can also be triggered by loud noises or a 5% dorsal lag in head control. Maintaining head control, therefore, not only allows children to view the world in a more adaptive fashion, but helps to prevent them from being thrown into more encompassing reflex patterns that are distracting and prevent attention to academic and social skills.

Feedback on Head Position in Mentally Retarded Children with Cerebral Palsy

Walmsley[12] and associates provided feedback on head position to five profoundly mentally retarded children with quadriplegic cerebral palsy and poor head control. The researchers used a head trainer consisting of a series of mercury switches that could be set in response to deviations from a set plane. Music was used as a signal to indicate head position and was continuously available when the head position of each subject was maintained within predetermined limits. Each child had unique obligatory reflex patterns and his or her own physical abnormalities. This required that each child had to pay attention in order to maintain an upright posture for the study, which was performed by the use of adaptive seating devices. Of the five subjects, music served as a reinforcer for three, who demonstrated significantly increased time in an adaptive vertical position. Leiper[13] and associates showed the generalization of this greater head control from a laboratory setting to the classroom. The researchers demonstrated that these increases could be sustained while children engaged in academic activities involving arm movement and with some destabilization of the trunk of their body. A head position monitor that responded to a deviation in the head from a vertical plane and concomitantly provided an analogue auditory signal resulted in all children increasing their ability to maintain their heads within proscribed limits. The extension of these laboratory findings to a setting in which academic skills are taught represents the goal of any interventional technique.

Identifying Point of Effective Intervention in Complex Chains of Behavior

Drooling

Adaptive behaviors are not single, discrete units of activities that occur in an "all or none" fashion. These behaviors are highly integrated chains, in which a response is a trigger which then physiologically bridges a preceding behavior to the next response in a synchronized pattern. Monitoring a complex chain that has been disrupted by the metaphorical "weakest link" can pinpoint where intervention is necessary. Drooling is a common problem occurring in the developmentally disabled and is a behavior that often signals cerebral palsy. This behavior, while hygienically undesirable, also carries a social stigma, which separates the person from his nondisabled peers. Drooling is not a unitary action; it is the result of pooling of saliva and the inefficient swallowing of this accumulation. Looking at the sequence required for this highly complex behavior, we see that it involves the sequential and patterned movements of lips, tongue, palate, jaws, and larynx, and the coordination of the respiratory muscles. According to Koheil[14] and associates, swallowing can be divided into three major stages: oral, pharyngeal, and esophogeal. In observing groups of nondisabled nondroolers and children with cerebral palsy who drooled, it was found that the C.P. child has a dysfunction in the requisite muscle coordination of the swallowing response. Postural problems contribute to drooling and the greater the postural abnormality, the greater the problem presented by drooling. The researchers evaluated 12 children with spastic and athetoid cerebral palsy. Their head control ranged from poor to good with eight having significant deficits in communication. All subjects were hypotonic, and while they all had the ability to close their mouths, a mouth-open posture was habitual. A combination of binary and analogue auditory feedback was used during this study. The researchers collected saliva through a quantification system while EMG was recorded simultaneously from surface electrodes placed over the infrahyoid muscle and the obicularis muscle. Children were initially given binary auditory feedback while observing themselves in the mirror. Low muscle tone was accomplished by the auditory signal, and an increase in muscle tone reduced signal feedback. The children were given different exercises of lip puckering, sucking, blowing, and swallowing, while monitoring themselves in the mirror. When they became capable of controlling the signal with an increase in muscle tone, an analogue signal was sounded. If the muscle tone was hypotonic, the sound level decreased. Every 40 seconds an alarm would signal the children to swallow. The signal was set to occur at this predetermined interval but was regulated if the interval was too long, as marked by increased pooling of saliva and drooling. As a result of the auditory feedback training, which helped to focus the subject's attention to the mouth-open position and drooling, all subjects showed a decrease in drooling behavior.

Bowel and Bladder Control

Other major deficits may be encountered in the person who has sustained spinal lesions such as those found in myelomeningocele. This congenital malformation of the vertebral column may impair neurological innervation below the level of lesion, affecting bowel[15–17] and bladder control. Volpe[18] indicates that as much as 72% of infants born with myelomeningocele show urodynamic deterioration. The use of augmented feedback has been demonstrated to increase muscle control affecting bladder activity in these cases as well as in bladder dyssynergia,[19] neurogenic bladder,[10] and general bladder incontinence. Biofeedback with bowel control problems resulting from such lesions as well as from anal atresia, another birth anomaly, has also been successful. Wald[16] indicates that rectal sensation, ability to contract the anal sphincter, and motivation are three key factors in achieving continence. Whitehead and associates used biofeedback training with eight children with spina bifida to attain bowel control. These children had lesions that ranged from as high as the ninth thoracic vertebra to as low as the third sacral vertebra. Before training, fecal control was attained through frequent bowel evacuation in order to avoid soiling. After the use of augumented visual feedback training, six of the eight children achieved control. The researcher cautions, however, that the initial incontinence resulted from poor external sphincter control, which was strengthened through repeated contraction exercise. Incontinence associated with the aging population often results from poor sensation arising from bowel distension, another a problem with a different etiology and not as "easily" amenable to training in this fashion.

Headache

Biofeedback has made an impact on the more severely developmentally delayed child. However, its application to more prevalent disorders found in childhood also represents an important application. A common complaint, and one that probably ranks second only to the stomachache in children, is that of a headache. While similar reports for children have not been observed in the literature, such disorders are not uncommon in the clinical setting. Children who report with frequent headache generally fit into two categories.[21] The first category of headache is associated with increased muscle tone and is experienced as a constriction around the forehead. This "tension" headache has been demonstrated to be amenable to treatment through electromyographic feedback. The second category, which is primarily vascular in origin, is classified as the migraine headache.[22,23] The migraine headache is treated by diverting blood from the brain to the periphery by means of peripheral vasodilation.[24–26] The reduction of blood allows less dilatation of the cerebral blood vessels and a return to their normal, narrower diameter.[27] The determination of nonmigranous headaches in children, which was reported as occurring in 48% of children age 7–15 in a Swedish cohort, has been suggested to be the result of tension.[28] Migraine headaches, which may at times be precipitated by tension responses, are essentially vascular and occur with a positive family history[29] in almost 90% of cases. The type of headache must be delinated, because the diagnosis will determine the applicable biofeedback treatment. Biofeedback offers a less invasive technique for dealing with the causes and discomforts of the headache then other treatments found in the medical literature. Common treatments include the use of aspirin, Fiorinal, Chlorpromazine, Dilantin, phenobarbital, and Elavil.[29] Children with migraine headaches also face the difficulties and complications of other chronic pain syndromes. These may include depression[30]; impairment of self-concept[31]; deficits in posture, mobility,[32] concentration, and memory; as well as helplessness and feelings of victimization.[33] The pervasiveness of headaches in the child's daily life compromises social and academic performance.

Labbe and associates,[25] citing the side effects of vasoconstrictive medication for migrane control, demonstrated a decrease in the number of headaches per week as well as headache intensity in three children ages 9, 12, and 13. Labbe's study was one of the first providing follow-up, although prior studies involving greater numbers of subjects have demonstrated the efficacy of skin temperature biofeedback as an effective alternative to pharmacological intervention. Waranch and associates have also demonstrated long-term follow-up of biofeedback effectiveness for headache in children using a population of 15 children ages 10–17. The researchers reported on 10 subjects with migranes; four had migraine with muscle contraction, and one experienced a clear muscle contraction headache. EMG training performed with the frontalis muscle as well as increasing peripheral skin temperature by thermal biofeedback appeared to maintain the reduction in 13 or the 15 children.

Attentional Deficit Disorder and Hyperactivity

More pervasive learning disorders associated with attentional problems have been treated through use of biofeedback. As indicated previously, a high frequency of studies have involved children who were regarded as hyperactive. Hyperactivity has generally been associated with attentional deficit disorder (ADD) and has appeared predominantly in boys. ADD and hyperactivity have a pervasive influence on the academic and social experiences of these children and cast them in a negative light both to themselves and to others coming in contact with them. These children are often shunned by their peers, experience rejection from teachers, and in general begin to see themselves as failures. They perform poorly in sports as a result of the clumsiness that they often demonstrate as well as their inability to inhibit their impulsive behavior.[34] These problems are compounded by the feedback that they receive on their academic productivity. Increased activity and poor attentional capacity prevent optimal interaction with their environment. These children often lack the ability to monitor their own behavior and cannot inhibit their distraction to extraneous stimuli. The extent to which this is seen as a problem by the professional community is witnessed by the attention given to these problems in the scientific literature. Relaxation training and biofeedback have both been seen as important, effective, and nonintrusive interventions. These approaches will become even more frequent as the public becomes increasingly reluctant to use amphetamines such as Ritalin in the treatment of these disorders. The side effects of retarded growth development and reports of psychomotor agitation seen with some medications may provide greater impetus for the use of behavioral approaches in treatment. The biofeedback procedures that are employed help the child to monitor his own behavior and thus retain control of himself. These techniques help the child become more aware of involuntary bodily activity, and a greater degree of control over behavior may become established. While biofeedback may be an effective approach to symptom reduction, it too must be used with caution. Lubar and associates[35] used the EEG feedback of sensory motor rhythm to increase its voluntary inhibition. Training of the sensory motor cortex resulted in generalization to other gross motor activity, with the result that the children were more likely to stay in their seats and, in general, fidget less. The children also improved in task-oriented skills such as classroom cooperation. Braud[36] made a comparison of EMG feedback with progressive relaxation exercises and no training in 15 hyperactive children. While both relaxation exercises and relaxation exercises with biofeedback resulted in reduced tension, a greater reduction accompanied biofeedback training. Both methods resulted in an accompanying reduction of hyperactivity, although there were no differences between the two groups. Others have demonstrated that behavioral change did not parallel the tension reduction that was achieved.[37] In an attempt to determine the variables that would predict successful EMG biofeedback training in hyperactive boys, Denkowski and associates[38] evaluated the effects of pretreatment EMG levels, degree of hyperactivity, and locus of control upon the effectiveness of biofeedback in reducing the activity levels of 59 hyperactive boys. After conducting EMG training, it was observed that internally oriented boys, those with an internal locus of control, were more proficient in modifying physiological processes. It was also noted that age did not appear to be a significant factor in predicting treatment effectiveness. These findings, however, were not born out by Omizo and associates[39] in a study involving 32 hyperactive boys. These researchers employed a Conners Behavior Rating Scale[40] to identify levels of hyperactivity in children before intervention. The children were then assigned to one of two groups, which were matched on the basis of Conners scores, with one group randomly selected as the experimental group. A visual discrimination test, the Matching Familiar Figures Test (MFFT), was used to assess impulsiveness and attention to the task, while the Nowicki–Strictland Scale was used to assess the locus of control. The researchers reported that locus of control failed to be identified as a significant variable, although there was a significant difference between the experimental and control groups in impulsiveness and attention to task as a result of relaxation training. Prolonged training may, however, be associated with changes in locus of control.

SUMMARY

Biofeedback has demonstrated its effectiveness in the treatment of childhood disorders over the cynicism of many clinicans. Its appropriateness to the pediatric population is not a function of the age of the subject, but of whether the disorder is amenable to treatment. To reiterate, not all disturbances are the same. Incontinence in the child with spina bifida may be different from incontinence in the aged. Hyperactivity in children, while often defined globally, has many concomitants, some of which help to determine the efficacy of biofeedback treatment. The instructions given are specific and easily understood and can be comprehended even by some of the youngest children. Biofeedback deserves to be considered as the treatment of choice, in a wide range of disorders occurring in childhood.

REFERENCES

1. PORTER, J. 1965. Guided fantasy as a treatment for childhood insomnia. Aust. N. Z. J. Psychiatry **9:** 169–172.
2. LEVINE, E. S. 1980. Indirect suggestions through personalized fairy tales for treatment of childhood insomnia. Am. J. Clin. Hyp. **23:** 57–63.
3. MELAMED, B. G., K. A. MATTHEWS, D. K. ROUTH & B. STABLER. 1986. Introduction. Health Psychol. **5:** 181–183.
4. LORD, J. 1984. Cerebral palsy: A clinical approach. Arch. Phys. Med. Rehabil. **65:** 542–548.
5. LINKENHOKER, D. 1983. Tools of behavioral medicine: Applications of biofeedback treatment for children and adolescents. Dev. Behav. Pediatr. **4:** 16–20.
6. MILLER, N. E. 1981. Behavioral medicine, biofeedback and homeostasis: New application of learning. Psychiatr. Ann. **11:** 111-14.
7. STERMAN, M. B. & L. FRIAR. 1972. Suppression of seizures in an epileptic following sensorimotor EEG feedback training. Electroencephalogr. Clin. Neurophysiol. **33:** 89–95.
8. FINLEY, W. W., H. A. SMITH & M. D. ETHERTON. 1975. Reduction of seizures and normalization of the EEG in a severe epileptic following sensorimotor biofeedback training: Preliminary study. Biol. Psychol. **2:** 189–203.
9. BAROWSKY, E. T., J. B. ZWEIG & J. MOSKOWITZ. 1987. Thermal biofeedback in the treatment of symptoms associated with reflect sympathetic dystrophy. J. Child Neurol. **2:** 229–232.
10. TALBOT, M. L. & J. JUNKALA. 1981. The effects of auditorally augmented feedback on the eye-hand coordination of students with cerebral palsy. Am. J. Occup. Ther. **35:** 525–528.
11. FINLEY, W. W., M. D. ETHERTON, D. DICKMAN, D. KARIMIAN & R. W. SIMPSON. 1981. A simple EMG reward-system. Biofeedback Self-Reg. **5:** 169–180.
12. WALMSLEY, R. P., L. CRICHTON & D. DROOG. 1981. Music as a feedback mechanism for teaching head control to severely handicapped children: A pilot study. Dev. Med. Child Neurol. **23:** 739–746.
13. LEIPER, C. I., A. MILLER, J. LANG & R. HERMAN. 1981. Sensory feedback for head control in cerebral palsy. Phys. Ther. **61:** 512–518.
14. KOHEIL, R. A. E. SOCHANIWSKYJ, K. BABLICH, D. J. KENNY & M. MILNER. 1987. Biofeedback techniques and behavior modification in the conservative remediation of drooling by children with cerebral palsy. Dev. Med. Child Neurol. **29:** 19–26.
15. OLNESS, K., F.A. MCPARLAND & J. PIPER. 1980. Biofeedback: A new modality in the management of children with fecal soiling. J. Pediatr. **96:** 505–509.
16. WALD, A. 1986. Fecal incontinence. Postgrad. Med. **80:** 123–128.
17. WHITEHEAD, W. E., L. H. PARKER, B. J. MASEK, M. F. CATALDO & J. M. FREEMAN. 1981. Biofeedback treatment of fecal incontinence in patients with Myelomeningocele. Dev. Med. Child Neurol. **23:** 313–322.
18. VOLPE, J. J. 1986. Neurology of the Newborn, 2nd edition. Saunders. Philadelphia, PA.
19. LIBO, L. M., G. E. ARNOLD, J. R. WOODSIDE & T. A. BORDEN. 1983. EMG biofeedback for functional bladder-sphincter dyssynergia: A case study. Biofeedback Self-Reg. **8:** 243–253.

20. SUGAR, E. C. & C. F. FIRLIT. 1982. Urodynamic biofeedback: A new therapeutic approach for childhood incontinence/infection (vesical voluntary sphincter dyssynergia). J. Urol. **128:** 1253–1258.
21. WARANCH, H. R. & D. M. KEENAN. Behavioral treatment of children with recurrent headaches. J. Behav. Ther. Exp. Psychiatry. **16:** 31–38.
22. BILLE, B. 1967. Juvenile headaches: Its natural history in children. *In* Headaches in Children. A. Friedman & E. Harms, Eds. Charles C. Thomas. Springfield, IL.
23. BROWN, J. K. 1977. Migraine and migraine equivalents in children. Dev. Med. Child Neurol. **19:** 683–692.
24. DIAMOND, S. & M. FRANKLIN. 1975. Autogenic training with biofeedback in the treatment of children with migraine. Ther. Psychosom. Med.: 190–192.
25. LABBE, E. E. & D. A. WILLIAMSON. 1983. Temperature biofeedback in the treatment of children with migraine headaches. J. Pediatr. Psychol. **8:** 317–325.
26. FENTRESS, D. W., J. M. BRUCE, J. E. MEHEGAN & H. BENSON. 1986. Biofeedback and relaxation-response training in the treatment of pediatric migraine. Dev. Med. Child Neurol. **28:** 139–146.
27. MACDONALD, J. T. 1986. Childhood migraine: Differential diagnosis and treatment. Postgrad. Med. **80:** 301–306.
28. BILLE, B. S. 1962. Migraine in school children: A study of incidence and short-term prognosis, and a clinical, psychological, and encephalographic comparison between children with migraine and matched controls. Acta Paediatr. Scand. **51**(Suppl. 136): 1–151.
29. PRENSKY, A. L. 1976. Migraine and migrainous variants in pediatric patients. Pediatr. Clin. North Am. **23:** 461–471.
30. HENDLER, N. 1984. Depression caused by chronic pain. J. Clin. Psychol. **44:** 30–36.
31. ARMENTROUT, D. P. 1979. The impact of chronic pain on self-concept. J. Clin. Psychol. **35:** 517–521.
32. WRIGHT, G. N. Total Rehabilitation. Little, Brown. Boston.
33. BAROWSKY, E. I. 1987. Factors affecting the impact of pain and painful experiences on the exceptional child. J. Spec. Educ. **21:** 109–121.
34. TAFT, L. T. & E. I. BAROWSKY. 1989. The clumsy child. Pediatr. Rev. **10:** 247–253.
35. LUBAR, J. F. & M. N. SHOUSE. EEG and behavioral changes in a hyperkinetic child concurrent with training of sensorimotor rhythm (SMR). Biofeedback Self-Reg. **1:** 296–306.
36. BRAUD, L. 1978. The effects of frontal emg biofeedback and progressive relaxation upon hyperactivity and its behavioral concomitanys. Biofeedback Self-Reg. **3:** 69–89.
37. DENKOWSKI, K. M., G. C. DENKOWSKI & M. M. OMIZO. 1984. Predictors of success in the EMG biofeedback training of hyperactive male children. Biofeedback Self-Reg. **9:** 253–264.
38. OMIZO, M. M. & W. B. MICHAEL. 1982. Biofeedback-induced relaxation training and impulsivity, attention to task, and locus of control among hyperactive boys. J. Learn. Disabil. **15:** 414–416.
39. CONNERS, C. K. 1973. Rating scales for use in drug studies with children. Psychopharmacol. Bull. **15:** 24–84.

Index of Contributors